# FORD MOTOR COMPANY:

## THE GREATEST CORPORATE TURNAROUND IN U.S. HISTORY

## GERHARD GEYER

ISBN:1-4609-7573-1
ISBN-13:978-1-4609-7573-2
LCCN: 2011903768

In memory of the late Professor Bernard Forest of Arlington, MA and his surviving wife, "Mother Forest." They opened their home to a penniless stranger in 1958. Through their generosity and kindness, I was able to graduate from Boston University with B.S. and M.B.A. degrees. It can only happen in America.

I am also grateful to the American people for allowing me to be part of this great country (the Attachment includes a brief synopsis of my vision of the "American Way of Life").

Lastly, although long forgotten in today's Germany, I wish to thank the United States of America for its extraordinary contributions and far-sighted vision in the rebirth of post World War II West Germany, my place of birth. The people who should receive special recognition include the late President Harry S. Truman, a true American icon and hero, and George G. Marshall, the primary force behind the Marshall Plan. DANKE SCHOEN.

I would also like to praise the unsung "All-Stars" of the automotive press who have kept me abreast of developments around the world since 1964. I continue to spend my Social Security checks on many automotive publications. The lifetime "Oscar" should be awarded to Keith Crain who is the principle behind the venerable bible of the auto industry–Automotive News with its superb staff. My other favorites are Phil LeBeau and Jim Cramer of CNBC, the auto writers of Motor Trend, Car & Driver, Road & Track and Ward's. The Wall Street Journal, Fortune and Forbes also have outstanding auto analysts who are the Deans of the auto press corps including Alex Taylor III, Paul Ingrassia, Dan Neil, Michele Maynard (PBS), and the late Jerry Flint. The new boys and girls on the block include Bill Saporito (Time), Keith Naughton (Bloomberg), Michelle Krebs (Edmunds.com), Rebecca Lindland (IHS Automotive), Rick Newman of U.S. News & World Report and Joan Muller (Forbes).

# CONTENT

Introduction ...................................................................i

Chapter 1 ............................................................... 1

• **This Is a Magic Moment So Different and So New**
• **Prologue**

Chapter 2 .............................................................. 7

• **Born in the U.S.A.**
- ☐ The Legendary Henry Ford
- ☐ Henry Ford II and Company

Chapter 3 ............................................................. 13

• **The Emperor Without Clothes**
- ☐ An Industry in Disarray
- ☐ Back-Office Outsourcing
- ☐ Impact on American Families
- ☐ America, Fight Back

Chapter 4 ............................................................ 29

• **The (Former) Pride and Joy of America**
- ☐ The Automotive Development Process
- ☐ U.S. Auto Industry Volumes
- ☐ U.S. Auto Industry Market Shares
- ☐ Vehicle Ownership

☐      Automobile Production by State

☐      Passenger Car Fuel Economy

☐      U.S. Gasoline Price Trends

☐      Passenger Car Horse Power

☐      Fortune 500 Rankings of U.S. Auto Companies

☐      U.S. Auto Industry in Crisis

☐      Impact of U.S. Job Losses

☐      Auto Industry Culprits

**Chapter 5.................................................. 55**

**• Marching Together to the Same (Sometimes Wrong) Tune**

☐      Background

☐      The U.S. Marching Band Until the Early 1970s

**Chapter 6.................................................. 73**

**• The Land of the Rising Sun's Invasion**

☐      The Early Years

☐      1970s and Beyond

☐      The U.S. Auto Companies' Response

**Chapter 7.................................................. 85**

**• Auto Companies Playing in the Same Sandbox (Buying the World)**

☐      Defense/Consulting Acquisitions

☐      Automotive Acquisitions

☐      Car Rentals Acquisitions

☐      Financial Acquisitions

## Chapter 8...................................................... 91

- **The Roaring 1990s (Flowing With Milk and Honey)**
  - ☐      Money, Money, Money
  - ☐      Jacques Nasser, Ford's Mr. Acquisition
  - ☐      Competitive Auto Company Acquisitions

## Chapter 9...................................................... 103

- **Ford's Transformation Process (The Ringing Grooves of Change)**
  - ☐      The "Ford 2000" Plan
  - ☐      The Contour Debacle
  - ☐      The Ford Focus

## Chapter 10.................................................... 111

- **The Ouster of Ford's CEO Jacques Nasser (Time to Leave)**

## Chapter 11.................................................... 121

- **Ford's 2002 "Revitalization" Plan (Carrying Too Much Sail)**

## Chapter 12.................................................... 123

- **Ford's 2005 "Restructuring" Plan (The Underbelly Is Still Soft)**

## Chapter 13.................................................... 127

- **Ford's 2006 "Way Forward" Plan ("Change or Die")**

# Chapter 14.............................................. 131

**• Ford's Status by Mid-2006 (At the End of One's Rope)**

☐ Declining Profits
☐ Deteriorating Balance Sheet
☐ Uncompetitive Cost Structure
☐ Rapidly Declining Sales
☐ Poor Product Quality
☐ Ford's Factories Lagged Behind Competition
☐ Senior Management Turnover
☐ Employees and Wall Street Lost Faith
☐ Unhappy Dealers
☐ Dissatisfied Suppliers
☐ Ford Missed the Boat in Asia

# Chapter 15.............................................. 147

**• Toyota's Status by Mid-2006 (My Cup Runneth Over)**

☐ Background
☐ The Overachiever

# Chapter 16.............................................. 161

**• The New Kid on the Block**

☐ Introduction
☐ Mr. Mulally Arrives at Ford

# Chapter 17.............................................. 173

**• Let the Magic Begin (Zauberer)**

☐ The Plans and the Goals

## Chapter 18........................................... 179

- **Mr. Mulally's "One Ford" (Miracle) Action Plan**
  - ☐ Ford's Mission Statement
  - ☐ Ford's Basic Thrust
  - ☐ Financial Plan
  - ☐ Balance Sheet Actions
  - ☐ Organization Plan
  - ☐ Product Strategy Plan
  - ☐ Rightsizing Facilities Plan
  - ☐ Flexible Manufacturing
  - ☐ UAW Agreement
  - ☐ Ford Supplier Strategy
  - ☐ Ford Dealer Plan

## Chapter 19........................................... 211

- **The Unstoppable Thundering Herd**
  - ☐ Background
  - ☐ Finance Plan and Improve the Balance Sheet
  - ☐ Restructure To Operate Profitably
  - ☐ Accelerate Product Development
  - ☐ Work Together Effectively As One Team

## Chapter 20........................................... 239

- **Mr. Mulally's "Whiz Kids/All Stars"**
  - ☐ The Original "Whiz Kids"
  - ☐ The New "All Stars"

# Chapter 21 ......................................... 245

**• The Job Is Not Done (Ain't No Half-Steppin)**

- Continue to Strengthen the Balance Sheet
- Passenger Cars
- Emerging Markets
- Asia
- South America
- Mexico
- UAW Agreement
- Lincoln Brand
- Former Visteon Corporation Plants

# Chapter 22 ......................................... 263

**• The Fifth Column in America**

- Washington's Job Saboteurs
- America, Wake Up
- The Ballot Box Still Works

# Chapter 23 ......................................... 285

**• The Cat With Nine Lives (Reborn Again)**

# Chapter 24 ......................................... 289

**• The Sleeping Giant Is Awakening**

- Introduction
- General Motors' Restructuring Plans

## Chapter 25 ................................................ 299

- **Who Has the Card Up One's Sleeve? (Ford vs. General Motors)**
  - ☐ Ford Vs. GM

## Chapter 26 ................................................ 307

- **The "Old Man" Still Has Muscles (General Motors vs. Ford)**
  - ☐ GM Vs. Ford
  - ☐ Analysts' View of GM Today
  - ☐ GM's November 2010 IPO

## Chapter 27 ................................................ 323

- **The $64,000 Question**
  - ☐ Introduction
  - ☐ Ata Boys for Mr. Mulally
  - ☐ The $64,000 Question
  - ☐ The Korean Threat
  - ☐ Ford's Next Phase

## Chapter 28 ................................................ 345

- **The Ford Renewal Seriatim (Eins, Zwei, Drei)**
  - ☐ Step by Step

## Chapter 29 ................................................ 349

- **Management Lessons to Remember**
  - ☐ "Creative Destruction"
  - ☐ Why Change Management Fails
  - ☐ Management Lessons to Remember

## Chapter 30........................................................ 365

**• Why "One Ford" Accomplished its Goals**

    ☐     Happy Days Are Here Again

## Chapter 31 ....................................................... 377

**• Walking on Thin Ice**

    ☐     Expert Opinions

    ☐     The Man with the "Golden Touch"

    ☐     Grand Cordon

## Chapter 32........................................................ 393

**• News Flash**

    ☐     Alan Mulally's Indy 500 Race

    ☐     Celebrations in Dearborn, Michigan

## Chapter 33........................................................ 401

**• Alan Mulally's Scorecard**

## Chapter 34........................................................ 405

**• Epilogue**

# Attachments......... 455

- **Ford and the American Way of Life**
  - ☐ The Decline of America?
  - ☐ The Positive Aspects of America
  - ☐ Hip, Hip, Hooray for America
- **The Rulers of this Century**
  - ☐ Overview
  - ☐ Economic Powerhouse
  - ☐ Chinese Automotive Industry
  - ☐ Not Everything Is Coming Up Roses

# Bibliography......... 487

# INTRODUCTION

This book was prepared without any support from Ford Motor Company although many chapters, especially discussing the Mulally era, sound like they were written by a paid Ford agent. To buttress my arguments why the company is the greatest corporate turnaround in U.S. history, I wrote a six-page letter in November 2010 to the Ford PR Vice President requesting certain non-proprietary information. Waiting on pins and needles, I finally received a one-paragraph response roughly four weeks later telling me that two other authors are writing a similar book and they won't supply any data. They didn't even have the courtesy to provide biographies of a few Ford executives who had been honored by Automotive News as 2010 "All Stars." I believe the PR people refused to provide support material because they didn't like a chapter, which reviewed Ford's disastrous status prior to Mr. Mulally's arrival in September 2006.

It was a painful defeat; I am sure they concluded that this old foggy-head would disappear into the woodworks and stop his work. The days of shaking in my booties when some VP speaks are gone. I am not on a scrap heap yet; therefore, I decided come hell or high water, they would not stop me because I am not a quitter.

The last time I checked, Ford was a publicly traded company. I don't believe it is kosher to play favorites by giving unfettered access to authors they like. In addition, the attitude of the PR people is contrary to Mr. Mulally's communicate, communicate, communicate philosophy. Moreover, I am a large individual Ford shareholder, and unwisely, 90% of my heavily under water holdings are in Ford stock. Further, I was inducted into Ford's "Ambassador Club" after sponsoring many friends and relatives to buy Ford products.

My whining that the Ford PR people stiffed me is nothing compared to a much more serious issue Ford's response seems to evidence–arrogance, cockiness and self-delusion (I experienced the euphoria of invincibility myself during the Ford boom periods). Voila, here we go again. Will Ford again be blinded by success? I am convinced that they are starting to believe in their own press notices and propaganda, which is a historic Ford trait after reaching Mount Everest. If this mindset starts permeating to the value-added, wealth-creating frontline Ford executives, this could eventually bring down Ford to earth, and we start the entire cycle of destruction again. No success (or failure) is final! (During the first two months of 2011, Ford recalled more than one million F-150 and Windstar vehicles. This is far more than for all of 2010. Moreover, "during the past year, Ford insiders sold $111 million worth of their company stock and insiders didn't buy a single share" according to a February 19, 2011 report by Brian Richards of Motley Fool.)

# CHAPTER 1

❁ ❁ ❁

## "THIS IS A MAGIC MOMENT SO DIFFERENT AND SO NEW"[a]

- "But Man, Ford Sure Looks Like the Smartest Kid in Class These Days." [1]

- "Ford, a U.S. Auto Maker Hitting on all Cylinders" [2]

- "This Is the Most Fantastic Turnaround in Human History" [3]

- "The Industrial Comeback of the Decade" [4]

- "An Astonishing Comeback." [5]

- "This is one of the most remarkable corporate comebacks in U.S. history." [6]

- "I can only marvel at witnessing one of the greatest single turnaround in American business history." [7]

- "They have been making all the right moves. It's been impressive. They just have an unbelievable amount of momentum right now." [8]

- "I've been studying the turnaround at Ford. The reason it has outpaced (GM and Chrysler) is because of the leadership and focus that Alan has brought." [9]

- "If it continues, Mr. Mulally will be credited with one of the great turnarounds in corporate history." [10]

- "Ford's Renaissance Man" (Alan Mulally) [11]

- "Ford's Comeback Kid" [12]

- "Mulally's Magic Works" [13]

---

**a Title of the famous 1960s song by The Drifters**

# PROLOGUE

With the survivability of his company in serious doubt, William Clay Ford, Jr., the torchbearer of the Ford clan, and Chairman and Chief Executive Officer of Ford Motor Company, dismissed himself as CEO in September 2006. Lacking viable internal candidates with proven turnaround skills, he appointed Boeing engineer Alan R. Mulally as President and CEO. Mr. Mulally came to Ford highly recommended because of his successful efforts at Boeing to turnaround the airplane giant.

To his great credit, Mr. Ford recognized that his company's business model was in shambles and required a radical overhaul. As Lee Iacocca stated in his 2007 book "Where Have All The Leaders Gone?" "His (Bill Ford) move took a lot of guts." [14] Not even the greatest optimists could have predicted the arrival of a new dawn for an American icon when Mr. Mulally jettisoned into Dearborn, Michigan, U.S.A. on a beautiful late summer day.

In the 2009 Harvard Business Review article entitled "Reinventing Your Business Model," the authors, Mark W. Johnson, Clayton M. Christensen, and Henning Kagelmann stated, "one secret to maintaining a thriving business is recognizing when it needs a fundamental change." [15] Ford's change was overdue, but at least it took place.

Mr. Mulally's appointment was risky because he had no automotive experience, and past efforts to hire outsiders at Ford were not successful. For example, "Bunkie" Knudsen left General Motors in 1968 when he was passed over for the presidency. Henry Ford II promptly hired him as president, but fired him nineteen months later. "It just didn't work out" was the explanation according to Robert Lacey's book "Ford, The Men and the Machine." [16] Other high level executives from GM and Chrysler also did not last long. This is not unusual; the 2009 McKinsey article in the Harvard Business Review entitled "When Growth Stalls" by Matthews S. Olson, Derek van Bever, and Seth Very stated "large companies have a fairly poor track record on incorporating new voices into senior management. Most studies agree that 35% to 40% of senior hires wash out within their first 18 months." [17]

The purpose of this book is to review how Ford Motor Company reinvented itself, and did not join GM and Chrysler into Chapter 11. It is the story of a crew on a leaking ship which almost sank to the bottom of Lake Michigan, but was rescued by a courageous Boeing pilot who appears to be direct descendent of the Great King Solomon. With tenacity, the virtually unknown executive rebuilt the decrepit boat into a highly admired ocean liner. It reminds me of the lyrics of the famous 1960's song by The Drifters: "This Is a Magic Moment So Different and So New." These words apply to the new Ford Motor Company, an American institution. The focus of the book is on Ford's North American business, with the heart of the story about CEO Alan Mulally's epic saga to reinvent a major American company. Ford Motor Credit Company, a highly profitable and strategic arm of Ford and the company's European Automotive Operations are excluded from the review because they have already undergone extensive and successful restructuring actions.

# CHAPTER 2

❃ ❃ ❃

## BORN IN THE U.S.A.

### The Legendary Henry Ford

Henry Ford founded Ford Motor Company on June 16, 1903 with eleven other investors and an initial capital of $28,000 ($660,000 in today's dollars). The company probably had more impact on 20th century life in America than any other company. Henry Ford who was named "Businessman of the Century" in 1999, was a true American original. Ford, according to Manufacturing magazine, was "once the symbol of modern industrialism." The Ford heritage includes:

• Introduced "the first affordable car for the masses."

• Introduced the automotive industry's first moving assembly line in 1913.

• Pioneered $5/day wages in 1914 or double the $2.34 a day earned by most factory workers for an eight-hour day. The wage hike reduced the disruption of extremely high levels of absenteeism. Steel workers were earning

$1.75 per day according to Douglas Brinkley's 2003 book entitled "Wheels for the World." [18]

- Pioneered "just-in-time" inventory management, which Toyota claims credit for.

- Introduced the Model T in 1908 (15 million built); Ford achieved a 50% market share in 1918. The Model T was named "Car of the Century" in 1999.

- Opened plants in Canada (1905), England (1911) and France in 1913.

- Established the Dearborn Rouge complex in 1918 employing over 100,000 people. (Raw material entered at one end and completed cars came out at the other end.)

- Produced 25,000 cars daily by 1925, and over 340 million vehicles through 2010 (possibly 400 million by 2020 and 450 million by 2050).

- Was slow in updating the Model T (discontinued in 1927), which allowed GM to overtake Ford in the late 1920's.

- Reluctantly entered into a labor agreement in 1941 with the UAW after violent confrontations.

- Became the "Arsenal of Democracy" (third largest defense contractor) during World War II by building thousands of B-24 bombers, M-4 tanks, jeeps, tractors, etc.

## Henry Ford II and Company

Henry Ford II took control of Ford Motor Company in 1945, with losses reportedly at one million dollars daily. Ford went public in 1956 with the biggest IPO ever ($700 million or $5.5 billion in today's dollars). The Ford Foundation, which owned 95% of Ford, became the largest philanthropic organization in the United States. Today, it has an endowment of over $10 billion, and donates more than $500 million annually to worthy causes.

Henry Ford II saved Ford Motor Company after World War II. He was an effective and powerful CEO for many years. Everybody in the company feared Mr. Ford, who was the only person out of 400,000 employees to be addressed Mister. Challenging Mr. Ford's decision was a sure bet of being banned to Siberia. He had no qualms of firing CEO's (Arjay Miller, Knudsen, Iacocca). He was the protector of the Ford family's financial interest in the company, which sometimes impacted on costly and risky new product decisions.

The Ford family has a great sense of civic duty, donating millions to charities. One of Henry Ford II's enduring legacy is the $500 million ($2.3 billion in today's dollars) Detroit Renaissance Center which is a 5.6 million square feet office/shopping complex. It was conceived by Mr. Ford in 1970 to rejuvenate downtown Detroit. He single-handedly pushed through the project, secured the necessary financing although Ford primarily underwrote the project. (GM has owned the seven connected skyscrapers since 1996, and spent $500 million in 2004 to renovate the center.)

Ford family members own about 71 million special class B shares. They effectively control Ford (40% of votes), and are still deeply involved in the company. In a one hour special on CNBC on November 10, 2010 entitled: "Ford: Rebuilding an American Icon," Bill Ford stated that the Ford family has an "emotional and financial investment" in the company.

In addition to Ford Board members Bill and Edsel Ford, three fifth-generation members work for Ford Motor Company. The New York Times stated the value of their holdings decreased to about $140 million during Ford's meltdown from $2.2 billion a decade ago. [19]

Henry Ford II's only son, Edsel, started his Ford career around 1973 at Ford's Product Planning and Research Staff I was associated with at that time. I remember Edsel as a smart and down-to-earth person with a wonderful personality. Edsel held many important positions in the company, including CEO of the highly profitable and important Ford Credit Company where he did an outstanding job. I was disappointed when he retired very early from Ford. My feeling is that he was not the mean-spirited, ruthless and "walk-over-dead" executive some people look for in CEO's. Edsel Ford can hold his head high; he is an honorable person, and was liked by all Ford employees. He is devoted to Detroit and was recently honored by the Urban Land Institute for his dedication to revitalize the city. I can't comment about Bill Ford, a graduate of Princeton and MIT, because I don't know him.

Edsel's oldest of four sons, Henry Ford III, joined Ford in 2006. He is rotating through various activities including a successful stint at a Ford dealership in California. He received an MBA from MIT. His professor called him one of the smartest students he ever had.

Ford remains a major world company with a number twenty-three position in the "Fortune Global 500" list, and eighth on "Fortune's Largest U.S. Corporation" list. [20 & 21] Following is a summary of Ford Motor Company's sales history since it's founding in 1903. Ford was the first company to sell over one million cars in one year (1,184,976 Model T in 1923).

| YEAR | WORLDWIDE SALES (000's) | MEMO: U.S. SALES (000's) |
|------|------------------------|---------------------------|
| 1903 | 2 | 2 |
| 1906 | 9 | 9 |
| 1910 | 20 | 20 |
| 1920 | NA | 464 |
| 1930 | NA | 1,237 |
| 1940 | NA | 778 |
| 1950 | NA | 1,773 |
| 1960 | 3,056 | 1,958 |
| 1970 | 4,770 | 2,794 |
| 1980 | 4,328 | 2,270 |
| 1990 | 6,023 | 3,286 |
| 1995 | 6,606 | 3,993 |
| 2000 | 7,424 | 4,486 |
| 2005 | 6,767 | 3,154 |
| 2009 | 4,866 | 1,677 |
| 2010 | 5,313 | 1,964 |

Source: *Automotive News; Ford Motor Company Annual Reports; Ford 10-K Reports; Fourth Quarter 2010 Ford Financial Results press release.*

Ford's 2010 worldwide sales and revenues totaled almost $129 billion compared with $116 billion in 2009. GM's 2010 sales totaled $136 billion. GM's worldwide unit sales in 2010 reached approximately 8.4 million units or about 3 million above Ford's sales. GM 2010 U.S. sales amounted to 2.2 million units, or roughly 265,000 units more than Ford's U.S. sales.

# CHAPTER 3

❈ ❈ ❈

# THE EMPEROR WITHOUT CLOTHES

## An Industry in Disarray

The story of America is similar to that of the former Roman Empire–devitalized. Our boat is sinking which is decimating the U.S. middle-class, which Professor Robert B. Reich in his book "Aftershock," defined as 40% of American families. Today the manufacturing sector accounts for 11.5% of GDP compared with 28% in 1960, 23% in 1980 and 18% in 1990. In a December 25, 2010 program on CNBW entitled "Rebuilding America" with Maria Bartiromo, this sector was described as "the soul of our great country." Manufacturing jobs account for less than 10% of all non-farm jobs compared with roughly 30% seventy years ago (22 % in 1980, 18% in 1990, and 15% in 2000). America has literally entered the stage of deindustrialization, which is inconceivable for the most powerful country in the world. There is no historic precedence for a country the size of the U.S. to literally become a service-sector economy without a decline in the standard of living, which is already taking place. It will eventually impact on our political freedom.

U.S. manufacturing reached its peak employment level in 1979 with 19.4 million people employed in this sector. Today, the number is around 13 million, and rapidly declining. Over six million middle-class manufacturing jobs have disappeared between 1980-2007. The Congressional Budget Office estimated the loss at 2.9 million jobs since 2000. [22] GDP growth during this period should have added millions of manufacturing jobs. For example, William A. Ward, Professor of Applied Economics and Statistics at Clemson University, estimated in his 2005 study "Manufacturing Productivity and the Shifting U.S. China and Global Job Scene 1990-2005," that 5.7 million manufacturing jobs should have been created from 1990 to 2004 as a result of the GDP growth. [23]

"Exports of manufactured goods from the United States rose by $334 billion between 1999 and 2007, imports grew by $692 billion-doubling the nominal trade deficit during the period." [24] The U.S. had cumulative manufacturing trade deficit of approximately $4.3 trillion between 2000 and 2009. [25] The trade deficit in 2010 was $500 billion. The major culprit is China, which has a tight grip on imports from other countries. The U.S. trade deficit with China was $275 billion in 2010–an unsustainable level.

According to a study by the Economic Policy Institute (March 23, 2010, report number 260 by Robert E. Scott), between 2001-2008 about 2.4 million U.S. workers, primarily low skilled, lost their jobs or were displaced as a result of the U.S. trade deficit with China. As David MacNeil, CEO of a major automotive supplier stated recently "recognizable American brands have been forced by shortsighted management and buyers at large national chains to build factories overseas just to save a lousy $.50 on a tape measure. To these ruthless buyers, it is all about the money. Rarely are product quality, the political system, human rights, animal rights and environmental costs to the planet considered, not to mention the cost to our society of exporting not only jobs, but an entire factory!"

However, despite the dismal trade deficits, U.S. exports totaled $1.8 trillion in 2010, and exports as a percent of GDP increased from roughly 6% in 1960 to approximately 15% today. In addition, capital goods represent the biggest U.S. export sector. Further, the U.S. still has the biggest manufacturing industry in the world and is the world's third largest industrial exporter. Moreover, CNBC's Jim Cramer stated on his January 12, 2011 program "American manufacturing renaissance has arrived." Lastly, the U.S. trade surplus in services increased from $75 billion in 2000 and $150 billion in 2010.

Economists claim that the U.S. manufacturing industry still produces a healthy $1.6 trillion in goods. Secondly, they argue that the sector's decline is simply transitioning from a manufacturing towards a service sector economy. They claim that it is a normal development in an advanced society and it is a natural trend for a postindustrial society to outsource low-skilled and environmentally hazardous sectors overseas. Further, they ask how can we compete when U.S. manufacturing wages are approximately $21 per hour (over $32 including benefits)? U.S. wages are more than 10 times above average Chinese levels. However, adjusted for inflation, U.S. hourly wages have been flat since 1960. Reportedly, Mexican total compensation costs average $4 per hour and Mexico can't compete with China anymore.

So, according to Wendy's old commercial: "Where's the Beef?" It's in the vital, but declining U.S. manufacturing sector. The U.S. infrastructure supporting the manufacturing sector is disappearing. Outsourcing of vital U.S. manufacturing jobs could eventually threaten our national security. For example, machine tooling made in China is 40% less expensive than American-made tooling, according to the September 24, 2007 issue of Automotive News. Many U.S. stamping companies are sourcing tooling to China. The U.S. is also sourcing components for nuclear reactors, ball bearings and sensitive electronic components overseas. According to Michael T. Snyder's September 26, 2010 analysis in "Seeking Alpha," the U.S. "has lost approximately 42,400 factories since 2001." The trade deficits mean that we have to borrow more money from China, Japan and other countries to pay our bills, which in turn results in their greater power over America. Eventuality we will all be singing the 1950s Tennessee Ernie Ford's song

"Sixteen Tons...Owe My Soul to the Company Store." We are in the midst of a paradigm shift in U.S. manufacturing, which bodes ill for millions of middle-class Americans.

Deloitte's 2010 Global Manufacturing study concluded, "The global competitive landscape for manufacturing is undergoing a transformational shift that will reshape the drivers of economic growth, high-value job creation, national prosperity, and national security" according to Deborah Smith of the U.S. Council on Competitiveness. Also disconcerting is Gary Shilling's December 20, 2010 forecast in Fortune magazine that we're "turning Japanese...real GDP will rise only 2% annually on average in the years ahead."

Germany, which is awakening from a long Schlaefchen (sleep), is again growing vigorously driven largely by its vibrant export sector, which accounts for over 40% of GDP. The key contributor of the growth is the powerful German manufacturing industry.  Germany recently blamed "the U.S.A. for living off credit too long, inflated its financial sector massively, and neglected its industrial base."

We are allowing our important manufacturing base to be destroyed, and we are effectively handing it over to our economic and military adversary on a gold platter (China). Even Japan is starting to be concerned about its manufacturing sector. In an intriguing article by Hans Greimel in Automotive News on November 12, 2010, he stated that there is great fear in the Japanese manufacturing sector of "Hollowing Out"– the problem the U.S. has experienced for the last thirty years in its manufacturing industry. With the Japanese tradition of lifetime employment, cutting workers at home would unleash a political outcry according to Mr. Greimel. However, he also stated "reports of the death of Japanese manufacturing are greatly exaggerated." (In late 2010, vehicles sales in Japan reached a 40 year low.)  James Simms wrote in the December 4-5, 2010 issue of the Wall Street Journal that a new Japanese survey shows that "Japanese manufacturers expect overseas production to account for 35% of revenues in three years...(versus) 23% a decade ago." Even Japan now realizes that outsourcing destroys jobs, tax revenues, the vitality of a country, its future well-being, etc.

## Back-Office Outsourcing

There has also been a growing outsourcing of U.S. back-office processing jobs including call centers, especially to India. Even product development activities are moving offshore with labor cost savings virtually the only fingerprints to transfer these jobs overseas. Some U.S. companies have also established large overseas R&D facilities employing thousands of PhD's. During the October 9, 2007 Republican "Presidential Candidates Debate," one of the moderators–the highly respected Gerald Seib of the Wall Street Journal–stated "five million jobs have been lost since 1989 due to outsourcing overseas." President Bush stated in an October 11, 2007 interview with the Wall Street Journal that "we have lost our confidence in the ability to compete internationally."

Many American companies have turned into marketing outfits, which are why we don't have a product safety-net anymore, and thus have constant product quality scandals from China. The outsourcing of value-added functions overseas deprives Americans of millions of jobs (examples include: Mattel, Nike, consumer electronic companies, furniture corporations, textile, etc.). U.S. companies spent <u>trillions</u> of dollars on outsourcing. An article in the September 3, 2007 issue of Fortune stated, "Americans and others in developed economies are selling the world's most expensive labor."

America is also losing knowledge-based higher-skilled white-collar functions to overseas locations because of lower cost and because distance in today's telecommunication system is no longer an obstacle. IBM already has 43,000 employees in India, according to Robyn Meredith's insightful book, "The Elephant and the Dragon: the Rise of India and China and What it Means for All of U.S." In an interview in the fall, 2007 issue of Bostonia, the alumni magazine of Boston University, Ms. Meredith stated that IBM runs information technology systems for 225 of its client companies entirely from India, and "Accenture has more employees in India than in the United States." On December 7, 2010, Bloomberg, citing the Wall Street Journal, stated that H-P is establishing three new outsourcing centers in India! Further, Ms. Meredith stated "by 2008, the United States will have moved 2.3 million service-industry jobs overseas." According to the same book, wages for overseas service-industry jobs are "typically one-half to one-tenth of Western rates," which is probably why Forrester Research, renowned for its research on future technology trends, estimated that by 2015 3.3 million service jobs would go offshore. Moreover, the world-famous University of California, Berkley, in an October, 2003 study stated that a ferocious new wave of outsourcing of white-collar jobs is sweeping the United States…the trend could leave as many as 14 million service jobs in the United States vulnerable."

## **Impact on American Families**

In a November 1, 2010 article in Time magazine by Fareed Zakaria entitled "Restoring The American Dream," he stated, "the grim reality is that technology and globalization are shattering the middle-class." Moreover, he pointed out "The U.S. is not the land of opportunity it was…relative income mobility of a generation over the previous one…is below Denmark, Norway, Finland, Canada, Sweden, Germany and France." (Heartbreakingly, I am experiencing this trend in my own family of six college-educated children, four of whom graduated from the prestigious University of Michigan, one from the University of California, and one from Western Michigan University which recently received a $100 million anonymous donation. Our two girls have Master's degrees and a third has almost finished her MBA requirements.)  PIMCO's Bill Gross stated in December 2010 that "job growth is moving inexorably to developing economies because they are more competitive… jobs, in other words, can never come back to the level or the prosperity reminiscent of the 1960s."

Professor Alan Binder of Princeton University summarized our "dickensian economy" (his term, December 17, 2010 Wall Street Journal): "Real average hourly earnings (excluding fringe benefits) now stand roughly at 1974 levels." Median household income (adjusted for inflation) declined from $49,244 in 1999 to $48,200 in 2006. Late 2010 data from the Census Bureau reveals a continuing

negative trend. Inflation adjusted median household income decreased from $50,600 in 2000 to $49,800 in 2009
(the poverty rate in 2009 was at the highest level since
1994). At the same time, however, productivity in the
manufacturing sector improved from 3.6% in 1995 to 5.0%
in 2005. Concurrently, the Labor Department stated that
"unit labor costs" declined by 1.5% in 2009 and 2010 while
productivity increased roughly 3.5% during these years.
Corporate profits increased from $438 billion in 1990 to
almost $1.4 trillion in 2005 and reached a record $1.7 trillion in 2007. While American workers are struggling, 2010
corporate profits are estimated near the 2007 record after declining to $1.3 trillion in 2009. Companies have ex-
tremely healthy balance sheets with cash and other liquid
assets in excess of $2 trillion. Corporate profit margins are
projected at "9.5%, on average, in 2011...and well above
10-year historical averages of 7.3%" according to the May
2011 edition of SmartMoney. Further, corporate taxes as
a percent of GDP are presently 2% compared with about
5% during the 1950s. In my opinion, American workers are
not getting their share of the pie.

In an October 29, 2007 interview on NBC's "Nightly News
with Brian Williams," a Harvard University professor stated
"today's two wage-earner middle class families are not
better of than a one wage-earner family a generation
ago." Even in 1886, President Rutherford Hayes candidly
acknowledged, "labor does not get its fair share of the

wealth it creates" according to Noel Jacob Kent's book, "America in 1900." Concurrently, the mega rich are earning undreamt-of sums of money. The New York Times stated in an October 16, 2010 article "the share of total income going to the top one percent of earners, which stood at 8.9 percent in 1976, rose to 23.5% by 2007, but during the same period, the average inflation-adjusted hourly wage declined by more than 7 percent." (Professor Sachs of Columbia University stated on the February 22, 2011 "Morning Joe" on MSNBC that the top 1% of the income bracket controlled 10% of total income in 1980 compared with 25% today.) Income inequality is now at the highest level since the Census Bureau started tracking household income in 1967, and the U.S. has one of the highest levels of income inequality among high-income industrialized countries. The average CEO earns 364 times as much as the average worker (August 30, 2007 "Fox & Friends" television) compared with 36 times in 1976 (October 31, 2007 NBC "Today"), and 24 times in 1965 (BNET, April 28, 2008).

## America, Fight Back

"It's Late and We Are Running Out of Gas" (Rick Nelson's song) because these are Malthusian predictions relating to future U.S. job losses with its negative impact on the livelihood of millions of Americans, especially with the projected slow economic growth. We're in the thick of a fray, which is destroying the fabric of our society. What economic sectors remain where we can experience a nucleus of job growth–low-paying Wal-Mart and McDonald jobs? This is why I consider Ford's Mr. Mulally's "shock-and-awe" display of American economic combat so vitally important. With lightning rod speed, and without taking the GM and Chrysler easy way out of misery, Mr. Mulally has taken a formerly floundering American icon out of "obscure darkness" and returned it once again to its historic place in the world automotive industry.

America, we can do it. Asia is waging economic war against us, which, of course, is all part of capitalism. We are in a hot war for survival, and can't expect help from our economic enemies. (China needs to generate in excess of 25 million new jobs annually. According to the CNBW report cited previously, roughly 30% of Chinese students study engineering compared with 4% in the United States. Attachment II provides further details about the rulers of this century.) (Even in my daughter's MBA class at a major university, all her professors are from overseas except one American finance professor.) We should be in a "State of Alarm" and should stop being worried about creating "frosty" relations once we finally decide to stand up for America. This is not a "Dr. Strangelove" affair because there is no such thing as "Soul Mates" between countries. It is a real Wirtschaftskrieg (economic war). Let's become "blunt and self-assured" which is how King Abdullah of Saudi Arabia is described in Wikileaks. We will eventually buckle under to these countries because our trade deficits and federal debt borrowings moves more and more power to the Asian nations.

I am tired of continuing to defend Japan and South Korea at our expense. Throughout most of the post-World War II period, Japanese defense expenditures have been below one percent of GDP. This allowed the Japanese to focus on economic development, which resulted in the "miracle" decades of the 1950s to the early 1980s. Since then, they have experienced "lost decades" of economic growth, which is no excuse not to carry their fair share of the Western defense burden. Even today, with the world ablaze in conflicts, Japan continues to spend less than one percent of its GDP on defense (ranking the country number 148 in the world behind such heavy-weights as Brunei, Panama, Bhutan, Burkina Faso, etc.). U.S. defense spending totals roughly $665 billion (14 times Japanese expenditures) or in excess of 4% of GDP.

Self-interest is the only thing that matters. The December 6, 2010 edition of the Wall Street Journal stated, "U.S.

public support for free trade has eroded amid the recession and the lack of Presidential leadership." I believe the Wall Street Journal is missing the real issue–we are sick and tired of being taken as one-way trade lackies. (Incidentally, December 6 is a big day for children in Germany when Saint Nicholas brings them gifts in his rucksack. I am not expecting any from our dear trading partners.)

First, let's have a level playing field, especially vis-à-vis China which has a "state-run economy" according to the February 23, 2011 "Dylan Ratigan Show" on MSNBC. Even a Boeing executive, who does a lot of business in China, stated on the same show that the playing field is tilting toward China. We must stop the Chinese currency manipulation and insist on two-way trade. Unfortunately, it is an unrealistic battle plan because the cards are stacked against us since we owe billions to our economic adversary.

The borrowings are putting America into the opponent's clutches, and we can't shake off the yoke. Begging Asians to end currency manipulation is useless and embarrassing. If we keep getting no actions from the Asians, we will have to institute trade restrictions, which Bill Gross of PIMCO claims is the wrong attack plan. Even Adam Smith in his 1776 book "Wealth of Nations" argued against protectionist tariffs. I also know from history that it is lose-lose for all involved, including America. The 1930 Smoot-Hawley high tariff legislation demonstrated it, and some experts claim that it made the Great Depression even worse. However, before we institute such drastic actions, we should give our trade negotiators one more chance to settle the score. Years and years of negotiations only resulted in empty Chinese promises. This time, I suggest we do to our trade negotiators what Hernando Cortez did in 1519 when he attacked the great, honorable, and civilized Aztec Empire, which ended in its destruction. He burned his boats; thus, it was a life or death struggle for the Conquistadors—win the battle or die!

Secondly, we have spent hundreds and hundreds of billions of dollars defending Japan and South Korea during the last 60 years. Have they sent any CARE packages to America as my beloved U.S.A. did after World War II to the starved Germans including myself? No, instead, they flood our open market with cars and created huge U.S. trade deficits. Our economic adversaries had Schadenfreude when America's pride and joy—the formerly powerful auto industry—sank to the bottom of Lake Michigan. To be honest, they didn't give a shit. Accordingly, effective in 2012, I would demand that Japan and Korea must pay the <u>full burden</u> of the defense expenditures we incur in defending our Asian "friends." I have no umbrage against them because I actually admire their work ethic. Also, this is not a repeat of the 1920s anti-Asian crusade; it is simply fairness for being taken as suckers (I traveled the world on business—I know what they think of us—"softies").

Unfortunately, it will never happen. There are 37,000 registered lobbyists in Washington pulling strings. The hired guns of these countries will assure that this idea will never be implemented because John Q – public has no effective and powerful voice in Washington!

# CHAPTER 4

❃ ❃ ❃

# THE (FORMER) PRIDE AND JOY OF AMERICA

## Automotive Development Process

Automobile development is a complex and costly process, with long-lead times. Today's vehicles require millions of software codes; the auto industry accounts for over 60% of the global market for microelectronics or electronic components (a typical car has more than 60 or more microprocessors on board).

A totally redesigned vehicle (new platform, new exterior, new interior, possibly even a new engine and transmission) often involves billions of dollars in expenditures, and over 3,000 parts. A new powertrain costs up to $1 billion and takes over 5 years to develop according to the Alliance of Automobile Manufacturers. Auto companies have developed extensive program control systems to follow the key measurable on a daily basis. The program status is constantly compared with the program objectives, and the plans for corrective actions are developed, if necessary. The programs include: quality, safety, fuel economy, performance, environmental issues, program timing, weight, styling, product image, new product features, volumes, manufacturing plans, expenditures, cost and profitability.

Development of a totally redesigned vehicle takes in excess of three years, and involves thousands of experts all working in sync, like an expensive Swiss watch. They include: program managers, designers, engineers, product planners, quality, manufacturing, purchasing, environmental, safety, technology, marketing, program timing, labor, human resources, information technology, communications and legal experts. (The oil and gas industry has the same long-lead time and costly investment.)

Product planning managers must anticipate the shifting consumer tastes, and the economic environment, including future gasoline prices, when planning a car to be introduced in approximately three years. The 1958 model Ford Edsel arrived at the worst time because the U.S. economy had entered into a recession, which negatively affected sales (many people also questioned Edsel's styling).

The second most extensive change is called "re-engineered." It includes major changes in parts, and possibly platform modifications to improve safety, fuel economy, ride, etc.

"Freshened" is the term used by Automotive News to reflect minor exterior changes. Generally speaking, they have a minor impact in generating increased sales.

A report from Booz &Co., summarized in the November 15, 2010 issue of Automotive News, stated that the worldwide auto industry spent $73 billion on R&D in 2009. This ranks the auto industry third behind computing/electronics and healthcare. Toyota Motor Corporation had the largest R&D budget with $7.8 billion. GM ranked number eleven with $6 billion and Ford was number twenty with $4.9 billion.

## U.S. Auto Industry Volumes

U.S. automotive sales reached a record-high of 17.4 million units in 2000. During the 2000-2007 period, sales averaged 16.8 million units. The economic meltdown since 2007 reduced sales to 10.4 million in 2009–the lowest level since 1970. In 2010, sales increased to 11.6 billion units.

In 1980, passenger cars accounted for 78% of U.S. industry sales. By 1990, the ratio was 66:32; in 2000 the ratio had narrowed to 52:48. By 2008, trucks outsold cars for the first time ever. However, the economic recession has reversed the trend because many typical truck and SUV buyers lost their job or business during the downturn. For example, according to Automotive News, Ford F-series truck sales decreased from 691,000 in 2007 to 414,000 in 2009. Ford Explorer sales declined from 138,000 to 78,000 during the same period, and Ford Expedition sales contracted from 90,000 to 32,000 units. Concurrently, the resale value of large SUV's collapsed (recovered since 2009).

Imports have steadily increased their sales and market share during the last fifty years. They reached record 6.7 million units in 2004 and 2006. Import penetration improved from 7% in 1960 to 13% in 1970, and 25% in 1980. In 1990, the import share declined to 21%, possibly because of stronger domestic small car entries such as the Ford Focus.

In the 2000s, imports increased their share to almost 50% in 2009 (49% in 2010). The average annual import volumes

were over 6 million units, which is equivalent to about 25
assembly plants (250,000 unit capacity per facility).

### U.S. VEHICLE SALES  (000's)

| YEAR | CARS | TRUCKS | TOTAL | MEMO: IMPORTS |
|------|------|--------|-------|---------------|
| 2010 | 5,988 | 5,602 | 11,590 | 5,699 |
| 2009 | 5,692 | 4,739 | 10,431 | 5,209 |
| 2008 | 7,042 | 6,204 | 13,246 | 6,163 |
| 2007 | 7,885 | 8,269 | 16,154 | 6,628 |
| 2006 | 8,131 | 8,430 | 16,561 | 6,712 |
| 2005 | 7,964 | 9,033 | 16,997 | 6,630 |
| 2000 | 9,005 | 8,397 | 17,402 | 5,993 |
| 1990 | 9,300 | 4,846 | 14,146 | 3,034 |
| 1980 | 8,979 | 2,487 | 11,466 | 2,884 |
| 1970 | 8,400 | 1,811 | 10,211 | 1,346 |
| 1960 | 6,641 | 963 | 7,604 | 536 |
| 1951 | 5,164 | 1,111 | 6,275 | 21 |

Source: American Automobile Manufacturers Association (1951-1990 data);
Automotive News (1990-2010).

## U.S. Auto Industry Market Shares

Around 1960, GM had a U.S. market share of about 46%, and Ford's share was approximately 30%, with Chrysler's share around 10%. Thus, the "Big Three" controlled around 85% of the market! GM's and Ford's share gradually declined in the 1960s and 1970s, with the loss accelerating in the 1980s and 1990s. The roof collapsed in the 2000's, with GM's share declining from 28% in 2000 and to 19.1% in 2010. Ford's share decreased from 23.7% to 16.5% between 2000 and 2010. However, for the first time since 1995 Ford increased its market share in 2010 back to back as a result of its highly competitive products.

The biggest winner has been Toyota, which increased its market share by almost eight percentage points between 2000-2009. Hyundai/Kia and Honda followed with over five percentage point gains. In 2010, Toyota suffered a setback as a result of its bungled recalls. The hottest car company presently is Hyundai with outstanding products, good quality and attractive styling, excellent management, and support from the Korean government.

## U.S. AUTOMOTIVE MARKET SHARES [a]

| YEAR | GM | FORD | TOYOTA | HONDA | HYUNDAI/KIA |
|------|------|------|--------|-------|-------------|
| 2010 | 19.1% | 16.5% | 15.3% | 10.6% | 7.7% |
| 2009 | 19.8 | 15.3 | 17.0 | 11.1 | 7.1 |
| 2008 | 22.1 | 15.1 | 16.5 | 10.6 | 5.0 |
| 2007 | 23.4 | 15.6 | 16.0 | 9.4 | 4.7 |
| 2006 | 24.1 | 17.1 | 15.0 | 8.9 | 4.4 |
| 2005 | 25.8 | 18.2 | 13.0 | 8.4 | 4.2 |
| 2000 | 28.2 | 23.7 | 9.1 | 6.5 | 2.3 |
| 1990 | 35.3 | 23.9 | 7.6 | 6.0 | 1.0 |
| 1980 | 44.1 | 20.5 | 6.2 | 3.3 | 0 |
| 1970 | 38.9 | 28.3 | 2.0 | 0.1 | 0 |
| 1961 | 45.7 | 29.3 | 0 | 0 | 0 |

(a)    Ward's data is somewhat different from Automotive News and company reports, but it provides a 50 year sales history not available from other sources.

Source: WardsAuto.com

# Vehicle Ownership

There has been a significant increase in licensed drivers in the U.S. during the last 50 years–from 87 million in 1960 to 220 million in 2010. Concurrently, vehicle registrations increased from 74 million to 250 million during the same period.

| YEAR | LICENSED DRIVERS (Millions) | VEHICLE REGISTRATIONS (Millions) |
|------|------|------|
| 1960 | 87 | 74 |
| 1970 | 108 | 108 |
| 1980 | 145 | 156 |
| 1990 | 167 | 189 |
| 2000 | 191 | 218 |
| 2010 | 220 | 250 |

Source: U.S. Department of Commerce

## Automobile Production by State

The Midwest has been the epicenter of auto production for the last 110 years. It remains the foundation for U.S. vehicle production, although its influence is declining with the emergence of numerous new foreign assembly plants in the South. This trend is expected to accelerate with three new transplants coming on stream.

### SHARE OF U.S. VEHICLE PRODUCTION

| STATE | 2009 | 2008 |
|-------|------|------|
| Michigan | 20.4% | 21.7% |
| Ohio | 14.0 | 17.4 |
| Indiana | 9.6 | 7.0 |
| Illinois | 3.1 | 5.0 |
| Sub-Total | 47.1% | 51.1% |
| All Other | 52.9 | 48.9 |
| Total | 100.0% | 100.0% |

*Source: Automotive News 2004 & 2010 Market Data Books, 1994 AAMA Motor Vehicle Facts & Figures.*

The North American Free Trade Agreement (NAFTA) between the U.S., Canada and Mexico, which became effective on January 1, 1994, eliminated trade barriers between the three countries. Canada and Mexico are accounting for an increasing share of North American vehicle production. In 1977, Canada's share was 12%; in 2010 it was 17% according to Wardsauto.com website. Mexico's share improved from 2% in 1977 to 19% in 2010 because of significantly lower labor costs.

# Passenger Car Fuel Economy

In 1975, primarily in response to the 1973 OPEC oil crisis, Congress enacted the first Corporate Average Fuel Economy (CAFE) legislation. In subsequent years, the CAFE requirements have been raised; it must reach 35.5 MPG by 2016. Average "Big Three" fuel economy has increased from 15.9 MPG in 1975 to 32.8 MPG in 2009, a 100% improvement despite more powerful and faster cars. The MPG improvements are probably the result of major powertrain technology advances, a roughly 400-pound reduction in curb weight, and the trend toward smaller cars.

### PASSENGER CARS MPG

| YEAR | U.S. DOMESTIC CARS | CAFE STANDARDS |
|------|--------------------|----------------|
| 1955 | 16.1 | - |
| 1965 | 15.9 | - |
| 1975 | 15.9 | - |
| 1985 | 26.3 | 27.5 |
| 1990 | 26.9 | 27.5 |
| 2000 | 28.7 | 27.5 |
| 2005 | 30.5 | 27.5 |
| 2009 | 32.8 | 27.5 |

*Source: U.S. Department of Commerce*

# U.S. Gasoline Price Trends

From 1950 to 1973, gasoline prices in the U.S. ranged from $0.27/gallon (about $2.20 today inflation adjusted) to $0.39/gallon. The 1973 Israel-Arab War, and the subsequent OPEC oil embargo, resulted in an almost 40% price increase in 1973 (official data show $0.39/gallon; I remember prices doubling to $0.50/gallon. OPEC, which was formed in 1960, increased oil prices from $3.60/barrel in 1970 to $8.55 in 1973 and to $38.00 in 1979). In 1980, gasoline prices reached the one-dollar mark for the first time ever ($2.66 in today's dollars). The $4 level was exceeded in July 2008, which resulted in a significant increase in small car sales, and a total collapse of the resale value of SUV's.

| YEAR | AVERAGE U.S. GASOLINE PRICES (Unleaded) | MEMO: GERMANY |
|---|---|---|
| 1950 | $0.27 | NA |
| 1970 | 0.36 | NA |
| 1980 | 1.25 | NA |
| 1990 | 1.16 | $2.65 |
| 2000 | 1.51 | 3.45 |
| 2005 | 2.30 | 5.66 |
| 2011 (March 1) | 3.20 | 7.90 |

Source: 1950-2005 data, U.S. Department Energy

# Passenger Car Horse Power

Fuel economy has improved sharply during the last thirty years; yet, average passenger car horsepower has also increased–from 132 hp in 1990 to 247 hp in 2009 or an increase of almost 90%. It appears that Americans still enjoy that feeling of power, which is difficult to understand since most interstate highways have a maximum speed limit of approximately 65- 70 mph. (The Autobahn has speed limits on only 50% of the expressway.)

| YEAR | AVERAGE CAR HORSEPOWER |
|------|------------------------|
| 1930 | 70 |
| 1955 | 140 |
| 1980 | 110 |
| 1990 | 132 |
| 2000 | 165 |
| 2009 | 247 |

Source: Autoblog

# Fortune 500 Rankings of U.S. Auto Companies

U.S. auto companies have historically been the largest corporations in America in terms of sales. From 1955 to 2000, except in 1975, GM was the leading company. Ford Motor Company, which was not ranked in 1955 because it was a private company, was always among the top five. The auto crisis of 2008-2010 reduced the ranking of Ford and GM to eighth and fifteenth position, respectively.

### U.S. AUTO COMPANY RANKINGS

| COMPANY | 1955 | 1965 | 1975 | 1990 | 2000 | 2009 |
|---|---|---|---|---|---|---|
| GM | 1 | 1 | 2 | 1 | 1 | 15 |
| Ford | NA | 3 | 3 | 2 | 4 | 8 |
| Exxon | 2 | 2 | 1 | 3 | 3 | 2 |
| GE | 4 | 4 | - | 5 | 5 | 4 |
| Wal-Mart | - | - | - | - | 2 | 1 |

Source: Fortune Magazine Website

## U.S. Auto Industry in Crisis

No industry had a greater impact on the post World War II American culture and way of life as automobiles (the same applies to computers starting in the 1970's). The demand for cars after the Second World War was insatiable. According to Automotive News, approximately 80 million vehicles were sold between 1950 and 1965. (The National Highway Act in 1958 created a solid highway infrastructure which encouraged automobile ownership.) Another 117 million cars and trucks were sold between 1966 and 1975. The car was not a toy for the wealthy anymore as before World War II. A new passenger car, in addition to a new house, was high on the priority list of Americans, with all the money they had saved during the war.

A car was very important in the mindset of Americans because people judged and identified themselves by the car they owned, with the Cadillac the ultimate status symbol. Demand was fueled by low levels of unemployment, rapidly increasing disposable income, two wage earner families, the trend toward the suburbs, low gasoline prices, and America's love affair with cars, even if they had tail fins in the 1950's. For example, "average income of workers virtually doubled between 1941-1945" according to DirecTV November 17, 2007 XM Music channel. Moreover, between 1947-1970, median family income increased at an annual rate of 3.7% above inflation according to James Quinn at "TheBurningPlatform.com." Professor Robert B.

Reich, in his 2010 book entitled "Aftershock," described 1947-1975 as the period of "Great prosperity." (Since then, the rate of growth has been around 0.3%).

The automotive sector remains the heartbeat of every industrialized country, and its most important element. China and India are the latest developing countries to embrace the automotive industry as the catalyst for industrialization. The bellwether, and the underpinning of the U.S. manufacturing sector, is the indigenous American automotive industry, which consumes roughly 13% of steel production, 35% of iron, 75% of rubber, 20% of zinc and 20% of aluminum according to the 1994 "Facts Book" of the American Automobile Manufacturers Association (the percentages are lower today because of the large increase of imported cars). [26]

- The U.S. auto and parts sector has over 1.8 million employees according to the Center for Automotive Research (CAR). According to the Executive Office of The President of the United States, "54 supplier-related bankruptcies occurred in 2009." [27]

- The U.S. auto industry has the second highest number of employees among 50 industry sectors in the United States; only retailing has more jobs. The auto sector is in chaos, as evidenced by heavy losses, many shuttered plants, and the elimination of hundreds of thousands of middle-class jobs. (The powerful German automotive sector is responsible for over 10% of jobs in Germany.)

- According to a 2010 study by the Center for Automotive Research, "the automotive industry spends 16 to 18 billion dollars a year on research and product development, half a trillion dollars on employee compensation, and is a major driver of the overall manufacturing contribution to the GDP." [28] The auto sector contributes about 2.2% to the GDP (one-half the share of the late 1970's).

- "Since 2000, the number of "Big Three" assembly plants in North America has dropped to 40 from 66." [29] More plant closings have been announced. Auto industry employment declined by 410,000 between 2000 and 2008. In 2008, the auto industry lost over 400,000 jobs. [30] The job losses are primarily related to U.S. "Big Three" sales declines, radical restructuring within the auto industry, and dramatic manufacturing efficiency improvements–from 13.4 vehicles per employee in 1992 to 23.4 in 2006, according to the Center for Automotive Research in Ann Arbor, Michigan. [31] The productivity improvements clearly demonstrate the positive mantra of change taking place in the U.S. auto industry, and that their mindset is not anchored in the past anymore.

- Over 200,000 auto <u>parts</u> production jobs have been lost since 2000. This is primarily due to the substantial sales decline in North America, plus the rapid growth in auto parts imports, which increased to $93 billion in recent years, an improvement of 300% since 1991. [32] Two of the U.S. auto supplier companies–Delphi (spun-off by

GM) and Visteon (spun-off by Ford) filed for bankruptcy in recent years, resulting in the closing of many plants and the loss of thousands of jobs (Visteon emerged from bankruptcy protection in October 2010). As late as 2004 the auto supplier industry employed almost 800,000 people. [33]

• UAW active membership has declined from 1.5 million in 1979 to 390,000 today in the auto, aerospace and agricultural sectors involving 1,700 employers. Some experts believe that unions are becoming an antiquated way of doing business. Every key industry in which unions play a powerful role, such as the airline, steel, rubber, automotive and auto parts sectors are in trouble. Overall union membership as a percent of the working population is 12% in the U.S. (28% at its peak in 1954), 19% in Germany, 68% in Sweden, 33% in Italy and 27% in the United Kingdom.

• The three domestic U.S. auto companies are major contributors to minority-owned firms. Ford Motor Company, General Motors and Chrysler each purchase more than one billion dollars annually from minority-owned companies. Ford alone purchased over $30 billion in the 2000s from minority suppliers. Who will support these minority-owned companies if we continue to outsource our manufacturing sector?

## Impact of U.S. Job Losses

The job losses in the manufacturing sector are creating a growing underclass in America because of disappearing prospects for unskilled labor. Moreover, three quarter of the people who lost their manufacturing jobs end up getting a lower-paying position. As Professor Robert Reich stated in his book "Aftershock," probably the "hardest loss for middle-class Americans will be giving up the expectation that the future has to be materially better. We're used to moving up in America, surpassing ourselves, trading up."

Outsourcing of U.S. manufacturing jobs could threaten our national security. For example, machine tooling made in China is 40% less expensive than American-made tooling. [34] Many stamping companies are sourcing tooling to China and the U.S. is also sourcing components for nuclear reactors, ball bearings and sensitive electronic components overseas.

Approximately the 3.3 million American job losses are predicted due to outsourcing by 2015 (not all are manufacturing jobs) in Robyn Meredith's compelling book, "The Elephant and the Dragon." [35] This could result in annual U.S. lost wages of $165 billion ($50,000 times 3.3 million), and an associated annual loss of roughly $25 billion of employer/employee Social Security contributions. Thus, an additional fiscal burden will be created.

The collapse of the domestic auto industry has a devastating impact on cash-strapped midwestern states, with Michigan having lost 800,000 jobs since 2000. People in the Heartland of America have little hope for a better future for their children (in the epicenter of the auto industry woes, Detroit, 5,000 people applied for 350 low-paying jobs at Wal-Mart three years ago). It is doubtful that U.S. hourly workers, especially in the Midwest, will ever see the blue sky again. This includes millions of black workers.

In addition, who will help the less fortunate and most vulnerable? U.S. based companies play a significant role, and it is an important tenet of their business philosophy. For example, according to the 2000-2009 Ford "Sustainability Reports," Ford's philanthropic contributions totaled $1,017,000,000 between 1999-2009!! The $10 billion Ford Foundation endowment donated over $500 million in 2010 to worthy causes, the second largest amount among the thousands of U.S. philanthropies in America. Ford Motor Company, General Motors and Chrysler have given hundreds of millions of dollars to the United Fund and similar organizations. (Despite its financial problems, GM announced in mid-December 2010 a record $23 million donation to United Way.) What's the record of Japan-based Toyota, Nissan and Honda's U.S. charity performance?

The near-demise of the entire U.S. automobile sector parallels the British auto industry's history. According to an article by Richard Northedge on May 13, 2009 in "CBS Moneywatch.com," entitled "When the Sun Set on the British Auto Industry," the U.K. industry was once very strong and controlled its home market. However, "the management of Great Britain's largest carmakers proved slow to adapt to changing markets and were handcuffed by their workers as well. Output at over-manned plants was hit by constant labor disputes from the 1950s, making them unproductive and unprofitable." Mighty British Leyland—the pride of the United Kingdom—was nationalized in 1975.

## Auto Industry Culprits

The two most destructive auto industry stakeholders are the bad decisions by CEO's (acquisitions, uncompetitive products, etc.), and the "take no prisoner" UAW. Both led their respective organizations to a path of self-destruction during the last thirty years. (I come from a union household and have no predisposition toward the union since my father, a skilled tool and die maker, belonged to the powerful German IG Metal Gewerkschaft).

What happened? The 1936-1937 sit-down strikes at GM by the newly formed UAW led to the unionization of the U.S. automobile industry. (The strike leader, Walter P. Reuther, stated in a 1950 "March of Time" newsreel shown on a January 1, 2011 TCM broadcast that "people are more important than profits." He failed to mention that without profits, there wouldn't be any jobs.) Governor Pawzenty of Minnesota stated it correctly in the December 13, 2010 edition of the Wall Street Journal "the rise of the labor movement...was a triumph for America's working class." However, as it happens to most of us, once we sniff power, we want more. For example, UAW leaders led members in a 113-day strike in 1945 to get their share of the pie. Based on the website of Local2209.org, Bill LeFever of the Wayne State University Walter P. Reuther Library is quoted as stating that there were 10 long strikes until the disastrous 2008 American Axle strike. The strikes I remember are the two months 1970 strike against GM, which ended with a 13%

pay raise (it was at the time when imports made big gains in America). The AP dispatch from Detroit at that time claimed that the strike cost GM $2.2 billion and pushed the country into a recession. The strike, which impacted me, was the UAW 1976 strike against Ford Motor Company, which shut down the company. (The 1982-1983 UAW strikes against Caterpillar "put the company on the brink of collapse" according to press reports.)

In a 1998 article in USA Today, Micheline Maynard stated that GM experienced "two dozen UAW strikes in the 1990s." What really illustrates the UAW's mindset is the 2007 UAW strike against GM. Flush with an $800 million strike fund, and beyond comprehension while "Rome was burning," the UAW launched a two-day strike in September 2007 against GM–a company in dire straights. GM also experienced costly local strikes.

In my opinion, the most militant UAW leader in recent times was the late Stephen Yokich (1995-2002) who marched to the beat of a different drummer. On various websites he was called a "militant firebrand with an explosive temper." He is one of the leaders blamed for the eventual demise of Saturn because during his tenure he authorized a strike at Saturn in 1998, which poisoned the atmosphere. (Launched in 1985, Saturn was the first new concept in the U.S. to fight imports with a unique labor agreement including elimination of work rules and reduced number of job classifications. Saturn achieved the highest quality among U.S. cars, and recorded the lowest absenteeism in the industry.) He also led the UAW on a 54-day bitter and crippling strike against GM during his presidency. However, he was highly respected by UAW workers. (Don Ephlin, the imaginative UAW leader at GM chose collaboration to confrontation.)

Rod Lache, the auto analyst at Deutsche Bank, calls strikes "lose/lose propositions" (the exact opposite of the "win-win" labor relations in Japan). Unionized American autoworkers appeared to have no fear of getting fired because the union protects them (almost like employees in the federal government where less than 0.5% ever get fired because of protection from powerful government unions). For example, according to Brink Lindsey's book "The Age of Abundance," "in the auto industry, absences from the job at Ford and General Motors doubled between 1961 and 1970. On a typical day in 1970, five percent of GM's workers were missing; on Fridays and Mondays absenteeism was more like 10 percent." This requires a costly relief pool. Mr. Brinkley also cited a Fortune magazine article about sabotage and vandalism (paint scratched, screws left in critical safety parts, etc.).

A 2003 Ward's report stated that absenteeism in the auto industry is 5% compared with 2.5% overall in the U.S. based on a 2006 CCH survey. A lengthy study by the National Academy of Engineering (NAE) claimed a "U.S. auto industry absentee's rate of 5.7% compared with 1.0%

in Japan." The U.S. data includes medical and personal absences. The NAE estimated "unplanned" absentees at 4.5% compared with 0.75% in Japan. According to a 2009 article in "Site Selection On Line Mexico," an executive of a Ford/Getrag Joint Venture, which is building a $500 million plant in Mexico, stated that "turnover and absenteeism rates are very favorable in Mexico." A 2004 report by "Workers Comp Insider" stated, "For every one percentage point change in absenteeism, the company (Ford) states that it spends $100 million." GM spends $125 million according to Search DetroitNews.com. (Hourly workers also receive 17 paid holidays and up to five weeks of vacation.) Reportedly, workers at Japanese transplants in the U.S. experience lower absenteeism rates.

The overriding power of the UAW can also be illustrated with the following anecdote. In October 1986 I completed a comprehensive review of a major Ford components operation. Division management had projected continuing roaring financial results in its Five Year Business Plan. My analysis came to a completely opposite conclusion, which I presented to a certain high-level Ford executive in charge of over 75,000 people. I proposed sale of the division ASAP with a conservative potential value of $1.2 billion. The plan never even reached first base because of labor issues (about 15 years later, the division was sold at a significant loss!). This illustrates union power, which is why 66% of respondents to a 2009 PEW Research Center poll stated that labor unions are "too powerful." (56% in 1999.) Moreover, an early 2010 PEW poll found that only 41% have a favorable opinion of unions compared with 58% in 2007. These results are consistent with Gallup poll findings–48% favorable in 2009 versus 59% in 2008.

The enormous power of the UAW can also be illustrated by the Chrysler bailout example cited in George Melloan's book entitled "The Great Money Binge." He claims that President Obama's auto task force "simply told the senior creditors that their rights would be subordinated to those of the UAW."

# CHAPTER 5

❈ ❈ ❈

# MARCHING TOGETHER TO THE SAME (SOMETIMES WRONG) TUNE

## Background

For over eighty years (except for strike affected GM results), General Motors held bragging rights as the "top gun" in Detroit. Ford Motor Company played second fiddle, and often felt intimidated by its much larger crosstown rival. During the glory days of the "Big Three," GM generally had a 2:1 market share advantage over Ford (roughly 50% vs. 25% and sometimes over 55%). Ford Division held its own against Chevrolet Division, however, the BOP's (Buick, Oldsmobile, Pontiac) totally dominated the medium-priced segment versus the Mercury Division, although the Mercury brand sold on average almost 400,000 units annually between 1960 and 1990, or 13% of all Ford U.S. sales of 122 million units during this period. Cadillac outsold Lincoln, and Ford did not have a counterpart to the GMC Division. To strengthen its position in the profitable medium-priced segment, Ford introduced a chrome laden Edsel in the 1958 model year (the car was named for Henry Ford's only son). The car sold poorly, and was discontinued in 1960 at a cost of $350 million. Timing was also unfortunate because of the 1957-1958 recession.

# The U.S. Marching Band Until the Early 1970s

Following is a synopsis of Ford's and GM's common history and practices:

• Both companies have a long history of over 100 years in Metro Detroit. (Before the 1930s Depression, the U.S. auto industry employed over 470,000 people.)

• Both are located within a stone's-throw of each other (GM in Detroit and Ford in suburban Dearborn). They are not too fond of each other. It is similar to the hockey battles for Commonwealth Avenue supremacy between Boston University (my alma mater) and the boys from Boston College, or the great annual football rivalry between the University of Michigan and Ohio State University. The fear of losing the game, and the associated humiliation is probably more overriding than winning the game.

• GM and Ford are the only companies (in addition to Chrysler) who survived the shakeout of the early years of the U.S. auto industry. According to "Free Database," there were "originally 500 auto manufacturers. By 1908, there were only 200; and in 1917 only 23 remained." Automotive News'1996 "American Automobile Centennial" listed 40 major nameplates with 178,000 sales in 1910 and 85 in 1920 with U.S. sales of 1.6 million units. John P. Kotter, in his book entitled "A Sense of Urgency" claims that "well over 90 percent of the car companies that existed in the early 1900s were gone by the 1940s." In the 1950s and early 1960, Packard, Studebaker, Hudson, Nash and Kaiser also ceased production.

- The auto and oil companies were the paramount sectors of the U.S. industry for many post-World War II years. GM and Ford were, and to some degree still are, the backbone of the once mighty U.S. manufacturing industry, which is vitally important "for its jobs, technology, wealth creation, trading balance, and prestige." [36] By 1992, according to the 1994 AAMA Facts Book, the 500 millionth vehicles were sold in the U.S. (worldwide, 614 million automobiles were registered at that time, an increase of roughly 500 million in about 30 years).

- The U.S. auto companies created the middle-class, especially in the Midwest–the Mecca of auto industry production. The companies offered generous compensation, which allowed workers to live in attractive homes in the suburbs. It also allowed the children of many of the hourly employees to move up the ladder by being the first generation to attend college. According to a 2007 BBC News report from Detroit by Steve Schifferes, "in the 1950s the Detroit area had the highest median income, and the highest rate of home ownership of any major U.S. city." Clearly, auto industry employees benefited from the industry's oligopoly position. Today, the Detroit Metro area is experiencing severe pain. The Detroit News reported in October 2010 that the median income in Detroit has declined by 21% between 2000 and 2009.

• The auto industry attracted the cream of the crop of college graduates because working in the auto industry was a dream job–excellent pay, great benefits, job security and solid promotional opportunities (I was promoted six times in eight years in the middle 1960s to early 1970s). Then the roof collapsed with the import invasion, and the whole milieu changed forever.

• Key Ford and GM executives lived in the same areas– mostly in prosperous and cultured Birmingham and Bloomfield Hills, with its upscale homes, elite schools (Cranbrook and Country Day), and fancy country clubs such as the Bloomfield Hills Country Club. It was the dream of most Ford managers to be able to move to "God's" country. (I had to be satisfied with a Tier 2 city– Farmington Hills.) Most executives were Caucasian and born in America. The salaried workforce was lily white; almost 100% of the salaried female employees were secretaries. Smooth-tongued up-and-coming analysts with an Eastern accent and well-dressed Ivy-Leaguers had an edge. However, American-born Ford executives only judged people by their contributions, and I never felt discriminated against because of my German accent.

• Everybody dressed like the famous 1960s IBM salesmen. The auto leaders had big egos and were arrogant, which is understandable with the power they wielded, and the employees they controlled (over 700,000 at GM and 400,000 at Ford).

- Companies were insulated and had a hauteur feeling. Executive promotions were strictly from within, and thus, no new visions originated (this was consistent with the mindset of U.S. manufacturing at that time. On December 13, 2010 the Wall Street Journal reported that giant Caterpillar was "long known for promoting senior executives from within"). There was very low executive turnover; employment in the auto industry was a prestige job, and corporate loyalty was a given.

- Hierarchy and dominance, which are core values in America, was the order of the day. At Ford, letters to top executives had to be on blue stationary (same color as "Situation Room" reports to George W. Bush). Having a large corner office at Ford World Headquarters was a sign that the executive was a "big man on campus," and "had arrived." The dining room on top of Ford's Headquarters was reserved for V.P.'s and above. (Steven Rattner stated that GM had an executive dining room on the 38th floor of its World Headquarters in Detroit.)

- The U.S. auto companies lived in utopia without external competitors and there was no upheaval in the industry at that time (the U.S. was at its peak in the late 1940s; Americans had the highest living standard in the world).

Therefore, innovation was not a word eulogized in Detroit in the 1950s, and even into most of the 1960s. Risk taking was not part of the repertoire, especially since nobody outside the U.S. threatened the "Big Three's" existence; the firms had an effective monopoly. Stephen D'Arcy, an automotive expert at PriceWaterhouse Coopers, stated in a 2005 CRS Report to Congress that "in the 1950s and 1960s, U.S. firms failed to innovate the design of cars, preferring to make money increasing the size and weight of their vehicles by adding extras like air conditioning, power steering, and fancy sound systems...the mass production system discouraged innovation because it was so expensive to introduce fundamentally new models." Tom Peters stated in his 1987 book "Thriving on Chaos" that "this all-American system-long production runs, mass operations-paid off with victory in World Wars I and II, and cemented subsequent U.S. economic dominance... but we won World War II with more tanks and planes, not, in general, better ones." M.G. Siegler, in a September 27, 2010 article in "TechCrunch" summarized it well: "there wasn't much innovation in the automobile industry in the 1950s and 1960s as big stagnant companies ruled."

• Making money was easy for U.S. manufacturing companies. The facilities of potential competitors' in Europe and Japan were destroyed during World War II or dismantled by the Soviet Union in the territories they controlled in East Germany. Moreover, they had neither money nor managerial talent to quickly rebuild. Japan was not even on the map because they didn't have a competitive car industry (Toyota's production in 1955 totaled only 23,000 units). Robert A. Lutz, then Chairman of GM North America, stated in a speech to the Automotive News Congress in January 2003 "when the American economy really powered up in the 1950s, it was the auto industry that led the way."

- The Kultur of the day was meetings, meetings, and meetings. Not in the world could an analyst present an argument, no matter how sound, which was contrary to the views of a superior, especially at the V.P. level and above. You are sent to the corner if you offered contrary views (ask Hal Sperlich, one of the greatest auto industry Product Planners ever who eventually got axed for being too aggressive with new ideas and his attitude toward superiors). Ford CEO Semon Knudsen discovered it quickly after arriving at Ford that it is dangerous to disagree with the boss! The same eventually happened to Ernest Breech who turned Ford around after World War II and was Chairman from 1955-1960. He was one of the most successful Ford leaders ever. Lee Iacocca was another CEO who was dismissed. In my opinion, certain senior company leaders sometimes exhibited a "my way or the highway mentality." In the mid-1970s I was a member of Ford's Product Planning & Research Staff. An interesting factoid was an assignment I received to study the viability of electric vehicles (EV's)—something nobody had looked at in 70 years! With technical assistance from Ford's Scientific Research Laboratory Staff, I prepared a lengthy strategy paper and presented my findings six months later to certain high level Ford executives. I recommended against E.V.'s, primarily because of high cost and the source of pollution was simply shifted from passenger cars to coal-fired power plants. Even today, coal represents the dominant fuel source with a 47% share. I recommended hybrids (hello Prius), which the Ford V.P. rejected. I was sent to "corporate purgatory" for defending my position and not being the usual yes person in dealing with "deity." The E.V. subject wasn't on anybody's mind for the following 25 years. (The fear of these pantheons of power permeated throughout the entire organization, including Finance Staff. They even scared the pants off of executives' one level below the vice president level—Executive Directors. For example, the executives from the Scientific Laboratory whom I worked with on the E.V. strategy paper had supported my conclusions. However, they suddenly switched allegiance in the meeting after they sensed that their boss didn't like my recommendations. I was knocked down, claustrophobic and felt like a "Poor Little Fool" (Ricky Nelson's 1960s song). However, with six children in private high school or in college, I picked myself from the floor remembering, "Gib niemals auf. Niemals" (Never give up. Never).

- GM was considered the gorilla in the zoo; Ford and Chrysler literally feared for their existence (not to speak of tiny AMC) because of GM's market dominance, and the associated economies of scale. Today, it is the opposite–Ford is in the driver's seat.

- An article by Tim Williams on June 13, 2009 in "American Chronicle" stated it succinctly "the American auto industry was like the Titanic, unsinkable." The U.S auto companies dominated the planet with over 75% share in1950, and still over 45% by 1965 according to Automotive News. The "Big Three" had a virtual monopoly position and a rueckwaerts (backward) culture. For example, Ford Motor Company earned an astounding $5.5 billion ($45 billion in today's dollars) between 1951-1960.

- American companies did not know what a challenge meant (same applied to steel, aircraft, etc.). As late as 1965, they controlled 95% of the U.S. market. The U.S. government even threatened to break-up GM in the1960's. Ford executives were very concerned about the impact of the break-up because two new entities would direct their guns at Ford.

- By 1970, the domestic companies still had an 87% market share, 76% by 1980, and still around 70% by 2000. The oligopolistic position was a normal post-world War II pattern. It also extended to steel, aluminum, rubber, oil, aircraft, cigarettes and cereal. The monopoly position generated large profits. For example, in 1955, GM's net income was $1.2 billion, which is equivalent to over $8 billion in today's dollars according to "TheBurningPlatform.com". It was the highest amount ever in U.S. corporate history. Further, according to Answer.com, "by the late 1960s, after-tax profits for the industry (auto) in general reached a 13 percent return on investment." Tom Peters and Nancy Austin, in their 1985 book entitled "A Passion for Excellence," called "the 1946-1973 period the Great Anomaly. It is as if the United States economy had a record of 28 "wins," 0 "losses," but all the wins were by forfeit." The auto executives probably felt that they lived in an era of "milk and honey," which we know from history, doesn't last forever.

- Even during the first half of the 1960s, GM and Ford were still swimming in money because there was no serious import competition. For example, according to Automotive News' "American Automobile Centennial" edition, GM earned $959 million in 1960 and $2.1 billion in 1965 ($14 billion in today's dollars!). Ford recorded income of $427 million and $703 million during the same period. Except in 1965, when Chrysler earned $233 million, the company was never a big-time profit generator during its first 50 years of operations starting with its inception in 1925.

- The U.S. auto companies believed their heritage gave them a right to exist. Former GM president Charlie Wilson is still quoted as saying "What is good for GM is good for

America" (actually, he said "What's good for America is good for General Motors, and vice versa").

- During the 1950s and 1960s, there was still the typical post World War II "nobody can beat us mentality;" the "Big Three" had the playing field to themselves with the demise of brands like Nash, Hudson, Tucker, Kaiser, Packard, Willys-Overland and lastly Studebaker (1963). This WASP "big power" belief dates back from the post World War II period—the "Golden Era" in America. There was the feeling of invincibility—"we are the most powerful nation in the world." There was no pressure to become more cost efficient and no need to conduct benchmark studies such as Toyota's continuous improvement philosophy or the "Honda Way" by Soichiro Honda, founder of Honda who's basic approach is "everyone working diligently and in unity to develop competitive products." These good old days are gone forever.

- Brand loyalty was a given. Switching from Ford to GM, or vice-versa, was very unusual, which is probably why there was seldom a big shift in market share. The arrival of imports changed brand loyalty because consumers now had a choice.

- Both Ford and GM were highly integrated through their automotive components divisions with tens of thousand of employees (both operations were finally spun-off about ten years ago; both eventually entered into Chapter 11).

• Executive turf wars and political infighting was a given. "Political acumen" and self-preservation was often more important than knowledge. Having one's "squawk box" connected to the "right people" was a status symbol.

• Many of the top auto executives were former "bean counters," a powerful position at Ford and GM and the "High Society" of the auto industry. At Ford, the former finance leaders included  "Red" Poling, Phil Benton, Ed Lundy, Robert McNamara, and Jacques Nasser. At GM, examples include Roger Smith (of Michael Moore's 1989 satire "Roger & Me" movie), Fred Donner, Thomas Murphy, Jack Smith and Rick Wagoner. The "elite corps" Finance Staffs overshadowed all other activities. Often, their focus was on profits at the expense of cutting-edge technology. It appears that GM had the same problems. In a 1992 essay by Ross Perot "How I Would Turn Around GM" in a classic entitled "The Challenge of Organizational Change," Mr. Perot stated: "starting today, the historic power struggles between the financial staff and car builders will not be tolerated. Financial people will be responsible for maintaining accountant information. People who know how to build cars and serve customers will make the product decisions." High Beam Research, in an article dated January 1, 1994 stated that "under Robert McNamara, finance became the cornerstone of corporate power at Ford, overwhelming manufacturing and product development...every decision had to be justified in financial terms, an unbending principle which, generated constant tension between finance and operational functions." In an extensive review of General Motors on November 15, 2010 in the New York Times, the paper stated "its (GM) Finance staff argued with product developers and marketers who pushed for aggressive spending on new cars and trucks."   I totally support the thesis, based on my thirty years at Ford Motor Company. The finance people always seemed to have more firepower and manpower than the rest of us. Mr. Mulally is a trailblazer who is demonstrating that executives with proven manufacturing and engineering experience can effectively manage a company of Ford's complexity and size.

• In an industry in which the product should be "Number One," product planners seldom reached the top of the ladder because they have to be risk takers and visionaries–two words unwelcome in the auto industry during the first 25 years after World War II. Playing it safe was the key buzzword. In Ford Motor Company's almost 110-year history, only Henry Ford, former CEO's Don Peterson and Alex Trotman were considered executives with product DNA. At GM, I believe only former vice chairman Bob Lutz can be classified as true product planner. Moreover, Ford never had a CEO with the critical manufacturing background until Mr. Mulally arrived at Ford in 2006 (Chrysler had one–Bob Eaton and GM had three–Bob Stempel, Jim McDonald and Lloyd Reuss).

- Blockbuster models seem to be born only every 5-10 years. It often takes a fearless product planner to push through totally new concepts (1955 T'Bird, 1965 Mustang, 1976 European Fiesta, 1978 Fairmont, 1986 Taurus, 1991 Explorer and 2000 Focus. Under Mr. Mulally, the pace has increased: 2009 Ford F-150, 2010 Ford Fusion, 2011 Ford Edge, 2011 Ford Explorer, 2012 Ford Focus). Once a vehicle is selling like hotcakes, everybody is the proud father.

- Outsiders snooping around the auto industry were definitely not welcome. In 1965, an unknown agitator named Ralph Nader unnerved Detroit, which resulted in unwelcome scrutiny. [37] His book "Unsafe at Any Speed" eventually led to Washington imposed auto safety legislation. As Douglas Brinkley stated in his 858-page bible "Wheels for the World," "Detroit was going through a revolution, learning to take orders from Washington."

- When the U.S. auto industry was confronted with major problems, the companies generally blamed the usual escape goats including Washington, OPEC via high gasoline prices, the UAW, Asian competitors, and Asian governments manipulating their currencies (Korea and China are the main culprit today).

- GM and Ford were unwilling to confront the UAW to gain concessions to aggressively enter the small car business. The "Big Three" gave away the store to the UAW. In my opinion, from the beginning of its founding in 1936, the

UAW has been an "us versus them" union. Subsequent contracts, during good times, actually increased the labor costs through "30 and out," Cost of Living Adjustments, Supplemental Unemployment benefits, very generous pensions and excellent healthcare benefits. One of the most contentious issues as part of the 2009-bailout negotiations was the "Jobs Bank" program. The plan paid UAW workers replaced by technological advances and plant closings up to 95% of heir take-home pay until they could be placed again in a plant, which could take years. The program cost the auto companies tens of billions of dollars without any value-added.

- Both Ford and GM kept factories running at full capacity because they considered the UAW-represented workforce as a fixed cost. Excess production was sold to low profit daily rental fleets, or sold with large rebates to generate sales. The Japanese companies did not employ such tactics, and their vehicles had higher residuals (trade-in-values). This, in turn, allowed them to premium-price their products.

- Being too far removed from the powerful corporate headquarters was a dangerous career move. People tend to be forgotten quickly in the hinterlands, based on my own experience in Mexico City, Sao Paulo and with Ford Aerospace in Newport Beach, California (after playing a key role as Director of Strategic Planning and Development in Ford Aerospace's successful $2 billion divestiture, I was welcomed back to the mothership with a salary grade reduction. (I shouldn't complain too much because only five out of 17,000 Ford Aerospace employees were allowed to return to Dearborn.) The same happened when I returned from a Ford/VW AG joint venture assignment in Brazil and Argentina with 52,000 employees. When I came back to Michigan, I went from a Director position to a Manager position in Ford's International Automotive Operations. The best ticket to punch was at the all-important Corporate Finance Staff, but that activity was impossible to penetrate unless certain people anointed you, and the employee attended certain universities (mostly Ivy League).

# CHAPTER 6

✕ ✕ ✕

# THE LAND OF THE RISING SUN'S INVASION

## The Early Years

Prior to 1955, U.S. auto manufacturers controlled almost 100% of the largest automotive market in the world (VW sold two cars in 1949 according to Automotive News). For example, with 1955 U.S. industry volume of roughly 8.5 million units, only 61,000 imported vehicles were sold in the U.S., mostly VW "Beetles" which were considered the antithesis of American cars (gasoline was $0.29/gallon). U.S. producers believed that a foreign company couldn't surmount the entry barriers of manufacturing cars in America. In fact, nobody dared the challenge of a U.S. manufacturing facility during the following 23 years until 1978. Moreover, it was easier and more profitable to simply ship the cars from their overseas plants.

Starting in 1957, import sales increased to 210,000 units, including some Japanese models. The son of Toyota's founder, Kiichiro Toyoda, visited Ford facilities in 1936 and bought Henry Ford's famous lean production system book entitled "Today and Tomorrow" according to David Magee's 2007 book "How Toyota Became #1." Eiji Toyoda and Shoichi Saito, both future Toyota Chairmen, toured Ford Motor Company facilities in 1950, and observed the company's production system. They reportedly returned to Japan with some good Ford ideas, which reportedly helped them to develop Toyota's widely acclaimed Toyota Production System.

Educated classes, and young people represented the key import buyer profiles. The 1960's was still the time when Americans listened to songs like: "Riding In an Automobile With No Particular Place to Go" by Chuck Berry, "Little Red Corvette" by Prince, "Mustang Sally" by Wilson Pickett, and "Fun, Fun, Fun Till Daddy Took the T Bird Away" by the Beach Boys. Americans still loved big U.S. cars.

Toyota opened its headquarters in the U.S. in 1957, followed by Honda, which opened a sales operation in 1959. Toyota's first car, the Toyopet, was underpowered and sold only 300 units in 1958 and was withdrawn from the U.S. market in 1961. Toyota then developed a car designed for the U.S., which was introduced in 1965. (Instead of focusing on the emerging Japanese threat, Ford Motor Company dabbled outside its core business by purchasing Philco in 1961 and a major tractor operation in 1962.) The first successful Toyota car was the 1965 Corona; 1966 Toyota sales reached 20,000 units.

Honda was the first Japanese company to establish a wholly owned plant in the United States in 1982 (VW was the first foreign company to build an assembly facility in the U.S. in 1978). Nissan established its first facility in Smyrna, Tennessee.

Toyota's first U.S. manufacturing plant was a joint venture with GM in 1984. I was part of Ford's Corporate Strategy and Analysis Staff at that time. We prepared numerous papers for the Justice Department's anti-trust group strongly objecting to a tie-up of two of the top three auto companies in the world. We also feared that GM would gain a competitive advantage by acquiring Toyota's famous way of doing business. According to J. Liker's 2004 book "The Toyota Way: 14 Management Principles from the World's Greatest Manufacturer," the Toyota philosophy included the following:

• Long-term thinking as a basis for management decisions.

• A process for problem solving.

• Adding value to the organization by developing its people.

• Continuously solving root problems drives organizational learning. [38]

Toyota established its first wholly owned manufacturing plant in 1986 in Georgetown, Kentucky. Today, Toyota has ten U.S. manufacturing facilities.

## The 1970s and Beyond

Tim Williams wrote an excellent article in "American Chronicle" in 2009 entitled "Why the American Auto Industry Failed." He stated that the U.S. auto companies "ignored the warning signs that the American public was beginning to purchase those foreign cars that were now of a better quality, more fuel efficient and more affordable." Thus, by 1970, U.S. imports reached about 1.3 million units, virtually all produced overseas. Foreign imports reached over 2 million units by 1973. Further, U.S. auto companies were unprepared during the 1973 oil crisis with fuel-efficient small cars. Gasoline prices increased from $.39/gallon in 1973 to $0.53/gallons in 1974 ($2.35/gallon in 2010 dollars) because of OPEC's refusal to sell oil to America. Thus, the U.S. auto companies were simultaneously confronted with two adversaries–OPEC and imports.

The 1973 oil crisis led directly to the establishment of the first fuel economy standards in 1975 (CAFE). It was the beginning of troubles in paradise. The U.S. monopoly position in the world's biggest auto market had come to an end. It put American auto companies into a defensive posture ever since. The carefree days of the late 1940s, 1950s and 1960s without imports were gone. In a January 2003 speech at the Automotive News Congress in Detroit, Robert A. Lutz, then Chairman of GM's North American Operations, stated that the 1950s and 1960s were the auto industry's "Golden Age." He also said "the 1970s were bad and the 1980s worse." According to a 2005 CRP Report to Congress, "the Big Three shed about 600,000 U.S. jobs since 1980."

To meet the new fuel economy standards, it became necessary to commence the costly downsizing of the entire U.S. product line-up with the associated billions of dollars in expenditures. In retrospect, CAFE forever changed the U.S. auto industry. From then on, Uncle Sam was the industry's unfriendly new partner. Moreover, CAFE played into the hands of foreign small-car producers who specialized in this segment because they already produced small fuel-efficient cars. The new standards led to the death of the U.S. dinosaur cars (late 1950's vintage Cadillac now sells at around $150,000 at Barrett-Jackson auctions).

By the late 1970's, imports had launched a full-laden attack; they achieved a 26% market share, with the Japanese companies accounting for 80% of the 2.4 million imports. The "Big Three's" 70 year long dominance of the U.S. auto industry had come to an end. This also ushered in a decline in influencing pricing, less clout in Washington, which was compounded by an ever more assertive UAW and more government regulations.

The flood of imports resulted in a massive U.S. auto deficit with Japan since American car sales in Japan totaled only a few thousand units annually, primarily as a result of Japan's highly effective tariff and non-tariff barriers includingmanipulationoftheyen,andlow-costgovernment financing (a weak yen makes Japanese exports less costly, and thus more competitive and profitable).

In 1980, GM, Ford and Chrysler lost billions of dollars and Chrysler faced bankruptcy. Ford Motor Company alone lost $2.7 billion between 1980-1982. Chrysler was bailed out in 1979 by a $1.5 billion government loan. Sales declined by almost three million units between 1979 and 1980 because of the recession.

There was intense pressure from Midwest politicians to impose import quotas. To forestall such a threat, in May 1981, "Japan announced that it would "voluntarily" restrain its shipments of automobiles to the United States during the next two years," according to Clyde Prestowitz's 1988 book "Trading Places, How We Allowed Japan To Take the Lead."[39] The initial quota was 1.68 million passenger cars, which increased to 1.85 million in 1984, and 2.3 million in 1985 and beyond. The restraints were eliminated in 1994. Economists claim that the import restraints resulted in higher consumer prices because of limited supply of the highly desirable Japanese cars. Reportedly, Japan had a $1,000-$2,000 cost advantage compared with the "Big Three" because of lower labor costs, and substantially higher productivity.

Ford and GM achieved record earnings during the early years of the "voluntary" restraints when imports were in limited supply. For example, between 1982-1990 Ford realized record earnings of $24.5 billion. (Steven Rattner, in his book "Overhaul," claimed that "Ford's stock price rose 1,500 percent between 1981 and 1987.) Unfortunately, the "Big Three" didn't utilize the "breathing space" restraint period to develop fully competitive small cars.

The impetuous for the establishment of Japanese operations in the U.S. may be related to the fear that the U.S. government would impose its own import quotas. Nissan opened a U.S. design studio in 1979. This was followed by the first Japanese auto assembly plant in 1982 (Honda in Ohio). Today, the Japanese operate dozens of highly efficient and ultra modern facilities, primarily in the southern United States (excluding Mitsubishi in Illinois and Honda in Ohio). These plants have been built with extremely generous state government grants. The facilities are non-unionized except for the UAW-represented Ford/Mazda joint venture in Flat Rock, Michigan, and the Mitsubishi plant in Illinois. The transplants have a roughly $20-$25 per hour cost advantage compared with domestic UAW-represented plants (the 2007 labor contract included a provision that up to 20% of newly hired UAW-represented employees would receive substantially lower entry-level wages). Since most of the Japanese plants in the U.S. are relatively new, the Japanese companies have virtually no health and pension legacy costs in America.

In 1986, Honda introduced the first Japanese upscale car (Acura), followed by Nissan's Infiniti and Toyota's Lexus line both in 1989. Initially, it was not considered a threat; the industry sneered at it. These companies only had a solid reputation for low-cost small cars. Who would buy a luxury car from such companies? The answer was millions of Americans. The same is happening with Hyundai's new 2011 luxury entry (Equus) which will compete against the Mercedes-Benz S-Class, BMW's 7-Series, and the Lexus LS.

In 2006, Toyota achieved its initial goal to beat Ford in the U.S. for the number two position. By 2009, the market share in the U.S. of all non-U.S. based companies totaled approximately 55%. The Japanese had a 40% market share! They had literally gained the upper hand, with the "Big Three" in an undisciplined almost warlike retreat. A new dawn in the world's biggest auto market had arrived. Toyota's dizzying worldwide success probably led to the arrogance the company has exhibited in recent years. An old proverb says: "When pride comes, then comes dishonor," which actually happened.

Toyota's forte is its well-crafted image and a perceived bias toward quality and safety. Its vehicles had high residual values, which gave them a competitive edge. This allowed Toyota to premium-price its products. Its reputation, however, is presently in shatters after Toyota had multiple recalls totaling about 8.5 million units. In a continuing series of glitches, Toyota recalled an additional 1.3 million cars in late August 2010. In October 2010 another 1.5 million units were recalled to fix brake-related problems, followed by 650,000 Prius worldwide in late November 2010 for heat risks and 110,000 all-new 2011 Toyota Sienna minivans in mid-December 2010 for brake system problems. An additional 1.7 million vehicles were recalled worldwide in late January 2011 followed by 2.2 million vehicles in late February 2011. Lawsuits have been filed claiming that Toyota secretly bought problem cars to hide unintended-acceleration problems. According to Automotive News (November 1, 2010), Toyota has recalled 15.4 million units worldwide, and "with Toyota Motor Corporation announcing fresh safety actions what seems like every week" (19.2 million units as of March 1, 2011). In mid-2010, the NHTSA fined Toyota $16.3 million for failing to report safety problems promptly; Toyota didn't contest the fine. Recalls are a way of life in the auto industry. However, as stated in a July 26, 2010 Fortune article by Alex Taylor III entitled "How Toyota Lost Its Way Conquering the Auto Market," "Toyota had known about some defects for years but strenuously resisted taking formal action." [40]

Having spent many months in Japan on business, I have a good understanding of the Japanese mindset. The highly nationalistic Japanese corporations are ruthless. Toyota's official motto is: "We Can and We Will." It means that the company will become the world's top automotive producer; absolutely nobody can stop the train. This is similar to a description of Digital Equipment Corporation in 1986. In a book by Clayton Christensen "The Innovator's

Dilemma," he stated, "taking on Digital Equipment Corporation these days is like standing in front of a moving train." [41] This is how U.S. auto companies felt. The Japanese companies unabashedly circled their U.S. competitors like vultures. In a November 18, 2002 article by Betsy Morris in Fortune magazine, William Clay Ford, Jr. stated in response to all the problems Ford was facing including the import invasion: "we're still trying to put the brakes on a freight train."

The U.S. Department of Commerce estimated that foreign direct investment in the U.S. automotive industry (assembly and components) has totaled approximately $45 billion. This includes $9 billion at Honda, $18 billion at Toyota and $4 billion at Nissan.

## The U.S. Auto Companies' Response

The constant adventures into noncore activities, to be reviewed in Chapter 7, kept the focus away from the emerging Japanese competition until they had established a strong dealer base with competitive products on the West Coast, followed by the East Coast, and then the South, and lastly the Midwest.

U.S. auto companies allocated insufficient funds for the development of highly fuel-efficient, top quality, low-cost and stylish small cars. The battle cry was "small car, small profits." Tom Peters in his 1987 book "Thriving on Chaos," quoted a highly respected auto expert from the University of Michigan who stated in a February 1987 article in Fortune: "the best of our are (now) about as good as the worst of theirs (Asian), and that is a tremendous achievement."

The top brass of the U.S. auto industry considered it almost "un-American" for consumers to purchase small cars. Only the fringe of society, at best 5%, would be potential buyers. This was the time when America had unchallenged world power status. The mindset was big cars, big houses, big skyscrapers, big roads, big suburbs, mega churches, and huge museums.

The absence of competitive "Big Three" small cars became highly visible during the first oil crisis in 1973. By 1975, imports captured 15% of the U.S. market compared with 5% in 1965. By 1980, their share had increased to 25%.

- In 1960, Ford introduced the Ford Falcon, followed in 1962 by a car somewhat larger than the Falcon called the Fairmont, which was highly successful. In mid-1964, Ford introduced the popular Mustang as a 1965 model.

- In 1970, Ford unveiled the sub-compact Pinto, which was followed in the late 1970s by the Ford Escort, one of Ford's most successful small cars. The Pinto offered excellent fuel economy, but not much else. The much-maligned Pinto had major safety-related issues. It had to endure comparison with the infamous Yugo.

- Escort's successor was the Ford Focus in 2000; it was Ford's first serious attempt to develop a "world car." The Ford Fusion was introduced in 2005 as a mid-size car positioned between the Ford Focus and the Ford Taurus.

- GM introduced the Vega in 1970, the Chevette, Cavalier and Sprint in the 1980s, an updated Cavalier in the 1990s, and Cobalt and Aveo in the 2000s. The quality of the Vega and Cavalier was considered very poor.

- Chrysler Corporation introduced several small cars including the Valiant in 1960, a pony car in 1964 (Barracuda) and the Neon in 1999.

To put it mildly, the U.S. efforts outlined above didn't move the needle in the "Big Three" favor. The march of the Asian rivals continued unchecked.

# CHAPTER 7

✠ ✠ ✠

## PLAYING IN THE SAME SANDBOX

During periods when the domestic auto companies' treasuries were as fat as a hog, and gushing with money, they went on costly acquisition sprees instead of focusing on their core business to reverse their rapidly declining market shares. Both Ford and GM copied each other's acquisition strategies, and even Chrysler sometimes followed suit.

### Defense/Consulting Acquisitions

• GM bought EDS in 1984 for $2.6 billion (spun-off in 1996). In 1985, GM outbid Ford to acquire Hughes Aircraft for $5 billion (name changed to GM-Hughes Electronics Corporation; Hughes Aircraft was sold in 1997 to Raytheon; Hughes Electronics sold to News Corporation in 2003).

• Ford Motor Company purchased Philco (1961), and subsequently acquired other defense-related companies such as BDM. The acquisitions were consolidated in 1986 into Ford Aerospace (FAC) with 17,000 employees and over $2 billion in sales (sold in 1990). In the late 1980s, Ford CEO Don Peterson attempted to acquire Lockheed Corporation for $3.5 billion because Ford had lost the Hughes Aircraft bidding war. However, Ford's Board of Directors and the Ford family didn't support the acquisition.

- Not to be outdone, Chrysler Corporation acquired Gulfstream, Electrospace Systems, and Technologies Airborne Systems in the 1980s (all defense-related companies; all sold subsequently).

## Automotive Acquisitions

Ford acquired Aston Martin, Jaguar, Volvo, Land Rover, and a controlling interest in Mazda (initial stake was 25% in 1979; subsequently increased to 33%, but reduced to 11% during Ford's financial crisis in mid-November 2010. Ford reduced its shareholding in Mazda to 3.5% in late 2010). In 1986, Ford also attempted to acquire Alfa Romeo, but was outbid by Fiat. The three European luxury brands and the medium-priced Volvo cars provided no economies of scale or synergies to Ford Motor Company. Moreover, they were relatively unimportant players in the global automotive industry. For example, in their most important single market, the U.S., Volvo's annual sales never exceeded 140,000 units and its highest share ever was 0.8%. Jaguar's share generally averaged around 0.1%; its best performance was in 2002 with 61,000 sales and a 0.4% market share. Land Rover's historic share was in the 0.2% range with its largest sales in 2005 with 51,000 units and a 0.3% market penetration. Aston Martin never sold more than 2,000 units annually in the United States. In retrospect, these were ill-timed and costly acquisitions. All were divested with significant losses.

To parallel Ford Motor Company, General Motors acquired Lotus in 1986 and Saab in the late 1980s after Ford's attempt to purchase Saab failed (sold in 2010). GM also acquired a 49% stake in Isuzu (sold in 2006), a 20% equity in Fuji Heavy Industries, which manufactures Subaru cars (sold in 2006), a 20% equity in Suzuki (sold in 2008), and a 20% share in Fiat with an option to purchase the remaining 80% between 2004-2009. GM had to extract itself from this obligation by paying Fiat $2 billion in 2005!

After GM disposed of its equity in Fuji Heavy Industries and Isuzu, Toyota Motor Corporation promptly acquired a minority position in both companies. Toyota also owns compact car specialist Daihatsu (800,000 sales annually).

# Car Rentals Acquisitions

• Ford acquired an equity in Hertz in 1987 and full ownership in 1994 (sold in 2005). Ford also acquired equity in Budget in 1989 (sold in 1997). GM acquired stakes in Avis (sold in 1997) and National Car Rental in 1989 (sold in 1995). Chrysler bought Dollar Rent-a-Car in 1990 and equity in Thrifty in 1991 (both divested in an IPO in 1997). Chrysler also owned Snappy and General Rent-a-Car, which were both sold in 1994.

## Financial Acquisitions

• GM established GMAC in 1919, and by 1958 the company had financed 40 million vehicles. In view of GMAC's success, Ford established Ford Motor Credit Company in 1959. Subsequently, Ford acquired several major finance companies including "The Associates" in 1989 with 15 million customers and 23,000 employees. Ford also purchased First Nationwide Financial, which, through acquisitions, became the fourth largest U.S. savings bank. The objective of the large-scale acquisitions was to smooth the cyclical nature of the automotive business. (The U.S. had about ten recessions during the last sixty years including 1953-1954, 1957-1958, 1960-1961, 1969-1970, 1973-1975, 1981-1982, 1990-1991, 2001, and December 2007-present.)

Buying and selling of companies involving thousands of employees often has a dramatic impact on the affected employees. Many consider themselves a pawn in a jigsaw puzzle. Many times, it has consequences on their professional career. Having been a Project Director on several Ford divestitures, I know of the human toll and upheaval it can take. As Neil Sedaka 1960s song clearly stated, "Breaking Up Is Hard to Do." Being tossed from the Ford "Blue Oval" to a much smaller enterprise, or buy-out specialists, was very foreboding (in one case outside the U.S., executives of a Ford subsidiary being divested threatened me because I was selling "their" company).

# CHAPTER 8

✵ ✵ ✵

## THE ROARING 1990s

### Money, Money, Money

Ford Motor Company and the other auto companies incurred significant losses in 1980, 1981, 1982, and 1983. An October 30, 1980 headline summarized it: "red ink floods auto industry." In April 1983, Ford Motor Company skipped dividends for six consecutive quarters. However, as with every boom and bust cycle, the auto industry improved strongly during the balance of the 1980's, like ABBA's "Money, Money, Money" song. Between 1984-1990, Ford's net income averaged a record $3.1 billion annually, with an all-time record of $5.3 billion in 1988 ($9.5 billion in today's dollars). Ford earned more than GM in 1986 for the first time in four decades, and during the subsequent two years, and bought back $4 billion in stock during the second half of the 1980s including $2 billion in early 1988 after eliminating 10,000 white-collar jobs starting in May 1986. (GM did well, too, earning over $16 billion between 1986-1989.) Ford U.S. sales averaged 3 million units annually during this period compared with 2.1 million units average annual between 1980-1982. The company's U.S. market share averaged 24% between 1987-1990; this compares with about 21% average annual between 1980-1986. In 1999, Ford outsold Toyota worldwide by 1.8 million units. Ford believed it was on top of the world, and outside analysts agreed. A 1989 Harvard Business School case study entitled "Transformation at Ford" stated that a Paine Webber automotive analyst wrote the following in 1989 about Ford "Almost everything in the world was right." Chilton's Automotive Industries "Report Card" gave Ford an overall grade of "A" in 1989.

This was, to use Ronald Reagan's 1984 campaign theme, "It's Morning Again in America." It is natural for executives to get carried away when money keeps flowing into the treasury and the trend line goes only one way–up, up, up. Thus, flush with success and money, Ford went on a buying binge by acquiring:

- New Holland (small tractors) in 1986 (sold in 1991 to Fiat).

- A majority interest in Aston Martin in 1987 (sold in 2008)

- An equity in Hertz in 1987 (sold in 2005 with a $1.5 billion gain)

- Jaguar in 1989 for $2.5 billion in a costly bidding contest against GM (Jaguar as well as Land Rover were sold in 2009 at a major loss). At the time of the acquisition, Jaguar was struggling. However, an UBS auto analyst was quoted as claiming that the purchase "will allow them (Jaguar) to compete in the 1990s" (November 3, 1989 AP dispatch from London).

- The Associates in 1989 for $2.7 billion (spun-off in 1998 with a one-time, non-taxable gain of $16.5 billion). According to Angel Investors (www.fundinguniverse.com), "Ford spent $5.5 billion acquiring assets for its financial services group...it made Ford the country's second largest provider of diversified financial services, ranking only behind Citicorp...Ford entered th 1990s with a $115 billion worth of banking related assets."

In 1991-1992, exactly as in the early 1980s, both Ford and GM sustained significant losses, primarily as a result of the U.S. recession, and significant charges in 1992 relating to a new accounting standard. In a repeat of 1982, Ford reduced its dividend in April 1991 as part of a $3 billion "belt tightening." Concurrently, Ford's credit was downgraded. (GM lost $23.5 billion in 1992.)

During the balance of the 1990's, again as in the 1980s, Ford's performance was phenomenal; in May 1994, CEO Alex Trotman characterized 1993 as Ford's "strongest single year for turnaround in our history" (Akron Beacon Journal on May 13, 1994). George Jones' lyrics said it well "It Don't Get Better Than That."

- Even excluding a $16 billion gain from the spin-off of The Associates in 1998, and the $6.9 billion negative impact of new accounting standards in 1992, Ford Motor Company's net income totaled $40 billion between 1993-2000.

• In 1999, Ford earned $7.2 billion ($9.2 billion inflation adjusted)–more than any other automotive company in history at that time (since 2006, Toyota held the title with almost $12 billion in profits for the fiscal year ending March 31, 2006, and $14 billion for the fiscal year ending March 31, 2007).

• 1999 sales of $163 billion established a new record ($121 billion in 2010). Worldwide sales totaled 7.4 million units in 2000, exceeding a prior recor reached in 1997 (5.3 million in 2010).

• Ford had an enviable net cash position of $10 billion in 1999 and Ford distributed $50 billion in cash and securities to its shareholders during the second half of th 1990's including about $24 billion in cash and stock as a special dividend according to an article in the April 15, 2000 edition of the Charlotte Observer. GM announced a $4 billion buyback in 1998; earned $6 billion in 1999, and in second quarter of 1999 GM's stock was trading at a record $95 per share. However, as Linda Killian of Renaissance Capital stated in a November 3, 2010 article in the Sarasota Herald Tribune, share prices are "like a photograph; they're a picture in a moment of time."

- In 2000, the Ford Focus and the F-150 were the world's top sellers. Five of the top ten best-selling vehicles in the U.S. were Ford products.

According to Paul Ingrassia's book "Crash Course," The Wall Street Journal featured a front-page article on January 8, 1999 declaring that the 21st century would be "the dawn of a new golden age for General Motors, Ford and Chrysler." [42] However, 1999 was the highpoint for the "Big Three" in terms of profits. They never achieved these levels again until Ford earned $6.6 billion in 2010.

In all fairness to the Wall Street Journal and Mr. Nasser's dizzying buying orgy described on the following pages, America was in a state of intoxication:

- In 1999, the U.S. economy was still in its "largest peacetime expansion in U.S. history" according to Christopher J. Waller of the University of Kentucky.

- The GDP was in the 4% plus range, and "the U.S. economy ended 1999 with flourish" according to an early 2000 statement by Decision Analysts, Inc.

- Unemployment was low.

- The inflation rate was low.

- Productivity was high

- There were real wage gains

- The S&P 500 Index increased at an average annual rate of 22% per year between 1995 through 1999.

- The U.S. had a budget surplus.

- Forbes' auto analyst, the late Jerry Flint, stated at that time "Ford is sitting on $30 billion or so in cash and securities. The money keeps pouring in...I think they should build some factories." However, Tom Peters stated in his 2010 book entitled "The Little BIG Things:" "That Which Goeth Up and Up and Up Doth Not Goeth More Up and More Up and More Up Forever and Ever and Ever."

## Jacques Nasser, Ford's Mr. Acquisition

With the economic environment outlined on the previous page as a backdrop, and Ford's financial success, again as in the late 1980s, Ford went on a buying spree. This time under CEO Jacques Nasser's leadership, who reportedly was called "deal-a-day Jacques." He apparently considered himself a "change maker" to fundamentally revamp the company. According to an article in the October 30, 2001 edition of the Detroit News, Mr. Nasser's objective "was to remake a century-old organization into a fast-moving consumer company to zoom past the Boom-Bust legacy of the auto industry into a new era of prosperity." Apparently, nobody at Ford studied the success rate of acquisitions. According to Tom Peters' 1987 book "Thriving on Chaos," he stated that a study by Michael Porter of Harvard's Business School concluded that, between 1950 through 1980, the thirty-three companies he studied, "subsequently unloaded 53 percent of all their acquisitions during this period and sold off a whopping 74 percent of their acquisitions in unrelated new fields." This turned out to be Ford's experience (actually 100%). Under Mr. Nasser, Ford Motor Company:

- Increased its stake in Mazda in 1996 to 33.4% from 24.5% (reduced to 11% in 2008 during Ford's financial crisis, and to 3.5% in mid-November 2010).

- Acquired Volvo's passenger car business in 1999 for almost $6.5 billion (sold in 2010 for $1.3 billion). Auto analysts claimed at that time that Ford overpaid for Volvo. Mr. Nasser even proposed buying Nissan; had the Ford family and the Board of Directors approved Mr. Nasser's fatal Nissan acquisition plan, which was then close to bankruptcy, it could have possibly led to Ford's own bankruptcy considering Ford's heavy losses in 2001 and 2002, and Ford's uninspiring performance during most of the remaining 2000s. Further, Ford did not have any proven turnaround executives, which Nissan urgently needed. Mr. Ghosn of Renault took control of Nissan in 1999 and saved the company.

- (In May 1998, Chrysler and Daimler AG merged in a $38 billion stock deal. I 2007, Daimler unwound the merger by paying Cerberus Capital Management $650 million to assume an 80% stake in Chrysler.)

- Purchased Kwik-Fit Holdings, a European car repair company with about 2,400 outlets for $1.6 billion in 1999 (sold in 2002 for roughly $500 million). Also purchased Master Service in Mexico and "B-Quik" in Thailand (all sold by 2002).

- Purchased "Think" Electric Vehicle Company in 1999 (sold in 2002).

- Acquired a major European interior parts supplier, Plastic Omnium, in 1999 for $500 million, and integrated the company into Visteon (Ford's component operation), which was spun-off one year later, and eventually filed for bankruptcy (Visteon emerged from bankruptcy in October 2010).

• Bought Land Rover from BMW in 2000 for $2.6 billion (sold in 2009 to Tatar Motors of India for $2.3 billion, including Jaguar). The objective was to gain a strong foothold in the growing high-margin luxury segment. In 1999, Ford formed a luxury division (Premier Automotive Group) to manage the diverse acquisitions. The goal was to sell one million luxury cars annually (today, only Lincoln remains with sales of less than 100,000 units in 2010).

• Acquired in the late 1990's, the following companies:

☐ Recycling companies
☐ Collision shops
☐ An extended warranty company
☐ Concierge services
☐ Entered into several E-business partnerships with Yahoo, Oracle, HP, and MSN CarPoint, to join the dot-com generation.

• Aggressively entered the retail automotive business through the formation of "Auto Collection" with the objective to consolidate dealerships. Auto Collection was defined as "Ford's new sales entities that are jointly owned by Ford and its dealers, servicing large metro geographic areas. This structure combines customer-driven retail, service and facility processes to create a total brand experience." This new business was strongly opposed by Ford Motor Company dealers because they believed that the company was directly competing with them (the venture was terminated after Mr. Nasser was ousted). (In mid-November 2010, VW AG acquired Europe's largest independent auto dealer group for $4.6 billion, according to Automotive News Europe.)

Moreover, Ford dealers in the West were very unhappy when Ford made a $5 million donation to the Sierra Club in 2000. Many Ford F-150 owners, who are in the logging business, refused to buy Ford trucks anymore because the Sierra Club kept threatening their livelihood. In 2000, when money apparently was not an issue, Mr. Nasser announced a $175 million program to provide a personal computer for 370,000 Ford employees worldwide. In a February 4, 2000 PBS interview with Ray Suarez, Mr. Nasser stated that this will "complete the circle of an integrated Internet strategy." Ford also spent millions establishing "learning centers" for UAW members.

It cost roughly $12 billion to acquire Jaguar, Land Rover, and Volvo, plus at least $10 billion required to rejuvenate the brands over many years. It would have been less expensive to develop highly competitive luxury vehicles from scratch. However, it would have taken at least three years to develop the new products. Moreover, executives consider it "sexier" to be involved in big-time acquisitions than the grind of the complex product creation process.

## Competitive Auto Company Acquisitions

The auto industry had many acquisition failures; the most prominent was the "merger" of Daimler AG (Mercedes-Benz) with Chrysler (Juergen Schremp, Daimler CEO, later admitted to the Financial Times that calling it a merger of equals was only a subterfuge to get Chrysler management support for the deal). The "merger" reportedly cost Daimler AG over $35 billion when it was unwound a few years later. Honda is the only major automotive company, which has never bought nameplates from another corporation, or purchased an entire company.

Daimler AG has made over 85 acquisitions during the last thirty years. This includes recent stakes in Renault-Nissan, Tesla Motors and KAMAZ in Russia. Companies often enter into acquisitions to achieve economies of scale, increase sales or market share, to diversify, to reduce costs through synergies, to achieve a sustainable competitive advantage, for prestige, etc.

Another Juergen Schrempp's debacle was the acquisition of a 34% controlling interest in 2000 of Mitsubishi Motors for approximately $2.5 billion. This purchase was part of his "Welt AG" (global company) vision. For several years after Daimler AG gained control of Mitsubishi, the Japanese company lost money, primarily associated with serious quality defects, which Mitsubishi had concealed (Toyota story). In 2005, Daimler sold its remaining stake in Mitsubishi.

As part of "Welt AG," Daimler also acquired a 10% equity in Hyundai in 2000, which also didn't work out. The failed Chrysler, Mitsubishi and Hyundai acquisitions eventually cost Mr. Schrempp his job.

The 1994 BMW takeover of British icon Rover (Land Rover) ended in failure in 2000. Analysts claim that BMW conducted little research prior to Rover's acquisition. It is the exact story of Ford's purchase of Jaguar; when Ford of Europe's top manufacturing executive, Bill Hayden, was finally allowed to visit the Jaguar plants after the sale, he was shocked by the primitive conditions in the plants. In 1999, BMW acquired Rolls Royce; it has been a successful purchase because Rolls Royce's sales are at record levels.

In addition to Ford and GM, Volkswagen AG is the biggest advocate of purchasing competitive brands. In 2009, Volkswagen bought Scania, Karman, 49.9% of Porsche, with a complete takeover scheduled in 2011, and a 20% stake in Suzuki for $2.5 billion. In 2010, Volkswagen AG acquired a famous Italian auto design company (IDG), and announced plans to purchase Alfa Romeo from Fiat, which Fiat has rejected. To date, VW owns Audi, (acquired in 1969), Seat (bought in 1986), Skoda (purchased in 1990), Bentley, Lamborghini, Bugatti, Scania, Karman, and has an equity in Porsche and Suzuki. The Audi, Skoda and Seat acquisitions have been highly successful.

# CHAPTER 9

## ❄ ❄ ❄

# FORD'S TRANSFORMATION PROCESS

## The "Ford 2000" Plan

As outlined previously, during most of the 1990s, Ford Motor Company had a strong balance sheet, achieved outstanding financial results, had a U.S. market share in the 25% range (Ford had five of the top eight best-selling vehicles in the U.S. in 1995), was the world's largest truck manufacturer, and the second largest vehicle producer. Ford employed almost 350,000 people, pensions were fully funded, and automotive cash and marketable securities were at record levels at the end of 1995.

To maintain the momentum, Ford Motor Company, under CEO Alex Trotman's leadership, launched a "comprehensive reprocessing of its business to achieve industry leadership in the 21st century ...it supported Ford's vision to be the world's leading automotive company." This strategy is consistent with an article in the June 2010 issue of the Harvard Business Review by Messrs. Vermeulen, Puranam, and Gulati entitled "Change for Change's Sake" which stated that "rather than wait for the heart attack to strike, executive should consider changing their firm's structures, rewards, and processes while performance is still good."

"Ford 2000" was the direct result of several years of comprehensive benchmarking studies focusing primarily on Toyota's way of doing business. Finally, in early 1994, my former boss, after many failed attempts with previous studies, convinced top Ford Motor Company management to "take the plunge."

Ford public releases at that time stated to "remake Ford into a very different company." Ford also announced "the reorganization is a fundamental change intended to provide customers with a wider array of vehicles in more markets, assure full competitiveness in vehicle design, quality and value, and substantially reduce the cost of operating Ford's automotive business. The new structure reduces duplication of effort and facilitates best practices around the world by merging Ford's North American Automotive Operations, European Automotive Operations, and the Automotive Components Group into a single global organization called Ford Automotive Operations." In 1996, Ford incorporated its Latin American and Asia Pacific groups into the new Ford Automotive Group (FAO).

To gain "leveraged areas of competitive advantage," "Ford 2000" included the following strategies for leadership:

- Achieve worldwide growth

- Achieve worldwide product excellence

- Lead in customer satisfaction

- Become the low-cost producer

- Nimble through process improvements, and

- Empower people

Ford created five engineering centers under the Ford Automotive Operations umbrella compared with at least ten centers previously. Four of the new centers were located in the U.S. and the Small Car center was located in Europe. The objective of each activity such as Product Development, Manufacturing, Quality, Finance, Sales and Marketing was to change from a local/regional to a globally integrated approach and mindset. To achieve the goals, Ford established a single set of worldwide processes and systems.

The global FAO structure included only one global product plan with the goal to achieve significant reductions in basic vehicle platforms, the number of engine and transmission combinations, and the number of unique components and systems. In its 1998 Annual Report, Ford claimed that "Ford 2000" achieved "best ever quality levels, billions of dollars in cost savings and faster product development." James Treece of Automotive News, in the 2003 "Ford 100"

Commemorative Edition stated, "In 1998, Ford Motor Company was on top of the automotive world. Profits were at an all-time industry high, Ford had the best-selling car and the best-selling truck in the United States, and its market share was rising as that of archrival General Motors was in free fall." [43] The company's stock reached a record high in 1999. According to Ford's 1999 Annual Report, "a recent CBS News poll showed that Coca-Cola and Ford Motor Company were the two companies Americans viewed as most likely to be around at the end of the 21st century- ahead of Microsoft and ahead of GE." [44] Alex Taylor III, in his book "Sixty to Zero," stated that Professor David Lewis of the University of Michigan, an authority of the auto industry, called "Ford 2000" the "biggest reorganization in the company's history." [45]

At the initiation of "Ford 2000" in January 1995, all Ford executives received a 216 page "Operating Guide" which is still difficult to comprehend today because of its enormous complexity. The name of a recipient was superimposed in large letters on each page to assure confidentiality. Key "Ford 2000" principles included:

• "Single profit center

• Global cross-functional mindset

• Efficient organization with increased spans of empowerment

- Affordable business structure

- Common business practices

- Top-down goals and strategies

- Metrics identified for each strategy

- Standardized world-class processes and practices

- Eliminate bureaucracy waste

- Bias for action

- Continuous competitive benchmarking"

## The Contour Debacle

The Contour, which was introduced in 1995, was a mid-size replacement for the Ford Tempo (in Europe for the Mondeo). The Contour remains the most expensive car program in Ford's history at $6 billion ($8.5 billion in today's dollars). Ford of Europe had lead responsibility for the car because it was its third best selling car after the Ford Focus and the Ford Fiesta. Auto analysts described the Contour styling as bland; it was a total failure because it could not compete effectively in the mid-size segment against the Honda Accord. Contour's rear-seat room was too small for the average American. The Contour was withdrawn from the market in 2000, without a replacement in place. Ford effectively abandoned a critical market segment; it was probably one of Mr. Nasser's worst business decisions.

Nevertheless, by 2000, Ford was on top of the world with 14 major brands–"Ford, Mercury, Lincoln, Volvo, Jaguar, Aston Martin, Land Rover, Mazda, Think, Ford Credit, Hertz, Visteon, "Quality Care," and Kwik-Fit. Ford's 1999 Annual Report was growling, "Ford Motor Company enters the new millennium with a clear vision to become the world's leading Consumer Company for automotive products and services."

# The Ford Focus

During "Ford 2000," Ford Motor Company developed the compact Ford Focus as a "world car." The car was launched in Europe in 1998 followed by U.S. introduction in October 1999. In the U.S., the Focus replaced the Ford Escort and Mercury Tracer. The Focus won North American Car of the Year award for 2000, and won European Car of the Year in 1999. The Ford Focus was the first attempt at globalization. The car was highly successful in Europe (500,000 annual sales) and in the U.S. However, the U.S. Ford Focus only had 20% commonality with the more up-scale European Ford Focus. Ford planners believed that the Ford of Europe content was too costly for the segment the U.S. Focus competed in. <u>The fundamental goal of "Ford 2000" to develop world cars with high commonality was not achieved.</u>

# CHAPTER 10

## THE OUSTER OF FORD'S CEO JACQUES NASSER

During record industry sales of 17.8 million units in 2000, Ford earned $3.5 billion under Mr. Nasser. However profits were down from $7.2 billion in 1999, and $6.1 billion in 1998. Mr. Nasser was voted Automobile Industries "Man of the Year" in 1999.

Entering into 2001, Mr. Nasser was still enthusiastic about the company's new business approach. In releasing fourth quarter, 2000 results, Mr. Nasser is quoted as saying: "we launched consumer driven 6-sigma and adopted new E-commerce initiatives across the organization that together have transformed how we do business on a day-to-day basis." The "Outlook" section stated that 2001 would generate positive cash flow, and deliver another year of strong financial results. Further, as late as April 2001, Mr. Nasser stated, "our earnings momentum is as strong as ever." By the middle of 2001, however, it became clear that Ford's "new company" strategy was a failure with operating losses of $1.4 billion in the second quarter, followed by $1.1 billion in the third quarter, and dropping precipitously to $6.4 billion in the fourth quarter of 2001. What happened?

- Mr. Nasser had entered into costly ventures outside Ford's core business.

- U.S. Ford sales declined by 600,000 units between 2000 and 2001.

- Ford's U.S. car market share declined from 19.9% in 1999 to 19.1% in 2000 and 17.7% in 2001 because of the absence of exciting new passenger cars, other than the highly successful Ford Focus. This reduced Ford's competitiveness (Toyota increased its U.S. market share from 8.5% to 10.0% between 1999-2001).

- U.S. marketing costs, including heavy discounting of cars, increased from 10.6% in 1999 to 11.1% in 2000 and 14.7% in 2001 to retain existing customers.

- Net vehicle pricing was over $2 billion unfavorable in 2001 (in the fourth quarter 2009 under Mr. Mulally, net pricing was $1.7 billion favorable).

- Provisions for credit and insurance losses increased from $1.5 billion in 1999 to $2.0 billion in 2000 and $3.7 billion in 2001.

• Ford product quality deteriorated according to J.D. Powers & Associates surveys of initial quality. Ford ranked number twenty-five in 2001 (GM ranked third behind Toyota and Honda; Chrysler was number twelve). Ford incurred billions in warranty costs. In a June 25, 2001 article by Fortune's Alex Taylor III, he quoted an anonymous Wall Street analyst as follows: "costs are up, productivity is down, and the value of the brand is sinking." He also stated that Ford "now produces vehicles with more defects than any of its six largest competitors according to J.D. Powers & Associates." Pat Dorsey in a December 2010 article in Money Magazine claims that "F-O-R-D stood for Fix Or Repair Daily" at that time.

• Ford Motor Company experienced a significant number of recalls in addition to the recall of 20 million Firestone tires which cost Ford over $3 billion (after an in-depth review, the National Highway Transportation Safety Administration subsequently exonerated Ford Motor Company). Disconcerting was the recall of the new 2002 Ford Explorer. Since 2001, there have been over 15 million vehicle recalls involving 2001 models of the Ford Escape, Ford Explorer, Ford Windstar, Ford Ranger, Ford F-350 and the Ford Excursion.

• There was a decline of the Ford productivity advantage as GM was closing the gap according to a June 2001 report by Harbour & Associates. Moreover, the "Big Three" continued to lag behind the Japanese competitors with

Nissan number one, Honda number two, and Toyota number three in productivity.

• Ford was unable to contain health-care costs, which were increasing at 16% a year over the last two years and totaled an estimated $2.4 billion in 2001 (equivalent to about $1,000 per vehicle according to a 2002 speech to Ford employees by Nick Scheele, who replaced Mr. Nasser).

• Ford's gross cash position declined from $25.4 billion in 1999 to $20.2 billion in 2000 and $17.7 billion in 2001.

• Ford's net cash declined from $10 billion to $3.9 billion during the same period.

• Ford Motor Company's stockholder equity decreased from $27.6 billion in 1999 to $7.8 billion at the end of 2001.

• Credit agencies lowered Ford's debt ratings.

• Ford's common stock price per share decreased from a high of $37.30 in the second quarter of 1999 to a low of $14.70 in the second quarter of 2001 ($6.90 in the fourth quarter 2002).

• Ford's relationship with its dealers was at an all-time low because of the ill-advised "Auto Collection" strategy and the plan to sell Ford vehicles on the Internet in competition with its own dealers.

• Mr. Nasser angered the UAW with the Visteon spin-off (in retrospect, it was an excellent strategy because it eventually allowed Ford to purchase components from more competitive suppliers).

• Morale among Ford salaried employees was low because of constant cost cuttings (Mr. Nasser was known as "Jac the Knife"), the frequent management changes, his controversial employee evaluation system forcing the bottom 10% out of the company, and his intolerance toward white employees (copying the over-hyped "rank and yank" Jack Welch way of management). He stated that Ford Motor Company was "too white and too male." Mr. Nasser's disdain for gray-haired white males led to lawsuits by hundreds of older Caucasian employees, which Ford had to settle in court with a $10.5 million judgment. In the Fall 2010 issue of Boston University's "Builders & Leaders" School of Management magazine Dean Ken Freeman stated "treating everyone with dignity and respect...spells the difference between having an optimistic, committed organization or a demoralized, disgruntled employee base that holds back progress."

• Mr. Nasser imported thirteen high-level senior executives at the coveted vice president level (many without automotive experience). It was very disruptive and didn't win Mr. Nasser the most popular man on campus title. Lastly, there were feelings that Mr. Nasser had become a little too imperious.

In 2001 and 2002, Fortune magazine published a series of excellent, and lengthy articles about Ford Motor Company. Alex Taylor III wrote three of the articles, (June 25, 2001, October 29, 2001, and February 4, 2002), and the fourth article was written by Betsy Morris (November 18, 2002). Following is a summary:

• The automaker's product quality is deteriorating.

• Ford's products are aging.

• Productivity is low.

• "Ford is likely the highest-cost big automaker in the world."

• Market share is declining.

• Ford instituted "lavish" incentives.

• Launch dates for new products are slipping.

• Ford's cash reserves are declining which slowed Ford's efforts to develop new cars, and forced Ford to cut the dividend.

• Employee morale was poor.

• There was a "flurry of employee lawsuits-mostly from middle-aged white males charging age and sex discrimination."

• Dealers were extremely upset with Ford's "Auto Collection" plan.

• Mr. Nasser "installed inexperienced outsiders in key posts."

• Ford's debt was downgraded.

• Mr. Nasser has a "frenetic" management style.

In an October 31, 2001 interview with the Australian Broadcasting Corporation (ABC), Alex Taylor III stated that Mr. Nasser's stewardship was:

• Marked by problems with quality control and a deteriorating market share.

• The Firestone tires controversy.

• Declining sales and profits because of the weakening economy.

• Pushing a large capital intensive "inbred company" too quickly.

• An abrasive nature.

• Trying to be a "pusher, cross cutter and a change agent and he tried to do all three of those things as CEO but you can't do that in a time when the basic business is deteriorating and you can't do that when you take your eyes off fundamental operations like manufacturing and product development, and you can't do that without the full support of the chairman and the board."

The day of reckoning finally arrived when Mr. William Clay Ford Jr. ousted Mr. Nasser on October 30, 2001 after less than three years on the job because he lost confidence in his judgment. This painful decision probably avoided an even more serious gathering storm, similar to what GM and Chrysler faced in 2009. Ford's stellar reputation was in shambles and Bill Ford faced severe headwinds. In an extensive October 30, 2001 CNN Money article entitled "Nasser Out As Ford CEO" by Scott Hill of Sanford Bernstein, he stated that "Nasser's been the primary architect of a failed transformation of Ford from its core automotive heritage to some expansive consumer-centric organization, which we think employees, dealers, suppliers and investors have found to varying degrees to be somewhat incomprehensible." Douglas Brinkley, in his 2003 book entitled "Wheels for the World" cited a Detroit News article by Daniel Howes which was published after Nasser's firing. It stated: "Ford under Nasser went from world-beater to doormat." [46] (Mr. Nasser is now Chairman of BHP Billiton. He is repeating his Ford "play-book." He made an unsuccessful $40 billion hostile takeover of Potash Corporation in 2010.)

Automotive Industries, in its November 2002 edition, summarized the Nasser era as follows: "no one could have imagined or predicted the flood of bad news that has inundated Ford in the year following the ouster of Jac Nasser. It took Roger Smith nearly 10 years to eviscerate General Motors, but Jac did it in three. He left behind a legacy of poor vehicle quality resulting in recalls and sky high warranty costs, non-competitive production and product development expenses, a lack of new models and enemies among dealers, suppliers and Ford employees."

Mr. Ford, who took over as CEO (he was already Chairman), stated in the 2001 Ford Annual Report "we lost track of the things that made us great." He also declared "we lost focus on the critical elements of products and people." Once mighty Sears faced a similar fate when it moved into unrelated businesses such as real estate and the financial brokerage business. Kmart made the same mistakes. They are "also rans" today. Anheuser-Busch's entry into the bakery and snack food business also wasn't successful.

# CHAPTER 11

�֍ ✖ ✖

# FORD'S 2002 "REVITALIZATION" PLAN

In January 2002 Ford announced a "Revitalization Plan" with the objective to achieve "$9 billion of pre-tax profit improvements by the middle of the decade," the closing of five plants, a 35,000 manpower reduction, and the elimination of the Mercury Cougar and Lincoln Continental. Concurrently, Ford returned to its historic management style by assigning total responsibility back to its key worldwide centers such as the Americas, Ford of Europe, etc. Ford Automotive Operation was dissolved, and Ford's regional operations (The Americas, Ford Europe, Ford Asia Pacific and Africa and Premier Automotive Group) again became directly responsible for their business, and held accountable to deliver on their goals.

According to the 2001 Ford Motor Company "Sustainability Report," following are auto analyst comments about Ford's "Revitalization" Plan:

- "Ford Motor's Restructuring Plan is credible and comprehensive, and meets or exceeds our expectations on most elements."

> – Wendy Needham
> CS First Boston (1/2002)

- "On paper, the plan appears largely credible. Execution will be key."

> – Steve Girsky
> Morgan Stanley (1/2002)

However, between 2002 and 2005, Ford profits remained unsatisfactory. Market share declined from about 23% in 2001 to a new low of 17% in 2005.

# CHAPTER 12

✁ ✁ ✁

# FORD'S 2005 "RESTRUCTURING" PLAN

In 2005, Ford redoubled its restructuring efforts because of heavy loses in the vital North American business, with initial emphasis on reducing health-care costs for U.S. employees and retirees, which totaled $3.5 billion, including $2.4 billion for postretirement health-care. Effective January 1, 2007 major health-care cost reductions were implemented for salaried employees, together with company-paid retiree life insurance benefits. These actions were projected to generate on-going annual expense reductions in excess of $600 million. (I made my contribution to the survival plan. My Ford executive life insurance policy was reduced from $352,000 to $25,000, although I had paid taxes on over $125,000 in taxable income for my share toward the policy value. In addition, Ford eliminated the health-care plan except for a small annual fixed contribution. Moreover, when Ford eliminated the dividend, there was an even bigger hit on my pocketbook.)

In December 2005, Ford reached an agreement with the UAW to establish a retiree health-care plan called "Voluntary Employee Benefit Association" (VEBA) Trust. Ford projected an average annual cost savings of $650 million.

Hertz was sold in 2005 to improve Ford's balance sheet. Furthermore:

• Ford announced the idling or closing of 14 manufacturing facilities in North America by 2012 including seven vehicle assembly plants. This would result in a reduction of manufacturing employment by 25,000 to 30,000 people. Also, 4000 salaried positions were to be eliminated.

• Ford restructured struggling Visteon Corporation, which was Ford's largest supplier (in 1997, Visteon had 74,000 employees, operated 83 plants and had annual sales of about $20 billion which placed it behind GM's Delphi auto component's unit as the second largest parts supplier in the world). Visteon was spun-off in 2000. Under the 2000 Agreement, Ford remained responsible for Visteon's UAW workers. In 2005, Ford effectively bailed out Visteon by taking back 24 Visteon facilities, and over 17,000 employees and spent in excess of $1.5 billion to assist Visteon to restructure its operations.

• Ford Motor Company initiated a major rationalization of the supply base, including a reduction of about 50% of the number of suppliers who would receive new business. Ford projected a net cost reduction of $6 billion by 2010.

Ford achieved profits of only $1.4 billion in 2005, its market share continued to decline, stockholder equity was down by over $3 billion compared with December 31, 2004, total shareholder return was a negative 45% in 2005, the dividend was eliminated in 2006, and Ford's and Ford Credit's long-term credit ratings were reduced in 2005.

# CHAPTER 13

✖ ✖ ✖

# FORD'S 2006 "WAY FORWARD" PLAN

Between 2000 and 2005, Ford's U.S. sales declined from 4.2 million to 3.2 million units. In a January 23, 2006 speech to auto analysts, Mr. Mark Fields, Ford Executive Vice President and President of the Americas stated, "since 2002, Ford has reduced capacity by one million units...our revenues didn't keep pace with higher costs." Ford projected a $17 billion cash outflow in the future. In 2000, Ford's U.S. market share was 24.2%; by 2005 its share had declined to 18.6%; it reached a record low of 14.7% in 2008 (Toyota's share in the U.S. increased from 9.1% in 2000 to 17.9% in 2009).

The U.S. auto industry was performing at record levels. It was Ford Motor Company, which had lost its golden touch and there was fear that Henry Ford's dream might go bust. Accordingly, in January 2006, Ford announced another restructuring plan called "Way Forward" with the objective to implement the "most fundamental restructuring in our history." The official "Way Forward" battle cry was: "change or die" (it sounds like Patrick Henry's 1775 declaration "Give Me Liberty, or Give me Death"). It was definitely a game-changing approach, yet some auto analysts claimed the restructuring was not tough enough. The plan included:

- "A renewed commitment to bold design, improved safety and technological innovation."

- New product investments using Ford's global architectures and scale to deliver more new products faster, including more crossovers, hybrid vehicles and new small cars, as well as increased spending to strengthen Ford's truck leadership, and launch products in new segments to reach more customers.

- More clarity for the Ford, Lincoln and Mercury brands.

- North American capacity realignment will be realigned to match demand–with 14 manufacturing facilities to be idled–resulting in significant cost savings and reduced employment of 25,000-30,000 employees. In addition, it would reduce 1.2 million units, or 26 percent reduction of capacity by 2008 (only one small assembly plant has been closed in Europe in 2008 compared with 18 in the U.S., according to a September 2010 Bloomberg report).

- Salary-related cost reductions of 10% in North America, with the reduction equivalent of 4,000 salaried positions. In addition, the company's officer ranks are being reduced 12 percent by the end of the first quarter, 2006.

• Material cost reductions, excluding special items, of at least $6 billion by 2010."

It appears that Ford Motor Company lacked focus on the business basics, and it had lost its mojo. Alarm bells were ringing as a signal of distress. Accordingly, Mr. Ford announced at the January 2006 meeting with auto analysts that Ford was "unleashing our spirit of American innovation." He said the company had "grown too conservative, too hierarchical, too resistant to change and new ideas, and frankly, accountability has not been our strong suit."

At the January 2006 auto analysts meeting, Mr. Fields stated, "Ford has let competition drive our investments and launch "me too" products, or worse, we invested in segments where our customers didn't care to follow."

By July 2006 the "Way Forward" restructuring plan ran into major financial troubles, and Ford was in serious financial straits. This situation could potentially affect the fundamental tenet of the plan to introduce many new products. This would have been a big blow to Ford because analysts claimed at that time that Ford products lacked style, and innovative technological features. This must have been the time when Ford executives remembered Franklin D. Roosevelt's famous words: "The only thing we have to fear is fear itself."

# CHAPTER 14

✕ ✕ ✕

## FORD'S STATUS BY MID-2006

Ford aggressively implemented the "Way Forward" restructuring plan. In April 2006, Mr. Ford also assumed the presidency of the company. By mid-2006, Ford Motor Company experienced its most serious crisis in its long history; the company was in unchartered territory. Gloom was too nice of a word to describe Ford's situation considering the plethora of problems and many missteps. David Magee stated in his 2007 book "How Toyota Became # 1," that "the harsh reality by the end of 2006 was that American automakers were out of touch with customers."

### Declining Profits

• Ford was unable to generate satisfactory profits despite record U.S. industry sales, which averaged 17.2 million units between 2002-2006. Ford's after tax losses during this period averaged $1.8 billion annually. Ford's Premier Automotive Group (PAG) had average annual pre-tax losses of $1.1 billion between 2002-2006, despite $27 billion in average annual sales during this period.

• Ford Motor Company was sustained in the 2000's by its finance subsidiary. Ford had, in fact, become a finance company. Moreover, Automotive Operations had a negative operating cash flow of $4.2 billion in 2006 compared with a positive cash flow of $5.4 billion in 2005 and $7.0 billion in 2004. Ford's Financial Services Group had a positive operating cash flow of $7.3 billion in 2006.

### INCOME/(LOSS) BEFORE INCOME TAXES

| YEAR | AUTOMOTIVE (Billions) | FINANCIAL (Billions) |
|------|-----------------------|----------------------|
| 2002 | $(1.0) | $5.0 |
| 2003 | (1.4) | 2.3 |
| 2004 | (0.2) | 4.3 |
| 2005 | (3.9) | 5.0 |
| 2006 | (17.0) | 2.0 |

• Ford lost $12.6 billion in 2006 ($30 billion between 2006-2008). Ford's loss was a far cry from its "Ford 2000" vision "to be the leading automobile company in the world." GM lost almost $100 billion during the five years prior to its June 1, 2009 Chapter 11 filing, including $70 billion in 2007 and 2008. Nevertheless, in 2006 GM CEO Rick Wagoner received $10.2 million in total compensation. In 2007 when GM lost $39 billion he received $14.4 million in total compensation! (Mr. Mulally is presently one of the highest paid CEO's in terms of total compensation. The UAW will loudly broadcast his earnings during the 2011 labor negotiations. However, he is getting his rightful rewards. Moreover, he has "skin in the game" because most of his compensation is related to option gains due to Ford's 1000% plus increase in the stock price.)

- Health-care costs increased from $2.8 billion in 2002 to $3.5 billion in 2005 ($5 billion at GM in 2005), but declined to $3.1 billion in 2006 as a result of having Ford employees and retirees assume a higher portion of their health-care costs. The health care burden was equivalent to roughly $1,200 per U.S. vehicle in 2006, or more than the cost of steel. A 2005 CRP Report to Congress stated that the total "Big Three" health care bill in 2003 was $10 billion. The CRP estimated health-care costs for transplants at $450 per vehicle (other sources claim it was $200 at Toyota in the United States). Ford provided coverage for over 500,000 people and GM for 1.1 million. In Japan, when auto company employees retire, they are switched to a government plan two years after their retirement.

- According to CSM Worldwide, North American automotive industry capacity was about 16% above production (14% in Europe), which put pressure on profits. The domestic industry had a historic philosophy to operate at full capacity, even if it resulted in the sale of excess production at high incentive levels.

- "The company had lost its competitive drive...but there wasn't a commitment to be the best in class" (Mr. Mulally's comments in the February 26, 2010 edition of the Seattle Times (blog.seattepl.com/aerospace/archives).

# Deteriorating Balance Sheet

- Ford had negative stockholder equity at the end of 2006 of $1.2 billion compared with a positive level of $17.4 billion in 2004.

- Operating-related cash flow was $5.6 billion negative in 2006.

- Automotive sector debt at the end of December 2006 was $26.9 billion compared with $13.4 billion on December 31, 2002.

- Net automotive cash decreased to $3.9 billion at the end of 2006 compared with $7.2 billion at the end of 2005. (Ford needs roughly $10 billion in cash or equivalent to operate the company.)

- Ford reduced its dividend to $0.25 per share in 2006 compared with $0.40 in 2005. The dividend was eliminated in the fourth quarter of 2006, and no dividends have been paid since then.

- Rating agencies downgraded Ford and Ford Credit to junk status (May 2005).

## Uncompetitive Cost Structure

- "The U.S. cost structure made it impossible for Ford to profitably build cars in this country" (Mr. Mulally's comments in the February 26, 2010 edition of the Seattle Times). Ford's total hourly compensation was about $71 per hour including $38 in benefits in 2006 compared with roughly $48 per hour at Toyota's U.S. facilities. Honda's hourly compensation was $43 and $42 per hour at Nissan. Ford, GM, and Chrysler literally gave away the store to retain labor peace or to settle disruptive UAW strikes.

- Estimated Ford Motor Company blue-collar healthcare liabilities for retirees and dependents totaled roughly $22 billion ($55 billion at GM).

## Rapidly Declining Sales

- Ford sales declined by $17 billion in 2006 from a record $177 billion in 2005; Ford was in the declining corporate life cycle (start-up, growth, mature, decline).

- Ford's U.S. market share decreased since 1995 and its share declined by four percentage points between 2002-2006 to 16.7%. The reduction is primarily the result of Ford's retail share decline—from 16.3% in 2002 to 11.8% in 2006. During the same period, Ford U.S. sales declined from 3.6 million to 2.9 million units, which materially impacted on Ford's financial performance because of the high proportion of the domestic auto company's costs are fixed.

- Toyota dethroned Ford in 2006 to become the number two-auto company in the world, and threatened Ford's number two U.S. position, which Ford has held since 1931 when it passed Chrysler Corporation.

- As part of the agenda to maximize profits, Ford overemphasized cash cow SUV's and trucks. This negatively impacted sales and profits when their popularity declined. Rapidly increasing gasoline prices reduced the demand for fuel hungry SUV's (gasoline prices increased from $1.36/gallon in 2002 to $2.59 in 2006). Ford Expedition sales decreased from 182,000 in 2003 to 87,000 in 2006. Ford Explorer sales declined from 373,000 to 179,000 during the same period (by 2009, Ford

Expedition sales decreased to 32,000 units, and Ford Explorer sales to 78,000 units according to Automotive News).

- The highly popular and high-profit SUV's and trucks like the F-150 masked the fundamental Ford and GM problems for many years. As late as 2000, Ford sold 450,000 Ford Explorers and over 900,000 F-150 trucks. U.S. companies had the market for these types of products largely for themselves. During these "Big Three" glory days, Toyota kept focusing on fuel-efficient cars, which led to the introduction of the Prius. (When U.S. gasoline prices are in the $2.50 range, hybrid sales collapse. Also, they have a long payback, and are very costly to repair according to a January 2011 article in SmartMoney.)

- Ford was underrepresented in the growing small car segment with only the Ford Focus until the arrival of the Ford Fusion in 2004. Ford did not have one small car among the top ten vehicles in America. The Toyota Camry, Toyota Corolla/ Matrix, Honda Accord, Honda Civic, Nissan Altima and Chevy Impala were on the top ten list. GM outsold Ford by 600,000 passenger cars in 2006. By 2009, only the Ford Fusion was on the top ten car lists. Japanese passenger cars accounted for six of the top ten entries.

- There was increasing reliance on low-profit fleet sales, especially to the daily rental fleets. Ford fleet sales as a percentage of total vehicle sales increased from 23% in 2002 to 28% in 2005, and 31% in 2006.

• Large rebates were required to sell vehicles, which reduced residuals.

• Ford products were mostly unappealing and lacked style and innovative features.

• There was a lack of focus on the core Ford brand.

• Ford Motor Company had too many brands–seven compared with three at Toyota, two at Honda and Nissan.

• The shortsighted mid-2000s decision to relegate two Ford flagship products–the Lincoln Town car and the Ford Taurus–to the rental fleet destroyed their image.

## Poor Product Quality

- Ford product quality lagged behind Japanese competitors. In the 2006 J.D. Powers & Associates Vehicle Dependability Study of original owners of 3-year old vehicles, the Ford brand ranked number twelve. The Ford brand ranked number fifteen (below average) in J.D. Powers & Associates initial quality survey in 2006 (2007 number ten; 2008 number eight; 2009 number eight, and a 2010 ranking of number five–ahead of Toyota, Honda and Nissan as a result of "One Ford"). Toyota's philosophy during weak industry sales was to invest heavily in quality; U.S. companies offered easy financing and/or major discounts.

- Ford recalled over five million vehicles in 2005 and 2006. Moreover, on April 14, 2011 Ford recalled almost 1.2 million 2004-2006 F-150 pickups for airbag issues.

- Ford's warranty costs totaled $4 billion in 2005 and $3.5 billion in 2006.

# Ford's Factories Lagged Behind Competition

- Ford's manufacturing complexity inhibited cost savings because of Ford's inflexible plants, which could produce mostly single products. The company was slow in switching to flexible facilities to meet changing consumer tastes.

- Ford productivity lagged behind competition. In 2005, it took Ford 37 hours to produce a vehicle in the U.S. compared with 28 at Toyota. On a worldwide basis, Ford produced 23 vehicles per employee, Toyota 31, GM 26 and Honda 25.

## Senior Management Turnover

- Ford had a high President/CEO turnover—four between 2000-2006.

- "I have never seen a company with the lack of consistency of purpose as Ford" (Mr. Mulally comments on May 9, 2007 "Ford CEO Mulally battles red tape, faces investors."(www.newsmax.com) [47]

- "The bureaucracy at Ford grew, and managers took refuge in the structure when things got tough rather than innovate or try new ideas that seemed risky." (Allan Gilmour, former Ford CFO in a 2007 interview "The New Heat on Ford"). (www.businessweek.com) [47]

- Ford's Finance Staff had a pervasive influence with Ford's top management. They overshadowed all other Ford functions by a wide margin, which sometimes impeded frank discussions. However, Ford's finance group was a "renowned incubator for finance executives" according to CFO.com.

## Employees and Wall Street Lost Faith

- Ford Motor Company employee's morale was low because of massive layoffs and a cloudy outlook.

- Ford had a poor reputation on Wall Street and lost its "blue-chip" pedigree. As late as 2007/2008, Ford was ranked last in survivability among the "Big Three." Ford common stock on the NYSE reached a record low of $1.01 per share in November 2008 compared with a record high of $37.30 in 1999 (adjusted for stock splits and stock dividends).

- Ford's public reputation was in shatters, which no ad campaign could repair.

## Unhappy Dealers

- Ford's relationship with its dealers was unsatisfactory, stemming from the "Auto Collection" fiasco described previously.

- Ford's dealer network in major metropolitan markets was too large which resulted in low-profit stores. Sales per dealers were significantly below Asian competitors.

- The Lincoln dealerbody and facilities were uncompetitive compared with Lexus, BMW, Mercedes and Cadillac dealerships.

## Dissatisfied Suppliers

- Key Ford suppliers ranked Ford last as the auto company they want to work with. Honda and Toyota were the preferred customers.

# Ford Missed the Boat in Asia

• Ford was underrepresented in the rapidly growing Asian markets although Ford Asia Pacific was established in 1970. In view of Ford's problems in the U.S. home market, Ford did not actively enter China until 2003. Today, Ford is not one of the top ten auto companies in China (2.6% market share).

It appeared that Ford had slid into an irrevocable decline because anything that could go bad did! The need for new leadership was urgent. Therefore, when Mr. Mulally joined Ford, he was confronted with a "leaking swimming pool" plus the menacing threat from Toyota, which had no qualm to make mincemeat of the company, and the other two U.S. based automobile manufacturers.

# CHAPTER 15

## TOYOTA'S STATUS BY MID-2006

### Background

I have the highest respect for the Japanese people who live in a land of peace and harmony. From my business trips to this lovely country, I observed well mannered, highly educated, friendly, very polite, orderly, and hard-working people who are totally dedicated to the advancement of their children including after-hour tutoring. Japan has a 1,300-year history, people are group-oriented, have great respect for the elderly, and they live in micro housing. The Japanese people are sensitive toward others, but are the opposite of the U.S. "embracing personality." They also enjoy beauty, especially nature. Further, they have a deep love for their country, and a high level of nationalism. In addition, it was wonderful to observe how the people relate to each other in a small, heavily mountainous country with 125 million inhabitants, the size of Montana (70% forested). In terms of comparing them to the many other nations I have been to in my lifetime, I would rank Japan close to the top on my list.

However, when it comes to international commerce, it is a survival of the fittest philosophy, especially since Japan has very few natural resources of its own. In my opinion, the Japanese strategy and juggernaut seems similar to the tactics of the famous Prussian military strategist Karl von Clausewitz who advocated the total destruction of the enemy. Another Prussian, Otto von Bismarck, favored an identical approach. It may sound mean-spirited and with a degree of envy, but I believe that Toyota and Japan Inc. are an embodiment of Julius Caesar (the great General) and Augustus (Rome's powerful emperor). They are the new Shoguns warrior class, which ruled Japan for over 700 years. They believe in the famous 1960s ABBA hit song "The Winner Takes it All." In view of the traditional lifetime employment, the dedication of Japanese employees' to their company is actually like a family. Their dedication to the "company family" can only be comprehended by somebody who has seen them close-up. Further, as Clyde Prestowitz, Jr. stated in his book "Trading Places," the companies in Japan "are structured along the lines of the ancient clan armies and there is a military aura about many of them." I have often witnessed with awe in my early 30s when the economic warriors departed for overseas battle from Tokyo airport with flags waving and all family members present and shouting the battle-cry Kudasai (do your best or work hard). Using a militaristic term, they looked like shock troops to me.

Encyclopedia Britannica defines economic warfare as "the use of, or the threat to use economic means against a country in order to weaken its economy and thereby reduce its political and military power." This is Toyota's philosophy. (I believe that the "War of 1812" (1809-1815) was the modern beginning in America of economic warfare.)

Toyota's economic strategy almost seems to be an embodiment of the 19th century economic powers represented by the Hudson Bay Company, the Dutch East India Company, and the British South Africa Company, as described in a new book by Stephen Bown entitled "Merchant Kings." Until Toyota's cataclysmic 19 million units worldwide vehicle recall, which served notice to consumers that Toyota was not walking on water with its unconquerable quality perception, Toyota's power in the global automotive industry wasn't far removed from the "Merchant Kings."

The Japanese auto invasion has caused undescribable pain and sufferings in the Heartland of America, with hundreds of thousands of job losses and the bankruptcy of hundreds of Midwest companies. (I readily admit that I see red when some countries make us look prostrate and feckless and it is all dismissed as part of unbridled capitalism.) (One-way.) Toyota follows the exact strategy Tom Peters recommended in his 2010 book "The Little BIG Things:" "grab your weakened competitors' customers ASAP." Toyota achieved it "as swift as a swallow flies."

The Japanese auto industry Kriegspiele (warfare) are identical to the philosophy employed by "Japan Inc."(It is a term used to describe the close relationship between the government and the business community, which remains to this day). It is, of course, the opposite in the U.S. because of Washington's tone deafness toward business. In the 1970s, America ceded first place to Japan in one manufacturing industry after another including the entire electronics sector (in the 1950s, Japan totally dominated the U.S. toys and textile business which has long ago moved from Japan to China, and will next move to Vietnam as China ascents the value added chain). Japan also devastated the U.S. high technology industries–from machine tools to semiconductors. Sadly, a quote from Clyde Prestowitz's 1988 book entitled "How We Allowed Japan to Take the Lead" epitomizes the U.S. government's attitude: "if our guys can't hack it, we ought to let them go."

The Japanese automotive companies were in the driver's seat and have used the classic conquer and destroy strategy. It started with small cars, followed by medium priced entries, then luxury cars. Finally, they achieved hegemony and a 40% market share in the world's biggest single auto market (until China dethroned the U.S. in 2009) by attacking the last bastion of the enemy–the highly profitable SUV and big truck segments. This was Toyota's coup d'etat and its planned coup de grace (death blow) against the formerly "Big Three." Concurrently, they kept protecting their home market with non-tariff barriers (Korea is following the identical strategy). They had one merciless target on their back: destroy the foe at any cost!

In my opinion, the Japanese, led by Toyota, would have lost no tears if they had succeeded in annihilating the entire U.S. auto industry, which they almost achieved. This includes the U.S. based parts suppliers (54 bankruptcies) because most Asian companies bring their own affiliated suppliers to the U.S. Today, two of the top three global OEM (Original Equipment Manufacturers) parts suppliers are Japanese-based and Toyota-affiliated. Two others in the Toyota Group are ranked number fifteen and twenty nine (no other automotive producer can make such a claim). The Toyota parts suppliers provide the parent company with new innovations first.  Historically, Delphi and Visteon were the top OEM suppliers until their recent bankruptcies and the decline of the U.S. auto market. The Japanese auto parts suppliers also have the "largest number of companies in the OEM supplier ranking, with 29 companies listed," according to Automotive News. They gained hegemony–almost like an octopus enveloped by its tentacles.

I have noticed over the years whenever Toyota had pushed the "Big Three" into the corner with the resulting negative press publicity, Toyota would imply publicly that they would "go soft" on the American auto companies (what an embarrassment to the one time world champion). People; let me assure you, it was all a façade. It is the same PR they used in Washington during the disastrous Senate Subcommittee hearings claiming that they expanded too fast, and would slow expansion. The exact opposite is actually happening with aggressive capacity expansion including China, Brazil, Russia, the U.S., Thailand, Argentina, etc. Fortunately, the world now knows that their highfaluting quality mystique included a lot of braggadocio and their products didn't walk on water.

In the fifty-year struggle between the old titans of the West, and the newcomers from the East, the latest casualty was Ford Motor Company; the mid-2006 period was Ford's worst crisis in sixty years. In a March 3, 2007 article in "The Market Oracle" entitled "The Demise of the American Auto Industry and the Rise of Toyota-Quality Vs. Quantity," Martin Weiss correctly called it a "clash of cultures." He stated that Detroit is losing:

• Economies of scale

• Loyal customers

• Their war chest is shrinking and, therefore, it is reducing their chances of catching up technologically.

The fight for survival has resulted in a clear winner: Toyota Motor Corporation, with their admirable "let's get it done attitude, and we want tomorrow now." Toyota was invincible; they won the demolition derby against the guys who honorably played by the rules. Toyota is a company not interested in taking prisoners in their relentless pursuit to totally dominate the world automotive industry. Toyota's unprecedented success, despite temporary minor recent setbacks due to the 19 million units worldwide recalls, has even left its Japanese auto rivals in the dust.

## Toyota's Status by Mid-2006

Toyota, which has over 660,000 stockholders, has achieved an enviable record:

- New income of $11.7 billion on sales of $171 billion for the fiscal year ending March 31, 2006 (Ford lost $12.6 billion in 2006).

- Ranked number eight on Fortune's 2006 "Global 500" list (in 1996, GM was number one, number two and Toyota number ten).

- Worldwide vehicle sales increased from 5.8 million units in 2002 to 8.0 million units in 2006 (Ford Motor Company sales declined from 7.0 million to 6.6 million units during the same period).

- Net income before taxes reached an astonishing $22 billion for the fiscal year ending March 31, 2007. Net income was $14 billion (Ford lost $2.7 billion in 2007). Reportedly, Toyota has never lost money between 1951 and 2006 according to "How Toyota Became # 1" (the book was published in 2007).

- Toyota dethroned Ford in 2007 from its historic number two position in the U.S.; in 2002, Ford had outsold Toyota by 1.9 million units! This was a defining moment with the old guard of the West being humiliated on its own home market. (In 2007, Toyota became the number one conquistador in the kanji (world).

- The top two passenger cars in 2006 were the Toyota Camry and the Toyota Corolla/Matrix (Ford's top entry was the Ford Fusion in number eight position).

- Toyota's perceived product quality was the envy of the industry, and was constantly trumpeted in its commercials. In J.D. Powers & Associates 2006 "Initial Quality Study," Lexus was ranked number two and Toyota number four; both brands captured eleven of nineteen segment awards in 2006. Now we know that behind the curtain, it was not true; they hid the facts. According to the January 2011 issue of Car and Driver, Toyota had five of the 10 biggest recalls in 2010 followed by GM and Honda with two each. Ford was not on the list. In mid-December 2010, Honda recalled 1.3 million Fit cars. (According to Bloomberg, Toyota announced on January 9, 2011 the establishment of a $50 million safety research center in Ann Arbor, Michigan.)

- Toyota was the industry benchmark in manufacturing productivity, according to Oliver Wyman's Harbour Report. However, the "Big Three" have substantially improved their productivity in recent years. They reduced the gap to around three hours to build a car when compared with Toyota's productivity. A 1995 Harbour Report cited by President Obama's "car czar" in a September 18-19, 2010 article in the Wall Street Journal, it took GM 46 hours and Ford 38 hours to build a car compared with 29 hours at Toyota.

- Toyota's average U.S. hourly compensation costs in 2006 totaled roughly $48 per hour compared with $71 per hour at Ford according to "Big Three Auto Procon.org" ($56 in 2011 according to Fox News on January 12, 2011 private sector wages averaged $25 per hour in 2006).

- Toyota has the highest customer loyalty rate in the industry.

- Toyota received Motor Trend's 2007 awards for: Truck of the Year (Tundra) and Car of the Year (Camry).

- Toyota was ranked eighth on Fortune's 2006 Top Ten "Most Admired" list.

- Toyota received rave reviews in the press:

  - "Toyota: The King of Automakers" and "Toyota is Winning the Auto War in the United States" (2008 article entitled: Understanding Business Strategy by Messrs. Ireland, Hoskisson and Hitt).

  - Other 2006/2007 Toyota headlines, according to "How Toyota Became # 1," included: "From Zero to 60 to World Domination" in the New York Times magazine, and "A Carmaker Wired to Win" in Business Week.

- The Toyota whirlwind wouldn't stop because they wanted to expand their booty. To further strengthen its hegemony and its massive assault on the "Big Three," Toyota opened a new truck plant in Texas (also an SUV plant in Canada in 2008). Toyota profits, of course, are going to Japan while chaos reigned in the U.S. Midwest. While Toyota overwhelmed Ford, GM and Chrysler, by mid-2006 other Japanese auto companies in the U.S. continued their aggressive expansion plans. Nissan Motor Company opened a $1.4 billion assembly plant in Canton, Mississippi.

Toyota gained the upper hand in every aspect of the automobile business. James P. Womack of MIT, one of the most astute auto industry experts, stated correctly in a February 13, 2006 article in the Wall Street Journal entitled "Why Toyota Won:"

- GM and Ford can't design vehicles that Americans want (today, Ford is proving this to be an old story).

- GM and Ford are clueless as to how to work with their suppliers (today, suppliers glamour to work with Ford because the company fundamentally changed its supplier relationship).

- GM and Ford have miasmic management cultures; he described Toyota employees as great team players (since Mr. Mulally's arrival in September 2006, Ford culture has radically changed).

- GM and Ford still treat customers as strangers (under the leadership of Jim Farley, an alumni from Toyota, Ford's sales, marketing and service approach is improving markedly and Ford is achieving significant sales gains).

- There is no mystery about the lean business model. Why can't GM and Ford embrace it? (Mr. Womack might wish to visit Ford Motor Company, especially the $500 million recently spent at a plant outside Detroit, which CNBC's Phil LeBeau called the first plant in the world to manufacture conventional, hybrid and electric vehicles under one roof. Professor Womack should also study the other Ford plants undergoing radical improvements under Mr. Mulally's "One Ford" Plan including a lean structure).

It is almost impossible to fully interpret the secretive mind of the Japanese despite having spent many months in Japan. Therefore, I rely on three Japanese authors of a book entitled "Extreme Toyota" for the six "secrets" of Toyota's philosophy which were listed in a November 2008 article on a website called "Reforming Project Management:"

- Set impossible goals

- Experimentation (the authors call it the "scientific method of learning")

- Founders' philosophies ("tomorrow will be better than today; everybody should win; customers first, dealers second, and manufacturer last")

- Nerve system ("everybody knows everything")

• Up and in ("competitors follow up our approach while Toyota keeps investing in training their staff")

Reportedly, "the six forces, in combination, create complex dependencies that strengthen each of the forces and keep Toyota in a state of disequilibrium, where radical contradictions coexist, generating healthy tensions and instability within the organization." Healthy tension in an organization is productive, although it was often carried to destructive internal warfare at Ford Motor Company.

To illustrate the David and Goliath battleground, Toyota's market capitalization was $170 billion in early August 2006 compared with Ford's $13 billion according to an August 3, 2006 article in Bloomberg BusinessWeek (on December 31, 2010 the value was $123 billion and $58 billion, respectively). However, as former President George W. Bush stated in his Decision Point memoirs, "you have to play the hand you're dealt." Therefore, Mr. Mulally decided, "It's My Turn to Touch the Stars and Nobody Will Stop Me" (Diana Ross song).

# CHAPTER 16

❧ ❧ ❧

## THE NEW KID ON THE BLOCK

### Introduction

Toyota was perilously breathing down Ford's neck and dealing a crushing blow. In addition, the company faced so many fundamental issues, which deteriorated almost daily. Thus, Ford was confronted with a crisis of confidence, and was at the crossroads of its existence. It appears that Ford had lost its compass with all key metrics pointing in the wrong direction, as described previously. There was a belief that Ford's doom was almost sealed because the company was facing monstrous problems of Shakespearean dimensions. There was real fear that the lights would go out at the company's World Headquarters, and that the freight train would stop in Dearborn, Michigan to haul away Ford's remaining valuable possessions. (It is exactly what is happening at the "Old GM;" GM calls it "predecessor"–which is disposing at auction hundreds of millions of dollars of "used" assets.)

It is understandable that the Ford family, Ford employees, Wall Street and other stakeholders such as dealers and suppliers hit the panic button because of the prospects of a potential bankruptcy. The Ford family and the Ford Motor Company Board of Directors had two strategic alternatives: sell Ford Motor Company, which would have been a fire-sale event, or fix the company. The former was unacceptable to the Ford family because as Rod Stewart's 1970s song lyrics stated: "Never Give Up On a Dream." Therefore, Mr. Ford sent an S.O.S. to the auto world; reportedly two of the most important European CEO's said: no, thank you. Thus, Bill Ford hired Mr. Mulally, a good "old" homegrown talent (no punt intended). The superman from Seattle was hired to lead the rebuilding and total makeover of Ford Motor Company. Fortunately, Mr. Ford didn't listen to the 1960s song "I Don't Need Nobody To Tell My Troubles To." Bold changes were required to turn the stranded ship around, which required a new buzz of energetic activity.

Some of Ford's mid-2006 problems can be traced to Mr. Nasser's misadventures. This included lack of focus on Ford's core business and spending billions of dollars of precious funds on questionable acquisitions. In addition, there was a continued lack of intense focus on passenger cars even after Mr. Nasser's departure (Ford's U.S. car share declined from 9.8% in 2000 to 6.7% in 2006). Moreover, despite continued heavy Premier Automotive Group financial losses, Ford kept funding these luxury brands instead of divesting the operations. According to David Magee's book "How Toyota Became # 1," Ford even paid bonuses to executives and hourly employees in 2006– in a year in which Ford reported one of the largest losses in the company's history.

Clearly, Mr. Mulally was confronted with "Mission Impossible" and it took more than guts to take on this assignment to pump oxygen into a seriously under performing company. Ford was boxed in by: $17 billion in Automotive debt ($144 billion including the company's financial sector), a deep slump in introducing high-volume and exciting new cars, and facing lower-cost aggressive Asian rivals. In addition, Mr. Mulally had no automotive experience, never held a CEO position, and Ford was not a "mom & pop" operation that could be nurtured back to health quickly. However, he had a crackerjack record at Boeing, which lent an "Aura of Legitimacy" to his appointment as Ford's CEO, and he was world-wise. However, he was in the sunset of his years when he entered a new industry. People questioned if a man in his 60's could rescue Ford. Moreover, there was no time for on-the job training. It seems that Mr. Mulally is a follower of the late Helen Keller who is quoted in Tom Peters' book "The Little BIG Things" as follows: "life is either a daring adventure, or nothing."

In an article published in 2009 by Beth M. Ramsay on a website called "Relationship Savy," she discussed "seven habits of highly unsuccessful people," which are summarized below, and several apply to some past auto industry executives:

1. Blind leading the blind

2. Charging credit on someone else's account (very popular trait in the auto industry–everybody was the father of the 1965 Mustang)

3. Yeah, but-ter (Yeah, it won't work)

4. Penalizing the messenger

5. Being a winner at all cost

6. I have it and you don't (withholding needed information)

7. Being an excuse-maker (blame OPEC, UAW, etc.)

Fortunately, these are not traits Mr. Mulally possesses. He has that uncommon American "can-do" spirit to persevere, with a 24/7 state of mind, and he practiced Pollyannaism (a forever optimistic attitude). It is exemplified in America's resilience to bounce back from wild storm clouds, and has happened many times since 1776. This survival, adaptability, forging ahead, and ultimately winning the battle was born in the wilderness of America, which lasted for over 200 years until roughly 1890 when the frontier vanished. The 1971 USDA Forest Service publication entitled "Search for Solitude: Our Wilderness Heritage" stated it perfectly "the wilderness shaped our national character

as our forefathers met and conquered its early challenge."
It remains to this day a basic American character. It was
this tenacity which Mr. Mulally brought with him when he
jettisoned in a Boeing airplane into Ford country in September 2006. His adrenal was pumping because he knew
of the job ahead, and he was ready to fight trench economic warfare to save an American icon, and was ready
to spearhead the story of the "Fall and Rise" of Ford Motor
Company. He had to ignore Ford's history, traditions and
culture because these characteristics had not passed the
muster of time. (His office on the twelfth floor at Ford World
Headquarters has no gold-gilded antique furniture).

## Mr. Mulally Arrives at Ford

As indicated in the prologue, William Clay Ford, Jr. took the unprecedented step in September 2006 to essentially fire himself as CEO and appointed Alan R. Mulally as President and CEO; it was a courageous act. (Giant computer company Wang Laboratories was also family controlled. Unlike Mr. Ford, the founder failed to act as his young son's management of the company ultimately led to bankruptcy, and I lost all my savings for my six children's college education which were in Wang shares.)

Prior to joining Ford, Mr. Mulally worked at Boeing for 37 years where he started in 1969 as an engineer. Reportedly, he was motivated by the late President Kennedy's challenge to send a man to the moon. Mr. Mulally's last position at Boeing was Executive Vice President of the Boeing Company, and President and Chief Executive Officer of Boeing Commercial Airplanes. Mr. Mulally was named Boeing's President of Commercial Airplanes in September 1998. Previously, Mr. Mulally served as President of Boeing Information, Space & Defense Systems, and Senior Vice President of the Boeing Company. Mr. Mulally is widely credited with Boeing's resurgence in the 2000's. He has been recognized for his contributions and industry leadership, including being named one of "The World's Most Influential People" by Time magazine in their 2009 "Time 100" issue, "Person of the Year" for 2006 by Aviation Week magazine, and one of "The Best Leaders of 2005" by Business Week magazine. He assumed responsibility for a storied company in a near-death spiral.

A native of Kansas, the home of the late Dwight D. Eisenhower, Mr. Mulally holds Bachelor and Master of Science degrees in aeronautical and astronautical engineering from the University of Kansas, and earned a Master's in Management from the Massachusetts Institute of Technology. In Ford Motor Company's almost 110-year history, Mr. Mulally was only the third CEO with a degree in engineering (John Dykstra and "Bunkie" Knudsen also were engineers; both were CEO's for only two years).

Peter Brown, Publisher and Editorial Director of Automotive News, stated in the June 16, 2003 Commemorative Edition of "Ford 100" that "the original Henry Ford had an optimistic, American vision of what people could become. It was mostly right and it changed the world." [48] Mr. Mulally also seems to have this exulting attitude–an "All-American" spirit. In a February 27-28, 2010 article by Paul Ingrassia in the Wall Street Journal entitled "Ford's Renaissance Man," Mr. Mulally is quoted as saying "there is no reason that America can't compete in a global economy, and I love being one small proof point in that." [49] Further, in an August 15, 2010 Time magazine article he is quoted as stating, "we are fighting for the soul of American manufacturing." [50] This is a message of an American patriot, which resonates in the Heartland of America. A commentator on the November 23, 2010 "Morning Joe" on MSNBC stated that Mr. Mulally is an "American Hero" who did everything right during the economic crisis! Mr. Mulally, unlike the CEO's of GM and Chrysler, is the highest practitioner of the U.S. style of capitalism.

Mr. Mulally is demonstrating to the world that U.S. companies can compete in the global economy. Mr. Mulally understands technology, studied Toyota's famous production system, knows how to upgrade plants because his forte is manufacturing, and has experience dealing with powerful unions based on his 37 years at Boeing. In addition, he brought with him to Ford a worldview, which was important because over 50% of Ford's business is outside of the United States. His Boeing skills were transferable because he faced similar problems at Ford. For example, according to an excellent December 2005 article in Business Week (images.businessweek.com), Mr. Mulally had difficult decisions to make after the September 11 terror attacks because "the attacks had sent the U.S. airline business into a tailspin." Production had to be reduced by over 50%, 27,000 workers had to be discharged, and concurrently, Airbus dethroned Boeing as number one in the world. "Since those days, Mulally, 60, has engineered a remarkable recovery. During the downturn, he focused religiously on cutting waste and streamlining Boeing's antiquated and inefficient airplane production lines. He then bet the company's future on a set of new technologies." This is the exact template Mr. Mulally has introduced at

Ford Motor Company. The Seattle Times, in a September 6, 2006 article stated that Alan Mulally "played a central role in restoring the company's (Boeing) luster, swagger and profits." The article also stated that Mr. Mulally reduced the number of Boeing models from 14 to 4–exactly what he is doing at Ford Motor Company.

In describing Mr. Alan Mulally when he was selected among "the 2009 Time 100," Steve Balmer, CEO of Microsoft stated "it is extremely rare for one leader to play a major role in two of America's top industries. Alan Mulally is that rare case. As president of Boeing's commercial-airplane business in the late 1990s, he revamped the company's product mix, transformed production and embraced digital technology. In the process, he made Boeing a model for global manufacturing. He also guided the company through the aftermath of 9/11, which dealt a nearly crippling blow to the aerospace industry. Fast-forward to 2009 and the challenges facing Detroit and the entire global auto industry are daunting. As CEO of Ford Motor Co., Alan, 63, is restructuring a 100-year old industrial powerhouse in the midst of a crisis that threatens the very survival of our auto industry."

A quote from the 2002 book entitled "The Ford Century" edited by Nancy Cash also seems to fit Mr. Mulally. It is from a fellow person from the Midwest by the name of Harry S. Truman who supposedly stated once: "men make history, and not the other way around. In periods where there is no leadership, society stands still. Progress occurs when courageous, skillful leaders seize the opportunity to change things for the better." [51] Yes, this is what Mr. Mulally is doing to revive an American icon which was in the midst of a historic turmoil when he joined Ford Motor Company. Henry Ford would have been proud of him. "Welcome to the Jungle" (Guns N' Roses song), I am sure, William Clay Ford, Jr. told Alan Mulally on his first day on the job.

Mr. Mulally's single-minded "let's make it happen" philosophy led to an immediate attack on Ford's fundamental problems despite the steep learning curve entering a new industry (it took countless Ford executives nine months in 1994 to develop the "Ford 2000" concept). However, he is not an executive who "shoots from the hip." In retrospect, it is quite evident that Mr. Mulally was like General Patton's military march into Germany–perfectly executed. (I remember the day when a seven-hour long column of American tanks and an array of indescribable support vehicles moved unopposed through my hometown of Bad Nauheim on March 29, 1945).

Mr. Mulally first established a clear vision for the new Ford corporate strategy and challenged the entire Ford way of doing business with a General Patton kind of fervor. Mr. Mulally conducted his own intensive research of the auto industry and Ford Motor Company prior to joining the company. He knew that his task would be unenviable, and he was determined to "Hit the Ground Running" (November

22, 2010 Forbes magazine title for the new Congress). This helped him identify the basic problems facing Ford, which led to the new business model. He outlined the issues to Alex Taylor III of Fortune magazine during their first meeting in 2006, "too much complexity, too little cooperation, and not enough transparency." [52] Mr. Mulally methodically prepared an aggressive business plan to correct the deficiencies, and established tough goals to achieve the reinvention of Ford Motor Company.

It was crunch time, with literally "having a gun held to his head," Mr. Mulally went to work systematically restructuring Ford without introducing eye-catching slogans. His was not a mosaic of dysfunctional approaches nor was it a Maerchen (fairy tale); he simply attacked all the key milestones ASAP. Since he had no automotive experience, he was able to think "outside the box." When asked "how are you going to tackle something as complex and unfamiliar as the auto business when we are in such tough financial shape?" He replied in a January 29, 2008 interview on MSNBC: "an automobile has about 10,000 moving parts, right? An airplane has two million, and it has to stay up in the air." He could have also mentioned that he is a manufacturing genius, which Ford desperately needed. Efraim Levy of Standard & Poor's stated that "Ford has a lot of parallel with Boeing ... Mulally has been able to put his vision and input into the culture and the execution." He made these comments on October 11, 2010 on

S&P "Market Scope" when his company upgraded Ford's stock and raised the target price.

Nobody could have ever imagined in 2006 that Mr. Mulally would eventually be celebrated as a game-changer, and toasted as the auto industry's new "super-star" in two of America's marquee industries. Clearly, Mr. Mulally followed Helen Keller's advice: "ONE CAN NEVER CONSENT TO CREEP WHEN ONE FEELS AN IMPULSE TO SOAR."

# CHAPTER 17

✖ ✖ ✖

# LET THE MAGIC BEGIN

## The Plan and the Goal

Like the worlds best starting pitchers such as Cy Young, Sandy Koufax or Tom Seaver, Mr. Mulally came on the scene with a blazing fastball. In a recent response to a Wall Street Journal story about George W. Bush, a reader stated, "it's not the hand you are dealt, so much as how you play it." That is how Mr. Mulally approached the job. The framework for the "One Ford" plan was a complete makeover of Ford, which centered on three fundamental building blocks–**ONE TEAM**, **ONE PLAN**, and **ONE GOAL**.

### "One Team"

"People working together as a lean, global enterprise for automotive leadership, as measured by customer, employee, dealer, investor, supplier, union/council, and community satisfaction." Mr. Mulally's leadership goal is a united team, and equally important, a stable management team. Except for the retirement of CFO Don LeClair in November 2008, and the departure of the Human Resources/Labor Affairs Group V.P., the only key Ford executive changes to date involved executive development moves. (GM had four CEO's in two years).

### "One Plan"

This plan will be described in detail in the following chapter.

### "One Goal"

"An exciting viable Ford delivering profitable growth for all."

A critical element was to establish the new basic parameters, which would set the stage for Ford's renaissance. This had to be accomplished "at one fell swoop" because the company was fighting an epic battle for survival. Without too much exaggeration, Asian vultures were already at his back and bivouacking at Ford's World Headquarters wallowing in glory at the company's demise and ready to "harvest" the company's valuable assets (many "old" GM auctioned assets are being shipped to Korea).

A list of expected behaviors was developed, including fostering functional and technical excellence, and becoming role models for Ford values and deliver results (details available on www.one.ford.com). The key element is WORKING TOGETHER.

- "Believe in skilled and motivated people working together.

- Include everyone, respect, listen to, help and appreciate others.

- Build strong relationships, be a team player, develop others and us.

- Communicate clearly, concisely and candidly"

Moreover, Mr. Mulally also created a business plan review process because he was operating in unchartered territory, and to use CNBC's tagline, Mr. Mulally was "navigating in choppy waters." Mr. Mulally meets every Thursday with his 16 direct reports (Mr. Sergio Marchionne, the CEO of Fiat Group/Chrysler, has twenty five direct Chrysler and twenty one direct executives at Fiat reporting to him). [53] Mr. Mulally's team includes the executives responsible for Ford's worldwide operations–the Americas (U.S., Canada, Mexico, South and Latin America), Europe, Asia Pacific/Africa, and Ford Motor Credit Company, and all staff activities.

Management gurus like Professor Rosabeth Moss Kanter of the Harvard Business School would define Mr. Mulally's "One Ford" reengineering as a "Bold Strokes" approach with top line leadership and rapid implementation. The other "change" management is described as "Long Marches" which represents a gradual restructuring. Mr. Mulally was against the piecemeal strategy, and attacked all central tenets of Ford Motor Company because a gradual "chugging along" approach would not have provided the vital medicine quick enough since the patient was already on a ventilator. Steven Rattner, in his 2010 book "Overhaul," claimed that former GM CEO Rick Wagoner "operated as an incrementalist, and a slow-moving one at that." He also stated that "there was no real urgency" at GM to fix its problems.

Mr. Mulally encourages an open forum. He also changed Ford's old ways of doing business, and nothing was too enigmatic for him. Historically, Ford executives making presentations at key meetings came prepared with five-inch back-up books. From my own experience, it used to take weeks to prepare such material. The likelihood was high that certain senior executives almost enjoyed embarrassing the presenter with often-unimportant details. Woe to the analyst who missed including the details in the back-up book. Under Mr. Mulally's refreshing philosophy, no back-up books are required because, as he stated in the 2009 Fortune interview, "I'm not going to grind them with as many questions as I can to humiliate them." Mr. Mulally has truly changed Ford's culture. Unlike certain previous Ford CEO's, he doesn't run the company by fear.

Professor Bill George of the Harvard Business School listed the following leadership characteristics (Harvard Kennedy School website):

• They should be authentic

• They should have integrity

• They need to adapt quickly to new realities, and

• The need the resilience to bounce back after devastating losses.

To date, Mr. Mulally has exhibited all these characteristics including a limitless confidence. Other attributes Mr. Mulally seems to have included the "ability to build, motivate, and maintain a team to a common goal, the ability to assert control of others to the right degree, in the right amount, at the right time" (Elmer, 2003).

It appears that Mr. Mulally's leadership also reflects many of the elements outlined in the 2009 article entitled "What is Leadership" by Michael Porter and Nitin Nohria:

• <u>Direction</u> – the strategy for the organization

• <u>Organization</u> – determining the organization's structure

• <u>Selection</u> – recruiting and developing senior managers

• <u>Motivation</u> – establishing financial and other incentives

• <u>Systems and processes for implementation</u> – processes to ensure implementation of the company's goals and strategy [54]

Mr. Mulally is a frontline soldier in Ford Motor Company's reengineering battle; he is actively involved in Ford's rebirth. He doesn't have time to play predictive computer model games to assess Ford's survivability. In addition, Mr. Mulally is not Bismarck, who sits on a throne and shouts out orders. Mr. Mulally's "One Team," "One Plan," "One Ford" thrust is not the usual PR slogan on plastic cards; it is real. He has similar characteristics the way Automotive News described former Ford Vice Chairman Allan Gilmour: "power of observation, attention to detail, analytical skills, and determination to make operations more efficient" (December 6, 2010 issue of Automotive News).

Mr. Mulally meets frequently with employees to instill enthusiasm. This is consistent with Tom Peters' belief of "enthusiasm begets enthusiasm." In addition, he is accessible to auto industry analysts and the U.S. business press community. Mr. Porter and Mr. Nohria article also stated that "to accomplish their agenda, CEO's have to communicate it relentlessly...it is almost impossible to over communicate," [54] As Mr. Mulally stated in the 2009 Fortune article: "communicate, communicate, communicate." [55]

# CHAPTER 18

✠ ✠ ✠

# MR. MULALLY'S "ONE FORD" ("MIRACLE") ACTION PLAN

## Ford's Mission Statement

Consistent with Mr. Mulally's laser focus in everything he does, he determined first what Ford's mission should be. In the late 1980s, Ford had a one-page mission, values, and guiding principles statement. The mission was as follows: "Ford Motor Company is a worldwide leader in automotive and automotive-related products and services as well as in newer industries such as aerospace, communications, and financial services. Our mission is to improve continually our products and service to meet our customers' needs, allowing us to prosper as business and to provide a reasonable return for our stockholders, the owners of our business."

Ford's 1995 mission statement as part of the "Ford 2000" was: "Ford Motor Company is the world's largest producer of trucks, and the second largest producer of cars and trucks combined. We are the world's only true full-line vehicle producer with products ranging from the subcompact Fiesta to the AeroMax heavy-duty truck. We also are one of the largest providers of financial services worldwide. The company's two core businesses are Ford Automotive Operations and the Ford Financial Services Group. (In 1995, Ford employed 346,990 people serving customers in more than 200 countries.) In all of our businesses, our focus is maximizing shareholder value through product excellence; customer satisfaction; efficient, low-cost operation and profitable growth."

Mr. Mulally has refined the "One Ford" mission statement into simple terms: "Ford Motor Company, a global automotive industry leader based in Dearborn, Michigan manufactures or distributes automobiles across six continents. With about 159,000 employees and about 70 plants worldwide, the company's automotive brands include Ford and Lincoln (Mercury was included in the original statement). The company provides financial services through Ford Motor Credit Company." There is no mention of "maximizing shareholder value." The most famous advocate of maximizing shareholder value was corporate turnaround specialist "Chainsaw Al" (Al Dunlap) in the 1990s. He joined Scott Paper in 1994 and immediately fired thousands of employees, closed plants, sold product lines without focusing on long-term restructuring. In 1995, he sold the company and pocketed $100 million. He tried to repeat the process at Sunbeam, but was fired after two years on the job as a result of a massive accounting scandal as he attempted to "package" Sunbeam for sale. The objective of these turnaround specialists is to "get in and out" quickly, which is the opposite of Mr. Mulally's philosophy. Mr. Mulally's vision is to build economic value through long-lasting restructuring. If successful, shareholder wealth will follow, as is happening with Ford's common stock.

## Ford's Basic Trust

After establishing the mission statement, the next step was to develop a plan Mr. Mulally called "One Ford." Clayton Christensen, in his famous 1997 book "The Innovator's Dilemma," stated that three groups of factors affect what an organization can and cannot do–its resources (money, people, technology, product design, brands, information, etc.), its processes (transforming inputs from people, equipment, technology, cash, etc. into products and services), and its values (ethics, rules employees must follow, etc.). [56] Following is the "One Ford" strategy, which Mr. Mulally has embraced consistently.

- **Finance our plan and improve our balance sheet;**

- **Aggressively restructure to operate profitably at current lower demand and changing model mix;**

- **Accelerate development of new products our customers want and value ...to deliver profitable growth for all.**
  - ☐ **Serve all markets**
  - ☐ **Complete family of products**
  - ☐ **Best-in-class-design, quality, green, safety, smart**

- **Work together effectively as one team, leveraging Ford's assets.**
  - ☐ **Partner with all stakeholders and each other**
  - ☐ **Have fun, celebrate**

Alan Murray stated in a Wall Street Journal article (August 21, 2010) "Managers are bureaucrats. Their fundamental tendency is toward self-perpetuation. They are, almost by definition, resistant to change." [57] Mr. Mulally's philosophy is the opposite.

Mr. Mulally has brought to Ford the historic American self-assurance and entrepreneurial spirit, which many large companies have lost. One of Mr. Mulally's secrets is that he thrives on change, and is not worried about the associated uncertainty. In addition, he did not have to focus on climbing the ladder at 65 years of age because he knew his place at Ford. He was so self-assured that he did not even bring any Boeing colleagues with him. Reportedly, one of G.E.'s Management Values is to "stimulate and relish change and not be frightened or paralyzed by it, seeing change as an opportunity, not threat." Some of G.E.'s other values closely parallel Mr. Mulally's basic philosophy:

- "Create a clear, simple, reality-based, customer-focused vision.

- Set aggressive targets, understanding accountability and commitment.

- Have a passion for excellence, hating bureaucracy.

- Have the self-confidence to empower others.

- Have enormous energy and the ability to energize and invigorate others."

## Financial Plan

Since the patient (Ford) was on death bed and urgently needed surgery, not only to survive, but more importantly, to become a productive member of society again, Mr. Mulally immediately developed a finance plan with highly respected Don LeClair, who was then the Chief Financial Officer. After months of intense negotiations, Ford announced on December 15, 2006 that it had reached agreement with a consortium of banks for what some auto analysts described as a $23.5 billion "home equity" loan package to finance the restructuring plan. This resulted in total automotive liquidity of about $46 billion at year-end 2006, which Ford believed should allow the company to fund the restructing and product development priorities, and provide the company with a cushion for a recession or other unforeseen events in the near term. This resulted in Ford's Automotive debt-servicing costs of approximately $350 per average worldwide vehicle sold between 2007-2009, compared with $160 per vehicle between 2000-2006 (Toyota's Automotive interest expenses for the fiscal year ending March 31, 2010 was about $50 per unit). As CNBC auto reporter Phil LeBeau stated in an November 10, 2010 one hour television special entitled "Ford: Rebuilding An American Icon," the $23.5 billion package was a "colossal gamble and Ford rolled the Dice." Car and Driver, in its January 2011 edition stated it as follows: "Mulally mortgaged everything in 2006 and 2007 in an all-or-nothing gambit to avoid bankruptcy." Truly, it was betting the farm; it can also be called "Brother Can You Spare a Dime?"

Ford virtually pledged all of its assets (excluding cash), including most of Ford's domestic manufacturing facilities, accounts receivables, and inventory, up to $4 billion of marketable securities, stock in most domestic and foreign subsidiaries including Ford Credit. Ford also had to pledge the treasured blue oval, Ford's trademark. There were also restrictions on paying dividends. Ford estimated the value of the eligible categories at $41 billion, including $8 billion in intellectual property and U.S. trademarks. The funding was required because Ford had projected a jaw-dropping $17 billion cash outflow between 2007 through 2009 with more than half to occur in 2007 which may have been the low point in Ford's survival struggle although the November 10, 2010 CNBC one hour special about Ford claimed that Ford "bottomed out in early 2009." (At the end of December 2008, according to Ford's 2009 Annual Report, and using December 2004 as a base period, the total return to Ford stockholders at the end of December 2008 was 17% compared with 81% for the S&P 500 Index and 89% for the "Dow Jones Automobiles & Parts 30 Index.") The Ford family, which controls 40% of the voting stock, must be given credit for not saying "we can't afford it," and not opposing the plan, which some observers called reckless. This single act of foresight saved Ford from following Chrysler and GM into Chapter 11. It provided Ford with the funds to implement the costly restructuring plan, and to launch its most aggressive new product revolution in history. Ford's competitors did not have the funds to match Ford, and thus lost market share because their products became dated. It also provided the funds to survive the subsequent global auto industry depression, and financial meltdown in Washington and on Wall Street. However, even Ford could not perceive at that time that it would lose $30 billion between 2006-2008.

## Balance Sheet Actions

By year-end 2007, Ford had total debt of approximately $27 billion with roughly $3 billion maturing in 2012. Ford's Automotive sector's net cash (defined as gross cash less total debt) was almost $8 billion. Gross cash and available credit facilities totaled $47 billion at the end of 2007. The major credit agencies such as Moody's and S&P changed their ratings in November 2007 from "Negative" to "Stable."

The transformation of Ford's business structure continued at a rapid base. By year-end 2008, Ford had exceeded its goal of reducing its cumulative annual North American Automotive operating costs by over $5 billion. However, the worldwide economic crisis starting in 2008, and the associated decline in automotive sales resulted in a significant decline in Ford's revenues. Ford sales decreased to $129 billion compared with $154 billion in 2007. Unit sales declined by over one million units to 5.5 million during the same period. Ford lost $14.7 billion in 2008 ($2.7 billion loss in 2007). Accordingly, even more drastic cost reduction actions were required to achieve a new target of $14-$17 billion cash improvement actions in 2009-2010.Therefore, Ford announced the following:

• Reducing North American salaried personnel-related costs by an additional 10 percent by the end of January

2009, in addition to personnel-related cost actions already taken or underway globally.

- Eliminating merit pay increases for North America salaried employees in 2009, and eliminating performance bonuses for global salaried employees.

- Reducing annual capital spending to between $5 billion and $5.5 billion.

- Reducing engineering, manufacturing, information technology and advertising cost through greater global efficiencies.

- Reducing inventories and achieving other working capital improvements.

- Continuing to develop incremental sources of Automotive funding, including divesting noncore operations and assets, and reducing debt.

- To generate funds, Ford reduced its 33% interest in Mazda to roughly 13% in November 2008 (subsequently to 11%, and to 3.5% in mid-November 2010).

- Reduced salaried post-retirement benefits effective January 1, 2007 with resulting cost savings of almost $500 million.

During 2009, Ford implemented the following additional actions, with the objective to achieve a fundamentally healthy balance sheet, and to provide additional liquidity.

- Negotiated with the UAW to amend the VEBA agreement to provide the option of paying up to approximately 50% of the VEBA obligations in Ford common stock, and to smooth payments over 13 years.

- Reduced automotive debt by about $10 billion by utilizing $2.6 billion in Automotive and Ford Credit cash and 468 million shares of Ford common stock.

- Raised $1.6 billion of equity in a public offering of Ford common stock.

- Raised $565 million as part of an equity distribution program begun in 2008.

- Entered into a U.S. Department of Energy (DOE) loan agreement to provide Ford up to $5.9 billion in loans, at favorable interest rates, under the DOE's Advanced Technology Vehicles Manufacturing Incentive Program.

- Issued almost $2.9 billion of 4.25% Senior Convertible Notes due 2016.

- Amended and extended the revolving credit facility under Ford's secured Credit Agreement—reducing the amount of the revolving credit facility from $10.7 billion to $8.1 billion, extending the maturity date of $7.2 billion of that amount from December 2011 to November 2013, and establishing a new term loan in the amount of $724 million maturing in December 2013.

• Registered an additional $1 billion equity distribution program in November 2009, and commencing sales in December 2009.

• Completed the UAW VEBA transaction on December 31, 2009 by transferring assets, consisting of cash and marketable securities, notes and warrants valued at $14.8 billion to the UAW VEBA Trust, thereby discharging Ford's UAW retiree health-care obligations.

As a result of the actions outlined above, Ford's Automotive debt at the end of 2009 was $34.4 billion compared with GM's $8 billion which had reduced its debt by 92% as a result of its bankruptcy filing. In 2010, Ford continued its massive efforts to improve its balance sheet by continuing to reduce Automotive debt.

## Organization Plan

The next step was to announce in December 2006 an organizational alignment to more fully utilize Ford's vast global assets. According to a June 2010 article in the Harvard Business Review entitled "The Decision-Driven Organization," "nearly half of all CEO's launch a reorg during their first two years on the job. Some preside over repeated restructurings." Unlike the "Ford 2000" plan implemented in 1995, which consolidated all regions into one single profit center, Mr. Mulally's plan was to retain the three automotive operations plus Ford Motor Credit as distinct entities with powerful executives. To be closer to the pulse of the business, Mr. Mulally eliminated a management layer outside North America. He also discontinued the position of Chief of Staff because Mr. Mulally likes to be in the trenches and hear the news unfiltered.

The position of Executive Vice President and President International Operations was eliminated and the business heads of the Americas, Ford of Europe, Premier Automotive Group and Ford Asia Pacific and Africa and Ford Credit now reported directly to Mr. Mulally. Concurrently, and most importantly, he created a single global product development organization headed by Derrick Kuzak (Executive Vice President, Global Product Development). All worldwide product development activities report to Mr. Kuzak. This philosophy has led to today's highly competitive and successful world cars such as the 2011 Ford Fiesta and the 2012 Ford Focus. Mr. Mulally also applied the same approach to other activities such as purchasing. Thomas Brown was appointed as Senior Vice President, Global Purchasing. Manufacturing, quality and other functions operate on the same basis. In August 2010, Ford appointed "Wunderkind" Jim Farley as Ford's Group Vice President of Global Marketing, Sales and Service.

A detailed business review process was also created. The most important is Mr. Mulally's Thursday's Business Review meetings with his 16 direct reports.

A car consists of over 10,000 parts, and about $1500 in electronics. It also contains roughly ten million lines of software code in an average Ford Vehicle. [58] The organizational steps outlined above helped to simplify a complex business. It allowed global sharing of vehicle platforms and components thus providing huge economies of scale. Commonality of components allows the full utilization of flexible manufacturing facilities because it allows a plant to produce several different models. Mr. Mulally also embraced Toyota's fundamental principle of continuous improvement (kaizen).

# Product Strategy Plan

From the beginning of his tenure, Mr. Mulally demanded that Ford offer a complete family of vehicles, which was a game changer at Ford Motor Company. The objective was to protect the company against constantly changing consumer tastes. One key element was to return Ford to its original roots of providing affordable transportation in the small car segment with a total focus on the Ford brand. This required products with leading-class fuel economy, quality, safety and technology to compete effectively against low-cost Asian producers who have dominated this important segment.

Mr. Mulally was aware of the motto that "small cars mean small profits." Nevertheless, the worldwide "One Ford" Ford simplification process improvements, the renovated flexible manufacturing plants, labor cost reductions resulting from the transformational UAW agreements, the speed-up of the new process to bring fully competitive new products to the market, and rightsizing of all aspects of Ford provided the company with confidence that it could achieve attractive small car returns. Thus, there will be heavy emphasis on the sub-compact and compact segments represented by the 2011 Fiesta, the 2012 Ford Focus and the highly successful Ford Fusion. In addition, Ford plans more crossover vehicles, and fuel-efficient trucks (starting with the F-150 in 2011). High-margin trucks and SUV's will also be part of "One Ford." The latest example of "One Ford's" global product planning is the new Ford Ranger which was introduced at the Australian International Motor show in Sidney on October 15, 2010. The truck will be sold on five continents and 180 markets.

Contrary to GM and Chrysler, Ford maintained an aggressive product development program during the auto industry depression. Between 2006-2009, instead of curtailing expenditures, Ford spent $24 billion on automotive capital expenditures. This illustrates Mr. Mulally's visionary mindset; Ford is now harvesting the benefits.

One triton among the minnows is "One Ford's" global product strategy. It includes a full line-up in all regions with a focus on best-in-class features.

• Bold, emotive exterior designs

• Superior product quality

• Innovative technology features

• Best-in-class fuel efficiency

• Great to drive

• Great to sit in (comfort and convenience; exceptional quietness)

• Leading safety features

• Superior performance

• Environmentally friendly

• All with exceptional value

The product agenda also includes an accelerated delivery of vehicles customers love. It is a striking change because it has been quite a few years since consumer loved Ford cars. Bloomberg's Keith Naughton in a November 15, 2010 report entitled "Ford Reaches Highest in 8 Years Before GM IPO," quoted Joseph Phillippi of Auto Trends as follows: "Ford is putting together a real terrific track record. The numbers are going to continue to get better because they have good product momentum."

Examples include the 2011 Ford Fusion, (ranked by Consumer Reports as its highest-rated sedan), the 2010 Ford Taurus (Kelley Blue-Books one of "Top Ten Most Comfortable Cars and also voted International Car of the Year" at the Los Angeles Auto Show), the 2011 Ford Fiesta, and the 2011 Ford Explorer with the world's first automotive product with inflatable rear safety belts. The 2012 Ford Focus and the 2012 Ford C-Max mini-minivan clearly demonstrate that the features outlined on the previous page are not the usual wish list characteristics. The Ford Fiesta was ranked first among 32 small cars in a U.S. News & World Report ranking, by its correspondent Rick Newman. Esquire magazine ranked the Fiesta "Compact Car of the Year." The Ford Fiesta represents Ford return to the subcompact segment since the Ford Pinto in 1980 (almost two million new Fiestas have been sold worldwide since its October 2008 introduction). Michelle Krebs of Edmunds.com stated that "automotive turnarounds are built on great products and Ford has introduced terrific new models, with plenty more in the pipeline."

In a Fortune magazine article dated October 18, 2010, by Alex Taylor III entitled "The Wheel Deal," he describes the inside of the totally new 2011 Ford Explorer as follows: "the interior is executed with the kind of attention to detail that has made them tops among the Detroit Three ... the Explorer's instrument panel is in a league of its own." It is Ford's unwavering strategy to accelerate the development of new products, which is why Ford is gaining U.S. retail market share. The aggressive product cadence will continue in the near-term. Further, every new Ford product has to be a proof point of "One Ford." The only disappointment has been the Ford Flex SUV, which was targeted at 100,000 units in annual sales, but is only selling in the 40,000-unit range (it made Consumer Reports "Top 10 Family Cars of 2011 list). However, a 750 batting average is very respectable and compares favorably to Toyota's record and exceeds Babe Ruth's.

In powertrains, Ford will offer hybrids, ethanol vehicles, clean diesel engines and an "EcoBoost" system offering a significant improvement in fuel economy. Electric vehicles are also part of the company's portfolio.

The integrated global "One Ford" cycle plan puts heavy emphasis on simplification in terms of the number of platforms used and the product's architecture. The objective is "low-cost and high-quality." In a December 5, 1994 Automotive News article from Tokyo by Richard Johnson, he outlined the Japanese auto industry "small step" approach:

• "Using more common parts between models,

• Cutting model variations,

• Reducing optional features,

• Improving operating efficiency and organization and

• Pressing suppliers for cost reductions." [59]

Mr. Mulally has thoroughly studied the Japanese strategy and adopted some of the features outlined above at Ford. He visited Japan several times while at Boeing and is a student of Japanese business practices. Mr. Mulally's focus is on "commonality of platforms, drivetrains and powertrains; this in turn will reduce complexity in Ford's vehicles and processes." (A platform is a rolling chassis on which a number of vehicles can be built). For example, the new 2012 Ford Focus will have ten various derivatives from SUV's to trucks, and a roughly 85% commonality between the worldwide Focus cars which will be produced in five key world markets (North America, Europe, Asia, South America) involving two million units. This has never been achieved at Ford Motor Company before. As the authors of "Reinventing Your Business Model" stated "successful companies have operational and managerial processes that allow them to deliver value in a way they can successfully repeat and increase in scale." [60] According A.T. Kearney consultant Daniel Chang (Automotive News' November 16, 2010 website), "by 2015, Ford's Focus platform is on track to be number three in the world, followed by GM's Cruze platform...no Detroit-based company is (presently) represented on the top ten list of global platforms."

Mr. Mulally is also a believer in process improvements. The continuous improvement philosophy and vehicle development efficiencies have reduced Ford engineering costs for a typical new vehicle by roughly 60% since 2005.

As part of Ford's "One Ford" plan to focus on its core business, Ford sold noncore businesses including Aston Martin, Jaguar and Land Rover in 2009. This is the opposite of VW's strategy, which has ten brands (GM has four brands and Chrysler five).

## Rightsizing Facilities Plan

The "Way Forward" plan, which was developed prior to Mr. Mulally's arrival, included a major capacity realignment to improve facilities utilization, and to achieve major cost savings. The objective was to "reduce and realign vehicle assembly capacity to bring it more in line with demand and shifting customer preferences"

Ford announced in 2006 the following capacity reductions to reduce North American operating costs by about $5 billion at the end of 2008 compared with 2005.

• Atlanta Assembly Plant (closed in 2006);

• Batavia Transmission Plant (closed in 2008);

• Essex Engine Plant (closed in 2007);

• Maumee Stamping Plant (closed in 2007);

• Norfolk Assembly Plant (closed 2007);

• St. Louis Assembly Plant (closed in 2006);

• Twin Cities Assembly Plant (closed in 2008);

• Windsor Casting Plant (idled in 2007);

• Wixom Assembly Plant (closed in 2007); and

• Cleveland Casting Plant (closed in 2010).

In addition, Ford stated that it would sell or eventually close 13 of the remaining component plants it took back from Visteon. At the end of 2007, four of these facilities have been closed or sold.

These actions reduced Ford's headcount by 35,500 compared with December 31, 2005. Ford's hourly and salaried personnel levels were 61,000 below 2005 levels by January 2009. Behind these emotionless, but mind-boggling numbers are 61,000 life-stories probably forever altered, often with little hope of finding a comparable job, especially hourly workers. As Jack Welch stated in his book "Winning," "almost no crisis ends without blood on the floors."

As part of Ford's emphasis on the growing trend toward small cars, Ford is converting three assembly plants producing SUV's and large trucks to small cars. In the future, roughly 50% of U.S. manufacturing capacity will be dedicated to small and medium-sized vehicles. Further, as described in the following section, by 2012, nearly all of Ford's U.S. assembly plants will have flexible body shops to meet constantly changing consumer preferences. Efraim Levy of Standard & Poor's stated on S&P "MarketScope" on October 11, 2010: "Ford's efficiencies from streamlining global production is progressing well–there has been much headway in economies of scale."

## The Importance of Flexible Manufacturing

According to Jim Tetreault, vice president, North American Manufacturing, (November/December 2010 issue of Ford's employee magazine), "traditional factories of yesteryear that mass-produced just one product are methodically being replaced by more nimble, flexible, technologically advanced operations capable of producing multiple vehicle models on a single assembly line – operations that could swiftly respond to unpredictable changes in customer preferences. In the past, the way Ford responded to shifts in consumer demand was to raise or lower production in one plant, and that's very problematic because people would either be on extensive overtime or we would have to lay off a shift. Today, the majority of our body shops have flexible capability to build several vehicles in one plant. This gives the company the ability to vary our model mix and more rapidly respond to the market."

Mr. Tetreault stated in the employee magazine "that the plants we have will produce much higher volume and multiple products. We've also been making steady, sizeable investment in our plants to create a manufacturing system that is both lean and flexible and capable of delivering best-in-world manufacturing quality." In addition to enabling Ford to better adjust capacity to match real demand, another important advantage to flexible manufacturing is the ability to introduce products without having to shut plants down to retool. With flexible manufacturing comes the ability to run higher-volume facilities. According to Mr. Tetreault, 100 percent of Ford's North American assembly plants will have some degree of flexibility by 2012, and nearly half of the company's transmission and engine plants around the world will be flexible.

According to the magazine article, the amount of money involved in the conversion is huge. For example, in 2005, the Ford Oakville Assembly Complex in Ontario began a $1 billion conversion to flexible manufacturing, including a state-of-the-art body assembly facility. Ford invested $3 billion in 2008 to develop three projects in Mexico. In 2009, Ford invested $550 million to transform Michigan Assembly Plant which formerly built the Ford Expedition and Lincoln Navigator into a lean, green and flexible manufacturing complex that will build the next - generation Focus along with a new battery-electric version of the Focus for the North American market.

For the first time in history, Ford is developing and manufacturing vehicles on global platforms. The first global vehicle–the sub-compact Fiesta–is already in the marketplace. The next-generation compact Ford Focus was launched in the first quarter, 2011.

CNBC's auto analyst Phil LeBeau stated on December 15, 2010 that Ford's plant near Detroit "will be the first in the world to build standard internal combustion, hybrid, plug-in hybrid, and electric vehicles in one plant. Why is this news? For starters, this is the first plant in the world where all models with different power train systems are being built under the same roof at the same time. More importantly, it shows the next level of flexibility in building cars and trucks."

## UAW Agreement

In November 2007 Ford signed a four-year agreement with the UAW; it was a watershed in the relationship between the two parties. The plan was projected to significantly improve Ford's competitiveness including more flexible work rules. The UAW agreed for the first time that up to 20% of <u>newly hired</u> workers would receive a significantly lower entry-level wages than currently employed UAW workers. Ford projected that the pay structure for the new employees would total approximately $26 to $31 per hour, which is roughly 50% of present levels. This would be a major long-term step to achieve competitiveness with U.S. plants of Japanese producers.

With the constantly rising health-care costs ($3.5 billion in 2005), Ford agreed with the UAW to permanently shift responsibility for providing health-care benefits to a new retirement plan funded by a new Independent Employee Benefit Association Trust (VEBA)." According to the UAW website, the Trust covers current retirees, eligible future retirees, their spouses, surviving spouses and certain dependents. Ford estimated the value at about $20 billion on its December 31, 2007 balance sheet. By the end of October 2010, Ford had prepaid the remaining $3.6 billion of debt owed to the VEBA Trust or significantly ahead of original plans (Ford didn't have to pay debt until 2022). This will lower Ford's ongoing annual interest expenses by about $330 million.

In total, the "Big Three" reportedly had about $86 billion in retiree health-care liabilities on their books according to a February 22, 2008 AP dispatch published in "Mfellows." GM's hourly health-care liabilities for retirees and their dependents totaled about $48 billion in 2006, and almost $16 billion at Chrysler. Reportedly, the "Big Three" are providing the Trust with $45 billion in assets–cash, bonds or stock. It will cover about 800,000 people; the UAW claims that the Trust "secures health-care benefits for retirees for 80 years, no matter what happens to the automakers' finances." For example, GM reportedly has over 500,000 people impacted by the VEBA Trust, and GM reportedly will have to contribute $33-36.5 billion into the Trust. The Trust became effective January 1, 2010. The VEBA Trust for each of the "Big Three" will be in separate accounts. Prior to the UAW assuming responsibility for the VEBA Trust, each of the "Big Three" had an internally VEBA Trust Fund to help pay for retiree medical benefits.

In February 2009, Ford reached agreement with the UAW to reduce benefits and provide for more flexible operating practices. The new agreement suspended the widely criticized and egregious "Jobs Bank" program. This boondoggle started over 25 years ago. Reportedly, at the program's height, roughly 15,000 UAW members were in the "Jobs Bank" getting up to 95% of their wages plus full benefits for doing nothing–often for years. Reportedly, Ford Motor Company paid over $3 billion between 2000-2008 for temporarily laid-off employees. An article by Professor Mark Perry of the University of Michigan on his website (September 2007) stated that for 5000-6000 "Jobs Bank" employees, it cost GM $800 million!!

On November 2, 2009, UAW members rejected an agreement supported by its leaders to modify the Ford-UAW collective bargaining agreement. It was similar to an agreement the UAW reached with GM and Chrysler. It would have precluded strike actions until 2015. Disputes regarding wages and benefits would have been resolved through binding arbitration. Ford's collective bargaining agreement with the UAW expires in September 2011.The contract rejection stokes fears regarding the mindset of rank and file UAW members going into 2011 contract negotiations. Many UAW members are already calling for restoration of the previous benefits, which would return the auto companies back to the "Dark Ages" of total uncompetitiveness.

# Ford Supplier Strategy

The U.S. supply base represents about 80% of Ford's North American purchases. During the economic meltdown and the associated collapse of the auto parts industry, Ford had to assemble SWAT teams to constantly assess the health of the surviving companies. Since the mid-2000's, Ford has reduced the number of suppliers eligible for major sourcing from 3,300 in 2004 to about 1,600 in 2009, and 1,500 suppliers in 2010. The long-term objective is 750 key suppliers. This philosophy is consistent with Tom Peters' "Thriving on Chaos" handbook, which describes 18 "Master Paradox" including the following: "more productivity ensues from having fewer suppliers."

Ford is also accelerating its "Aligned Business Framework" (ABF), which was launched in 2005. It is, in essence, a partnership relationship. Under ABF, Ford provides commitments including long-term sourcing. In 2009, approximately one-half of Ford's global production purchases were sourced to ABF suppliers (34% in 2006). The long-term objective is 65% of Ford's $50 billion global parts budget. In 2010, 67 production and 22 non-production ABF suppliers were part of ABF.

The ABF has 25 principles, including the following:

• A phase in up-front payment of engineering and development costs, extended sourcing for the life of a program or platform, improved commonality and early supplier involvement in the product development process.

- A bilateral commitment to competitive costs.

- A supplier commitment to bring leading-edge technological innovations to Ford.

- Continued sourcing emphasis to minority and women-owned suppliers.

Ford purchases about 10% of its requirements from minority-owned and female-owned suppliers. In 2007, when North American vehicle sales reached a record 19 million, Ford Motor Company spent $4.2 billion with minority-owned suppliers, and $1.2 billion with female-owned suppliers. In 2009, Ford purchased $2.7 billion due to significantly lower industry volumes. Thirteen minority-and women-owned suppliers are among the 89 companies in the ABF network. (GM has over 400 "certified" minority and women-owned suppliers).

Ford also projected that its move toward global vehicle platforms and increasing component commonality will allow suppliers to produce greater volume of similar components thus generating significant economies of scale.

Ford's new purchasing philosophy has changed Ford's perception among the supplier community. In a 2007 survey of U.S. auto parts suppliers, Ford was ranked dead last. Recently, Ford was ranked third, only behind Honda and Toyota. [61]

## Ford Dealer Plan

Ford's annual market share decline in the U.S. has resulted in a totally overdealered situation in major U.S. metropolitan areas. Ford brand volume per dealer is significantly below Toyota and Honda dealerships. This has resulted in unsatisfactory dealer profits and low, if any, "blue sky" for Ford Motor Company dealers wanting to sell their business. However, potential prospects were willing to pay astronomical "blue sky" for Toyota, Honda and Nissan dealerships. According to Ford Motor Company "Sustainability Reports," the overall dealer attitude (Ford brand) toward Ford has declined in recent years–72% in 2005 to 66% in 2009, but is up from 61% in 2002. According to the same reports, Ford brand retail customer satisfaction with dealers increased from 75% in 2002 to 82% in 2009.

Ford has reduced the number of Ford, Lincoln and Mercury dealers. At the end of 2008, The Ford Motor Company dealer network in the U.S. was reduced to about 3,800 from 4,400 at the end of 2005. By the end of 2009, Ford had 3,550 dealers in the United States, and 3,424 in 2010. The objective is 3,000 dealers.

To further reduce Ford's dealer overcapacity, Ford initiated a plan with its dealers to "downsize, consolidate and restructure" its dealer network in its largest 130 U.S. markets. The objective is healthy and profitable dealers. The goal is to achieve at least 1,500 average annual sales for

Ford dealers and more than 600 units for Lincoln Mercury dealers. Jim Farley, Ford's Group Vice President of Global Marketing, Sales and Service stated recently that Ford's relations with its dealers has improved.

The announcement in June 2010 to eliminate the Mercury brand by the end of 2010 will result in the potential closing of additional Lincoln Mercury dealers. Ford estimated its cost at roughly $500 million. Ford is providing funding as part of the dealer consolidation. Mercury's demise is primarily related to Ford's product neglect. Road & Track magazine described it as "an example of poor badge engineering" on its September 22, 2010 website. The elimination of the Mercury brand will result in a stronger Ford and a weak Lincoln network because of the loss of about 50% of its business. In contrast, VW has ten brands, and is trying to acquire Alfa Romeo from Fiat. VW claims that it will be producing ten million units on three platforms by 2018. GM has four brands (Chevrolet, Buick, Cadillac, GMC). Fiat/Chrysler has five brands (Dodge, Jeep, Ram, Chrysler, Fiat).

# CHAPTER 19

✠ ✠ ✠

# THE UNSTOPPABLE THUNDERING HERD

## Background

Primarily as a result of Mr. Mulally's clutch performance, Ford Motor Company has turned the corner in its survival struggle. The "Ford One" team has rescued a company smitten with death. "Morning Has Broken" (Gaelic song) for an American icon. As Time magazine stated in its August 2010 edition, Ford is "pulling off the biggest turnaround of the great recession." [62] However, as late as 2008, auto analysts insisted that Ford was in "the most precarious financial position." [63] Even astute observers as Global Insight concluded in May 2007 that "GM is most advanced in its cost cutting plan...because of product strategy, GM ranks at the top, Ford at the bottom, and Chrysler in the middle." [64] Therefore, it appeared that the day of reckoning had arrived for Ford Motor Company. Even Kirk Kerkorian, who acquired approximately one billion dollars of Ford stock in April 2008, liquidated his holdings only six months after indicating a loss of confidence in the company (report-edly, at a roughly $700 million loss). Good riddance; I con-sider this person a speculator. He also played this game with GM. In June 2005 he started acquiring GM stock; eventually he controlled 9.9% of GM shares. By December 2006 he had sold all his shares being dissatisfied with the company's turnaround efforts. In April 2007, he made an unsuccessful $4.6 billion bid for Chrysler. In 1995, he joined Lee Iacocca in attempting a takeover of Chrysler. He sold his stake in 1996.

The U.K. Guardian's dispatch on October 9, 2008 stated that "in a course of a few hours, GM's shares crashed by 31% to close at $4.76, their lowest level since 1950, while Ford's stock plunged by 21% to a 20-year low of $2.08 on mounting concern that both companies are at risk of bankruptcy." Ford's value was less than $5 billion, and its credit rating had reached "junk" status. In addition, the New York Times reported on October 21, 2008 "the finan-cier (Kerkorian) joined the growing ranks of investors who have soured on Detroit's prospects because of plummet-ing sales and mounting losses."

Moreover, Ford's common stock reflected the negative outlook and Ford's imminent demise. In November 2008, Ford's stock traded at $1.01 on the NYSE. This was probably when the company's recovery efforts slipped under Wall Street radar. As late as March 2009, highly regarded Bar-clays Capital auto analyst Brian Johnson stated in Fortune magazine "our target (Ford) is $1 a share." One year later, in the same publication, Chris Ceraso, another well-known auto analyst at Credit Suisse, concluded "it (Ford) could decline from $11 now to $10 in the next year." One voice in the wilderness, however, perceived a ray of sunshine. The late Jerry Flint stated in a May 25, 2009 article in Fortune: "There's still a Ford in our future."

It seemed that almost everybody "pooh-poohed" Ford's efforts. Accordingly, Ford had to put water on the doubters, and sandpaper – away the constant negative publicity. Therefore, according to a May 8, 2008 AP dispatch, CEO Mulally stated, "Our plan is working" (apparently not in jest), and he knew that the turning point was right around the corner. This man is truly a bird of a different feather. He probably remembered author Tom Peters' remarks "gloom is the ultimate weapon of mass destruction in tough times, and to avoid negative people." Even today, analysts continue to underestimate Ford and Mr. Mulally's restructuring capability (people also underestimated two of my favorite presidents–Mr. Truman who save Western Europe after World War II from communism, and the former Hollywood "B" film actor who defeated the Soviet Union). In raising Ford's corporate credit rating for the fifth time in 13 months in October 2010, Moody's stated that Ford's business model "is more robust, more profitable, and more sustainable than we had expected."

Ford had many skeptics because the company's previous turnaround efforts failed. In addition, Mr. Mulally's lack of automotive experience, and his turnaround of Ford with largely inside people, didn't generate confidence in the automotive community and on Wall Street. Lastly, there have been few examples of successful permanent auto industry restructurings. Carlos Ghosn is one of few executives who achieved long-term success. He saved giant Nissan from total collapse in 1999 by instituting the "Nissan Recovery Plan." It included plant closings and layoffs (unheard of in Japan), product quality improvements, a reduction in the number of platforms, and a restructuring of the historically cozy supplier relationship (keiretsu). Mr. Mulally was confronted with many of the same problems Nissan experienced in 1999. He adopted Winston Churchill's mindset: "a pessimist sees the difficulty in every opportunity; an optimist sees the opportunity in every difficulty." Clearly, to quote from the Dave Clark Five hit song of the 1960s, Mr. Mulally "You Got What It Takes." It is real, and not a Maerchen (legend).

Mr. Mulally was determined to achieve his goal of truly transforming Ford Motor Company with the "One Ford" restructuring efforts. Manufacturing magazine, in its March 7, 2010 article entitled "Ford CEO Alan Mulally: The Turnaround Specialist," summarized it succinctly. "Successful leadership hinges on such crucial skills as communication, collaboration and judgment. Alan Mulally has shown us how to embody these skills in an extraordinarily high-pressure environment. He has transformed Ford's culture since arriving at the firm and has fostered cooperation among divisions and regions that used to compete with each other for resources. He's also modeled transparency, meeting regularly with employees and instituting a dashboard system that makes key metrics about sales and market share more visible to the organization."

The demise of Ford Motor Company would have had a devastating impact on the company's retirees. Ford has about 550,000 people participating in Ford's pension funds, including 325,000 in America (I literally had a heart attack when Ford's stock hit $1.01 per share). Ford had roughly $56 billion in assets in its worldwide pension in late 2010, and paid $5.4 billion in 2009 to retirees in pension benefits.

Why did the "One Ford" global reinvention achieve its objective, and "Ford 2000" did not? Following are some of the possible reasons.

• Between 2006 and 2008, Ford lost $30 billion. During "Ford 2000," the company earned $48 billion between 1995-2000. Thus, there was less urgency to implement the tenets of "Ford 2000." Ford's survival was directly related to the success of "One Ford." The "Way Forward" slogan of "change or die" applied in the initial four years of "One Ford." Moreover, a total reengineering of a giant company seldom achieves its objectives unless the company is experiencing cataclysmic financial losses, which Ford Motor Company experienced.

- Since 2006, "One Ford" had stable senior Product Development management compared with three "Ford 2000" product chiefs between 1995-1998.

- During the last 15 years, U.S. cars have become more "Europeanized," which makes it easier to develop commonization worldwide.

- The "Ford 2000" process seemed more complex. It required a 216 page "Operating Guide" which I still have a hard time today to fully comprehend.

- The architect of "Ford 2000," CEO Alex Trotman, retired at the end of 1998. His successor, Jacques Nasser, may have had a "Ford 2000" "NIH" syndrome.

Even society has no guarantee of perpetualness. In all of recorded history, no empire has survived forever! This includes the great Egyptian (it lasted 3000 years) and the Roman empires (it stood for almost 700 years, stretched from Scotland to Syria as the height of its power, and controlled 25% of the world which constitutes 36 modern countries today). In addition, other dynasties such as the Mongol (the world's biggest land empire in the 13th century), Byzantine, Mayan, Inca, Aztec, and Ottoman empires didn't survive. The British Empire was the wealthiest and most powerful country in the world (19th century) and reached its pinnacle during the Victorian Age (1850-1900) when it controlled 25% of the world's population. Today, it is a shadow of this period. The Soviet Union was the latest empire to collapse. Presently, countries such as Greece, Ireland (the former "Celtic Tiger"), Spain and Portugal are struggling to survive. Many critics even question the survival of the "American Empire." My beloved America has, however, an historic ability to bounce back. We are far from the "Eve of Destruction," the song that Barry McGuire made famous in the 1960s.

The following pages outline the present status of "One Ford's" restructuring efforts.

# Finance the Plan and Improve the Balance Sheet

• Secured $23.5 billion in financing in December 2006 ($2.4 billion interest costs in 2007, $2.1 billion in 2008, $1.5 billion in 2009). Automotive sector gross debt was $27 billion at the end of 2006, $19.1 billion on December 31, 2010, and debt was reduced by another $3 billion in March 2011.

• Eliminated over $10 billion in Automotive debt in March 2009 through the exchange of cash and stock.

• Transferred to the UAW Ford's retiree health-care liabilities to the UAW Retire Medical Benefits Trusts (VEBA). This increased the company's debt by $7 billion, but it removed a substantial health-care liability from Ford's balance sheet. Concurrently, Ford prepaid $500 million of debt the company owed to the VEBA Trust, and in October 2010 prepaid its remaining $3.6 billion debt. The VEBA Trust will significantly improve Ford's competitiveness.

• Repaid $7 billion in debt in the second quarter 2010 consisting of about $4 billion to the UAW VEBA Trust and a $3 billion repayment of Ford's revolving credit facility. This will reduce annual interest costs by $470 million.

• Reduced its debt by $7.3 billion in the fourth quarter, 2010. Ford's Automotive debt was reduced by $14.5 billion in 2010 saving the company roughly one billion dollars in annual interest expenses.

• Credit rating agencies have been consistently increasing Ford and Ford Motor Credit Company's credit ratings.

## Conclusions

Ford Motor Company remains overlevered, especially compared with GM which has $28 billion in cash and only $11 billion in debt at the end of 2010 as a result of its Chapter 11 filing. Ford has adequate liquidity and access to the capital market. Ford Motor Company will take further actions to improve its balance sheet. Ford achieved net Automotive cash position at the end of 2010. This will allow Ford to further strengthen its balance sheet which would materially reduce the cost of funds borrowed.

# Aggressively Restructure to Operate Profitably at Lower Demand and Changing Model Mix

- Reduced North American structural costs by more than $10 billion. Downsizing the company, and simplifying the entire business process have reduced operating costs. This has significantly improved productivity. This is consistent with Tom Peters' philosophy of "simplify systems, constantly," which he outlined in his book "The Little BIG Things."

- Closed 12 manufacturing facilities in North America since 2005 in line with lower demand level, and to improve capacity utilization. Worldwide, Ford has 73 plants including 38 in North America as of December 31, 2010.

- Plans to close three additional plants between 2011-2012.

- By the end of 2011, Ford will have reduced production capacity by 40% as part of the "rightsizing" of facilities.

- Introducing highly efficient flexible body shops in almost all U.S. assembly plants by 2012 in response to rapidly changing consumer trends (Ford was slow in switching to flexible plants).

- Expects to achieve significant economies of scale from its supply base through Ford's aggressive consolidation of vehicle platforms–from 27 in 2007 to 15 different platforms in 2012. GM is implementing a similar strategy.

- Reduced the number of production suppliers eligible for new vehicle business from 3,300 in 2006 to 1,500 in 2010. Long-term objective is 750.

- Expanded its "Aligned Business Framework (ABF) by sourcing about 50% of its global production purchases to ABF suppliers. ABF includes long-term sourcing commitments, and additional sharing of future products, and manufacturing plans.

- In a July 26, 2010 article in the Honolulu Star Advertiser, Rod Lache of Deutsche Bank is quoted as stating: "At Ford, revenue in its North American operations is down by $20 billion since 2005, but instead of a loss like it had that year, the unit is expected to earn more than $5 billion in 2010. In large part, that is because Ford has shrunk its North American workforce by nearly 50 percent over the past five years." Ford Motor Company is clearly a more nimble company today.

### Conclusions

Since the launch of "One Ford" in 2006, Ford Motor Company has undergone the most fundamental restructuring in its history. Henry Ford encountered innumerable road-blocks when he established the company in 1903. He had the relentless perseverance, and the can-do spirit to overcome the obstacles.

Under "One Ford," the break-even point was materially reduced. Even with industry sales at a thirty-year low, which exacerbated Ford's recovery efforts, Ford earned a profit in 2009-it's most pivotal and historic year since WW II.

Ford is growing and profitable company again, and has regained its old luster. When sales return to the 15-16 million unit range, Ford and the other auto companies will sing hallelujah. Moreover, the up cycle could last several years.

## Accelerate Development of New Products Ford Customers Want and Value

Ford is undergoing a product revolution never experienced in the almost 110 year history of this American icon. Ford now has a vastly improved product line, which is truly world-class competitive. The company has a complete product portfolio, which was Mr. Mulally compelling vision when he developed the "One Ford" strategy.

The decision in December 2006 to "bet the farm" with a $23.5 billion loan allowed Ford to initiate an aggressive product innovation program. This was at a time of a worldwide economic meltdown, U.S. industry sales at thirty year lows, and Ford's $30 billion in losses between 2006-2008. Ford now leads GM and Chrysler with the highest vehicle replacement rate (freshest product portfolio).

Mr. Mulally's "One Ford" global focus is the primary driver of the product renaissance. The foundation is the new global development organization with a global product strategy, and a global product cycle plan. Concurrently, the company made the decision to focus exclusively on the Ford brand by selling Aston Martin, Jaguar, Land Rover and Volvo. Further, Ford is determined to have highly competitive products in all segments of the market, including the long-neglected, but growing low-profit small-car segment.

The global product strategy has allowed Ford to sub-stantially simplify and commonize its vehicle production. This has reduced fixed costs and achieved economies of scale. For example, according to Ford's 2009 Annual Report, Ford has "reduced the number of global name-plates from 97 in 2006 to 59 in 2008, with further reductions planned." In September 2010, Mr. Mulally announced that Ford plans to reduce the number of models to 30 during the next few years. Typical new vehicle facilities and tool-ing costs have been reduced by 40% between 2005 and 2008, with ongoing continuous improvements.

Furthermore, to achieve major savings, Ford plans to utilize 12 core platforms by 2013 compared with 27 in 2007 (GM has also launched a similar plan). By 2014, Ford projects about 1.6 million units annually from the global "B"compact segment car platform (Fiesta). The global platform and part commonality strategy is significantly reducing Ford's engineering and capital costs–60% and 40%, respectively, between 2005 to 2008. The efficiencies in global processes is allowing Ford to reduce R&D expen-ditures ($5 billion in 2010 compared with $7 billion in 2008).

Regional component commonality on the 2012 Ford Fo-cus is about 85%; this compares to less than 20% for the previous generation Ford Focus as part of the attempt to build a world car under "Ford 2000." The 2011 Ford Fiesta has about 65% common parts.

Ford's global product strategy is to offer "best-in-class fuel economy, quality, design, green vehicles, safety and smart features." These are not "pie in the sky" PR slogans. Ford plans to be the leader in every segment. In 2009, for the first time since 1995, Ford gained market share in the United States, which it repeated in 2010. In Canada, Ford Motor Company is the market leader for the first time in 50 years.

Automotive News, in its August 2010 Ford Product Review, stated: "The new Ford has learned to think' ... 'Ford goes green, small, high-tech." [65] "Autoblog," on October 7, 2010, said the "Blue Oval Boys Bet Big By Going Small." In a report from the Detroit Auto Show, CNBC's reporter stated, "Ford is firing on all cylinders. Ford's vehicles are drawing rave reviews" (January 11, 2011).

The bellwether of Mr. Mulally's mindset was his foresight in 2006 to insist that Ford Motor Company field a total product team, including small cars. This clearly demonstrates the mind of a visionary. For example, the U.S. small car segment actually declined from 18.3% in 2002 to 17.1% in 2005 based on Ford 10-K filings. Since then, the segment's share of the total U.S. passenger car market has increased to 23.7%. Concurrently, the medium segment increased from13.1% to 16.1% during the same period. Ford's small cars now account for 14% of total vehicle sales compared with 11.6% in 2005, and medium car sales represent 12.8% versus 8.2% during the same period.

Ford's new product machine and prowess can be illustrated with the new 2010 Ford Fusion, which was named Motor Trend magazine's "Car of the Year." In addition, the new Ford Transit Connect, an import from Turkey, was awarded the "2010 North American Truck of the Year" at the 2010 Detroit Auto Show. The 2011 Ford Explorer was named 2011 "Truck of the Year" at the 2011 Detroit Auto Show. In awarding Ford Motor Company "2010 Marketer of the Year," Advertising Age, in October 2010 stated, "the Company's (Ford) products are better than ever." In selecting Mr. Kuzak to its 2010 "All Star" list, Automotive News indicated that he "transformed Ford's lineup from a hodgepodge of forgettable vehicles into one of the industry's most fuel efficient, and visually coherent, fleets." In my opinion, during the last forty years, the U.S. auto companies had two product geniuses–Bob Lutz (of BMW, Ford, Chrysler, GM), and Hal Sperlich (formerly of Ford and Chrysler). I am including Mr. Kuzak into my U.S. "Product Planner Hall of Fame." He has accomplished product miracles at Ford. Bob Lutz is the brain behind the new wave of exciting new GM products. Hal Sperlich is the true father of many highly successful Ford and Chrysler products including the minivan, which he conceived at Ford. In 1972-1973, I passed by the minivan prototype everyday on the floor I was working on in the Ford Design Center. Embarrassingly, it made no impression on me. After Mr. Sperlich was fired, he took the concept to Chrysler and created auto history. He was also responsible for the birth of Ford Fiesta. I was the Business Planning Manager for the program when it was initiated in September 1972. Over fierce Ford of Europe opposition, the car was approved and formally transferred to Europe in October 1973.

Mr. Mulally's first babies under his "One Ford" plan are the 2011 Ford Fiesta, the 2012 Ford Focus, and the 2011 Ford Explorer (the lead time for "all-new" vehicles is around three years). The Fiesta is Ford's initial entry into this growing sub-compact segment long dominated by Asian competitors. There will also be a major effort on hybrids and electric vehicles in 2011.

Ford is now squarely setting its flag on enemy territory with an "out and out" assault on the previously neglected small car segment. Importantly, Ford has decided to assume control of small car development. The company effectively abandoned its thirty-year relationship with Mazda and reduced its stake in Mazda to 3.5% in mid-November 2010. Previously, Mazda had lead responsibility for Ford and Mazda small cars. There are several core imperatives in the auto industry that should never be outsourced, including powertrain and vehicle development responsibility.

Ford is rapidly becoming the leader in innovative breakthrough consumer technology product features. In 0CNBC's hour-long November 2010 special entitled "Ford: Rebuilding an Icon," reported Phil LeBeau stated that Ford is "in the bulls eye" of technology innovations and is "leading the pack."

- Ford Motor Company is the only automaker ever to be featured on Fast Company magazine's annual top 10 lists of the "Most Innovative Companies in Mobile Technology." Ford was recognized for its industry-first mobile device connectivity technology, SYNC, and the new "MyFord Touch" driver interface.

- The Taurus received Edmunds.com Technology Breakthrough Award. The car has ten class-exclusive features.

- Ford set a precedent in the Popular Mechanics 2010 Automotive Excellence Awards. It recognizes the best in execution and technology by winning more categories in a single year than any other automaker in the history of the awards. MyFord Touch won the Magazine's Editor's Choice Award.

- Ford also received Popular Mechanics' 2011 "Top 10 cars of 2011 awards" for the Fiesta, Mustang and F-250 Super Duty truck.

- In mid-November 2010, Ford Motor Company won the two 2010 "Best of What's New" awards from Popular Science.

- In late December 2010, " Global Green USA" awarded the Lincoln MKZ Hybrid with its award.

Following are examples of the ever-expanding Ford signature technologies which Ford believes differentiate the company as a leader in innovative and practical technology: next Generation Keypad, SYNC Generation 2, Sony Branded Audio, enhanced THX Audio, "My Key," Blind Spot Mirror, "MyFord" and "My Lincoln" features. Each year since 2007, the Ford brand signature content technology has expanded.

The tsunami of good news continues. The technologically sophisticated Ford products are winning awards. My Ford Touch won:

• CNET best of CES in "Car Tech" category–"People's Choice" and "Best of Show" (2010 Consumer Electronics Show.)

• Popular Mechanics – "Editor's Choice" Award

• Popular Science – "Product of the Future" Award

AutoBlog had the following comments: "besides all the little details, the big picture we took away from MyFord Touch is Ford is serious. These people knew going halfway wouldn't be good enough. The screens are beautiful. Before seeing MyFord Touch, we already thought that Ford had the best navigation/entertainment stuff in the industry (SYNC is really, really good – especially with Sirius Travel Link). MyFord Touch brings Ford a generation (or two) beyond the competition. In other words, no one could even compete with Ford's old stuff. How on earth will they manage against MyFord Touch?"

David Silver of Wall Street Strategies stated in an October 2010 research report that Ford is "really pushing the envelope with respect to technology that are in their vehicles." Motley Fool Stock Advisor contributor John Rosevear claims that Ford resembles Apple Inc. His colleague, Tim Beyers, believes Ford is more like Google with the approach Ford is utilizing with its SYNC in-car technology. Alan Mulally received the prestigious Edison Achievement Award in April 2011 in New York City in recognition of the "boldness of vision and leadership he has brought to the Ford Motor Company" (the Edison Award is one of America's leading innovation awards).

Ford is also in the forefront in developing fuel-efficient vehicles. The Ford Fusion Hybrid is second after the Toyota Prius among 2010 models. Compared with the Camry Hybrid, which is Fusion's facing competitor, the Ford entry offers significantly better fuel economy. The Ford Escape is number seven on the top fuel economy list. None of GM's and Chrysler's cars are on the top ten EPA list.

In late August 2010, Forbes ranked Ford second among America's "Best Car Brands" ahead of Honda, Chevrolet, BMW, Cadillac, Lexus and Mercedes. In addition, Ford received five segment awards, more than any other brand, in J.D. Power and Associates 2010 Automotive Performance, Execution and Layout (APEAL) study. The survey measures customer satisfaction in design, content and vehicle performance. The "American Customer Satisfaction Index" survey released in August 2010 ranked Lincoln highest in customer satisfaction.

In mid-2010, the Ford brand achieved the highest initial quality among all non-luxury brands in J.D. Power and Associates 2010 Initial Quality Study (IQS), and fifth overall (22 in 2000). There was no magic quality pill; it was a laser focus on improving quality and assigning top priority to it. Consistency, determination and skill were critical elements to the quality improvement journey. In honoring Mr. Mulally, "2010 Industry Leader," Automotive News stated that Alan Mulally "has steered the once-struggling automaker into profitable seas this year. Perhaps more valuable for the long term, Ford has become a favorite, and its vehicles have climbed steadily in product quality rankings." In selecting Mr. Mulally "North American CEO," the publication noted: "His steadfast plan to turn Ford around is bearing fruit in impressive fashion."

GQRS conducts quality surveys that measure "Things Gone Wrong" (TGW) per 1,000 vehicles after three months in service. In 2000, during Jacques Nasser's leadership, TGW was an embarrassing 2,300 per 1,000 vehicles. With quality being a super-focus as part of "One Ford," TGW's have improved from about 1,575 in 2006 to 1,300 in 2008, and 2010 level of 1,100. In 2000, only 69% of Ford, Lincoln and Mercury with satisfied with the quality of their vehicles; today it is 83%. Warranty costs have been reduced from $4 billion in 2005 to $2.2 billion in 2010.

According to Ford's "Sustainability Reports," Ford top safety picks from the Insurance Institute for Highway Safety (IIHS), totaled two in 2005, six in 2006, eight in 2007, fourteen in 2008 and nineteen in 2009. In addition, in June 2010, the 2010 Ford Flex, Ford Fusion, Lincoln MKZ and MKT earned the "Top Safety Pick" ratings from the IIHS. This gave Ford eleven top ratings for 2010 models–the most of any auto company. Further, in late August 2010, the 2011 Ford Fiesta received the "Top Safety Pick" rating by the IIHS and in late December, the 2011 Ford Explorer was added to the list.

Ford's number of safety recalls is moderating. In 2000, the company had 59 safety recalls involving 7.2 million vehicles. By 2007, recalls totaled 15 involving 5.5 million vehicles. In 2009, Ford announced 8 recalls with 4.5 million units.

Ford is now the "most considered" brand among potential new car shoppers. Secondly, in a December 6, 2010 press release from J.D. Power & Associates, Ford Motor Company was tied with Honda for first place in "owner retention," with a 62% 2010 retention rate.

Automotive News reported on January 5, 2011 that a Consumer Report's magazine survey showed that Ford Motor Company matched Toyota "as the most favorably viewed auto brand." For Ford, it was a giant 35-percentage point increase, and for Toyota a 46-point decline! Ford's score of 144 is 42 points above Chevrolet, 78 points above Cadillac, 75 points ahead of Lexus and 51 points higher than BMW. However, Toyota's staying power can't be underestimated because, as Doron Levin pointed out in the January 7, 2011 CNNMoney.com website, Camry is still the number one selling car in the U.S., very few of its cars go to the rental fleet, the company still has the highest number of most reliable vehicles, and its R&D budget is one of the largest worldwide.

Ford's highly competitive product portfolio is changing Ford from a discount brand, sold primarily on price, to a company offering superior products–the Japanese strategy. Ford's new way of marketing under the leadership of "boy genius" Jim Farley (Group V.P., Global Sales and Marketing) and U.S. V.P. of Sales and Marketing Ken Czubay (both Toyota alumni) is shown below.

• Implementation of a disciplined incentive strategy with lower rebates. Together with outstanding products, this has led to a critically important increase in residual value, which has historically been Ford's competitive disadvantage. When consumers trade-in their vehicles, a high resale value reduces they're cost of purchasing a new car. Toyota, Honda and Nissan have been the leaders with high resale values, which allowed them to premium-price their products.

- Introducing a new pricing philosophy. The company is premium- pricing products by adding content and offering highly fuel-efficient, technologically advanced, stylish, and top safety rated vehicles. It is generating over $2,000 per vehicle in incremental revenues compared with 2009. This has added billions of dollars in revenues. Today, according to an August 23, 2010 article in Automotive News, Ford average transaction prices exceed Japanese competition ($23,000 for the new 2010 Ford Fusion versus $22,500 for 2010 Toyota Camry; $16,300 for used 2010 Ford Fusion versus $15,800 for a 2010 Toyota Camry). Historically, Ford lagged behind Asian competitors.

- Instituted a disciplined dealer inventory management system so as not to flood dealers with vehicles. The objective is to match demand and supply. Historically, to keep factories operating at capacity because labor (UAW) is essentially a fixed cost, Ford often overproduced. This led to higher sales, but required heavy discounting, which impacted resale values. Today, dealers complain that they can't get enough of Ford's hot selling products. Ford is also carefully managing sales to low-margin daily rental fleets. Dumping returned rental fleet cars on the used car market often reduced residual values.

## Conclusions

Ford's "One Ford" product strategy, launched in 2006 with its focus on what consumers really want and value, is rapidly changing Ford's perception among consumers. Ford's new products are leading to increased market share, and higher residual values. The sleek styling, premium content, together with leading edge technology, and fuel-efficient vehicles is generating high transaction prices with a commensurate increase in profits.

## Work Together Effectively As One Team, Leveraging Ford's Assets

When Mr. Mulally joined Ford Motor Company in September 2006 as President and Chief Executive Officer, the company urgently needed a massive reengineering. Mr. Mulally's direct reports were all Ford insiders who held key positions during Ford's darkest hours in mid-2006. Tony Schwartz, President and CEO of The Energy Project, outlined in an October 13, 2010 Harvard Business Review article several capabilities every great leader needs including "great leaders recognize strengths in us that we don't always yet fully see in ourselves." Similarly, in Tom Peters' "Little BIG Things" series on leadership, he stated, "the business of leaders at all levels is to help those in their charge develop beyond their dreams." This is one of Mr. Mulally's fundamental métier. How else can one explain that he achieved miracles with essentially the same team, which was part of the mid-2006 Ford crisis? Having created a team spirit, and a positive atmosphere is a new phenomenon at Ford Motor Company. It has been a key aspect of the revitalization at the company.

Mr. Mulally did not bring other Boeing executives with him. The Harvard Business Review article entitled "Are Leaders Portable?" by Boris Groysberg, Andrew McLean, and Nitin Nohria stated, "Eight of the 20 former GE executives we studied brought in at least one former colleague, though only four brought along three or more." [66]

Importantly, during the critical early weeks on the job, Mr. William Clay Ford, Jr. said in an August 2010 article in Time magazine that some executives came to his office "to complain about the new guy." Mr. Ford refused to listen to them. [67] This immediately provided Mr. Mulally with important legitimacy, which a new outside leader requires. This illustrates the palpable tensions at that time; Bill Ford could not tolerate a rebellion within his ranks as the ship was sinking. According to a 2009 Harvard Business Review article by Michael E. Porter and Nitin Nohria (now Dean of the Harvard Business School) entitled "What is Leadership," the authors concluded that "legitimacy" gives a CEO the license to lead ... legitimacy creates trust. Trust, in turn, is a powerful resource in any organization." [68]

Legitimacy is only one aspect of a leader who is simply defined as "an individual who influences others to follow him or her" according to Professor Jay Lorsch's article in the Handbook of Leadership Theory and Practice, entitled "A Contingency Theory of Leadership." [69] Professor Lorsch also claims that charisma is important as a source of a leader's power. According to Ford insiders, Mr. Mulally possesses this characteristic. He is also driven to succeed. Further, "getting reliable information on what is truly going on in the organization is surprisingly difficult" according to the Messrs' Porter and Nohria article, cited previously. For the information hungry Mr. Mulally, that's not a problem because he reportedly has hundreds of data point performance charts in his "war room," which he and his top team of 16 executives constantly review.

## Conclusions

Based on Ford Motor Company insiders, Mr. Mulally has fundamentally changed the culture of the company. Instead of the usual turf wars, Mr. Mulally has forged a team, which is effectively working together because he nurtured and molded the team. Mr. Mulally will not tolerate schism.

# CHAPTER 20

⊠ ⊠ ⊠

# MR. MULALLY'S "WHIZ KIDS/ ALL STARS"

## The Original "Whiz Kids"

According to Douglas Brinkley's book "Wheels For the World," there was great concern in Washington in 1943 that the critically important Ford Motor Company was without effective leadership. [70] Ford, with over 130,000 employees, was totally dedicated to war production. Edsel Ford had died on May 26, 1943 and Henry Ford II joined the company in August of that year. It was his first job. The government had the following comments about Henry Ford and Henry Ford II: "One was past his prime, the other untested." [70] Moreover, Mr. Henry Ford suffered a stroke in 1945; he died on April 7, 1947.

After World War II, Ford returned to producing vehicles under Henry Ford II's leadership who became CEO in September 1945. Reportedly, Ford was losing $1 million per day at that time. In late 1945, ten highly educated U.S. ex-Air Force officers from the Statistical Control Office in Washington, including Robert McNamara, Arjay Miller (both Ford Presidents some years later) and Edward Lundy (Ford's long-time legendary Finance Chief) joined Ford. They helped to first stabilize, and then revolutionize Ford in all aspects of the business. They have been forever known as the "Whiz Kids." Ernest Breech, a former GM executive, also played a leading role in the rebirth of the company.

## The New "All-Stars"

Mr. Mulally also has surrounded himself with a group of senior executives who are truly reinventing an American icon, and are rightfully the successors to the original "Whiz Kids."

Automotive News, the long-time and highly respected bible of the auto industry, annually compiles a list of "All Stars." In 2010, ten Ford executives, an industry record, received such honors. [71] Two are African-American and one is a female. One of Ford's historic tenets is to actively foster diversity. In his book "The Little BIG Things," Tom Peters listed 51 "commonplace advices" including number twenty-four–"diversity always wins." In addition, in Motor Trend's "2011 Power List," four of the top 15 world leaders were Ford executives (Messrs. Mulally, Booth, Kuzak and Farley).

Alan Mulally, "Ford's Comeback Kid" (Fortune, May 25, 2009) [72] was named 2010 "Industry Leader of the Year," and "North American CEO." In 2009, Sergio Marchionne, CEO of Fiat/Chrysler, was named "Industry Leader of the Year." In 2009, Mr. Mulally was named "North American CEO." [73] Automotive News also publishes annually a list of top females in the automotive business (U.S., Canada, Mexico, auto producers, suppliers, union and dealers). The 2010 "100 Leading Women in the North American Auto Industry" included a record 17 Ford executives (Director level and above). Toyota and Nissan each had five, and Honda two honorees. [74] Ford publicly honored the women in a full-page advertisement in the October 30-31, 2010 edition of The Wall Street Journal.

| Category | Name/Title | Date/Comments |
|---|---|---|
| Finance | Lewis Booth, Executive V.P., C.F.O. | Second Straight "All Star" Award |
| Purchasing | Thomas Brown, Group V.P. Global Purchasing | B.S., joined Ford in 1989 from United Technologies, second straight "All Star" Award |
| Public Relations | Raymond Day, V.P. Communications | B.S., joined Ford in 1989 second straight "All Star" Award |
| Marketing | Jim Farley, Group V.P. Global Sales, Marketing and Services | B.S., M.B.A., joined Ford in 2007 from Toyota |
| Minority Business | Burton Jordan (title not available) | Third straight "All Star" Award |
| Product Development | Derrick Kuzak, Group V.P. Global Product Development | Second Straight "All Star" Award |
| Engineering | Barb Samardzich, V.P. Powertrain Engineering | Second straight "All Star" Award |
| Manufacturing | Jim Tetreault, V.P. North American Manufacturing | Not available |
| Design | Freeman Thomas (Title not available) | Not available |

There are many other high-level Ford executives at the group vice president level who are making Herculean efforts toward reengineering the company, and leading Ford to continuing profitability and world leadership. The most visible are:

• Mark Fields, Executive V.P. and President, The Americas.

• Michael Bannister, Executive V.P., Chairman and CEO, Ford Motor Credit Company (a reliable profit contributor).

• John Fleming, previously Chairman of highly successful Ford of Europe and Executive V.P., Manufacturing & Labor affairs (unlike many competitors such as GM in Europe, Ford of Europe, with its highly efficient facilities and attractive products is a consistent profit generator).

• Bernie Fowler, Group V.P., Quality. Ford now is the quality leader in the United States; he should have been on the 2010 "All Star" list.

• Joseph Hinrichs, Group V.P. and President, Asia Pacific and Africa. Until 2009, Mr. Hinrichs was Group V.P. Manufacturing and Labor Affairs. He led the Ford U.S. manufacturing revolution and successfully closed many plants, and the buyout of over 30,000 hourly employees in 2007-2009 without major disruptions. He was transferred to Asia to gain international experience where he will quickly move Ford up the ladder from "also ran."

Most professional turnaround specialists rightfully focus on solving today's crisis. To his credit, Mr. Mulally is working on succession planning. Mr. Mulally has already initiated a development program for several senior executives as part of his plan to groom possible replacements, and to provide them with international experience. In his widely acclaimed 1982 book "In search of Excellence," Tom Peters stated, "leaders don't create followers, they create more leaders."

# CHAPTER 21

✠ ✠ ✠

## THE JOB IS NOT DONE

### Continue to Strengthen the Balance Sheet

Ford's turnaround is one of the greatest stories in U.S. corporate history, but competition is unrelenting. Mr. Mulally, along with Mr. Henry Ford II, will be remembered in the annals of Ford's history as iconic figures and the savior of Ford Motor Company. The "One Ford" team has passed the required core curricula with a grade "A+," but it is only a preamble, and not the end game, and Ford's "Dawn of a New Age" must continue. The next step is moving toward the "Promised Land" of world automotive leadership. Obstacles remain including the following:

• Mr. Mulally and his finance team have stated that Ford's balance sheet is a distinct competitive disadvantage compared with General Motors because GM was able to eliminate most of its debt through the Chapter 11 process. Ford's debt is Achilles' heel; at the end of December 2010, Ford's debt totaled $19.1 billion ($16 billion on March 1, 2011), while GM eliminated 92% of debt when the company filed for bankruptcy. This gives GM the financial resources to aggressively launch a comeback. The new GM CEO, Dan Akerson, already announced in mid-September 2010 that GM would now switch to an attack mode. He is virtually implementing the "One Ford" (nice complement to Ford).

• Restoring Ford's balance sheet to investment grade level is a key priority because it significantly reduces the cost of borrowing funds, reduces Ford's annual interest expenses, provides the funds for continued aggressive product actions, and to strengthen the company's position in emerging markets which requires billions of dollars in new funds. Further, it offers a cushion in the event of continuing long-term weaknesses in the economy, with impacts auto sales. Toyota Financial Services, which has an investment grade rating, reportedly pays on average of 2.51% on its debt compared to Ford Motor Credit Company's $4.7%. [75] At the October 26, 2010 third quarter 2010 earnings conference call, Ford CFO Lewis Booth stated that Ford Credit's interest cost is 4.5%.

• Remarkably, Ford achieved a net cash position at the end of 2010 because of higher revenues, the most competitive product line-up in its history, higher prices associated with the new products, and continuing efforts to reduce costs as part of "One Ford." However, a significant shift (10+ percentage points) toward the relatively low-profit sub-compact and compact segments could affect profits. The segment shift could be as a result of a major increase in gasoline prices toward the $5 per gallon range because of continuing Middle East political developments (Egypt, Libya, Yemen, Tunisia, Algeria etc. unrests, as well as embargo, blocking of key oil channels, terrorist bombing of Saudi Arabia or Kuwait oil facilities, war between Israel and its neighbors, etc.).

## Passenger Cars

In 2008, Ford's U.S. passenger car market share as a percent of total U.S. automotive sales reached a record low of 5.5%. Ford is now an "also ran" in the U.S. car business with an embarrassing number four ranking in its home market in 2010. Even in Canada, where Ford achieved industry leadership in 2010 for the first time in 50 years, the Company only ranks fourth in cars (# 1 in trucks) and fifth in Mexico.

However, returning to the 2000 level of 9.8%, the lowest in Ford's history at that time, will require several "killer models" such as the 1965 Ford Mustang, the Ford Fairmont, Ford Escort, or the early 1990s Ford Taurus with 400,000 plus in annual sales.

A return to the 1960s-1990s Ford car share levels is totally unlikely because of the entry of powerful Asian imports. In addition, the truck share as a percent of the total industry sales has increased from about 20% to roughly 50% of the U.S. market since then. Although not shown on the next page, Ford Motor Company has consistently remained a strong number two in the truck business.

| YEAR | FORD U.S. INDUSTRY SHARE | | | FORD U.S. CAR POSITION |
| --- | --- | --- | --- | --- |
| | CARS | TRUCKS | TOTAL | |
| 2010 | 6.2% | 10.8% | 16.9% | # 4 |
| 2009 | 6.1 | 10.0 | 16.1 | # 4 |
| 2008 | 5.5 | 9.6 | 15.1 | # 4 |
| 2000 | 9.8 | 14.4 | 24.2 | # 2 |
| 1990 | 13.2 | 10.0 | 23.2 | # 2 |
| 1980 | 13.6 | 6.2 | 19.8 | # 2 |
| 1970 | 21.5 | 5.9 | 27.4 | # 2 |
| 1965 | 21.8 | 3.6 | 25.4 | # 2 |

Source: *Automotive News*

In the small and medium car segments, Ford has improved its market share in recent years as a result of aggressive product actions. However, Ford's performance in the U.S. large and premium passenger car segments remains very weak, which could be a potential engine of growth for Ford Motor Company.

Lastly, to really improve its small car position; the company has to invent a new market niche. The best example is the 1965 Mustang when Ford created a large-volume sporty segment. How about a sexy two seater "baby" Mustang–an inexpensive sporty car smaller than today's Mustang?

# Emerging Markets

## Asia

Ford Motor Company is only in the second inning in Asia. Ford did not actively enter the Chinese auto market until 2003. GM, which established it's first link with SAIC in 1995, outsells Ford four to one in China, and has a much broader line-up, and a stronger dealer body. [76] Chinese sales account for 24% of GM's worldwide sales. GM is creating a $250 million research center in Shanghai. [77] Ford's market share was 2.5% in 2010 of the rapidly growing Chinese market, and 2.6% in India.

According to a recent report by "Market Watch," Ford Motor's Group Vice President for Asia Pacific and Africa stated in a news conference that Ford is projecting industry sales for his area of responsibility to increase to 35 million vehicles by 2018. [78] This compares to 16 million in 2009. [79]

In India, Ford was also a late entry (Ford began operations in India in 1996). Suzuki Motors is the leading auto company in India with over 1.5 million in annual sales. Other competitors are rapidly expanding in India.

With significant progress in reengineering Ford's U.S. operations, Ford can now launch an aggressive effort in Asia. Ford's recent investment in Asia and Africa is shown on the next page.

| COUNTRY | INVESTMENT (Billions) |
|---|---|
| China | $2.5 (e) |
| India | 0.5 |
| Thailand | 0.5 |
| South Africa | 0.4 |
| Total | $3.9 |

According to a Zacks Equity Research report dated December 6, 2010, "Ford expects 70% of its sales growth to come from the Asia Pacific/African region in the next 10 years." This will require billions of dollars in incremental investment in these regions to achieve a top five position. Unless Ford China can be self-funded, will Ford's European and North American operations generate the profits and cash flow to sustain their own requirements, and fund the emerging market funding needs? (Ford recently announced a $2.4 billion investment in the United Kingdom during the next five years.)

## South America

In late 1995, Ford and VW AG dissolved their highly profitable Autolatina joint venture in Brazil and Argentina with 52,000 employees, $8 billion in annual sales, and a 50% market share in Brazil (having been at a director position at Autolatina at that time, and knowing all the facts, I continue to consider the dissolution a major mistake). At that time, Ford's share was 15% of the Brazilian auto market. New entries such as Toyota and Hyundai have reduced Ford's share of the Brazilian market to 10.4% in 2010.

In South America, Ford has announced a $2.6 billion investment in Brazil and an almost $500 million investment in Argentina, primarily for capacity expansion (Ford hired 1,300 engineers in Brazil during the last two years). Concurrently, GM, Renault, Fiat and VW will invest in excess of $10 billion to meet growing demand in Brazil. [80]

Ford is a distant fourth in the Brazilian market behind Fiat (23%), VW (21%), and GM (20%). Again, as in Asia, will Ford generate the cash flow required to fund billions and billions of dollars of investment required to meet North American, European, and emerging market needs?

## Mexico

Another market of major concern is Mexico. Ford's performance in Mexico has been unsatisfactory for many years, even during my three years as Business Development Manager at Ford Mexico between 1979-1981. Ford remains in fourth place behind Nissan, VW and GM. In Canada, Ford Motor Company became the leading auto company in 2010 for the first time in 50 years.

## UAW Agreement

The "Big-Three" continue to face a competitive disadvantage compared with the non-union foreign companies with U.S. facilities although the gap is shrinking. The present four-year contract with a UAW expires in September 2011. During the U.S. auto industry collapse, which resulted in GM and Chrysler entering Chapter 11, the UAW agreed to concessions (GM had 300 separate job classifications versus a few at Toyota). UAW President Bob King claims "UAW members who work for U.S. automakers have each given $7,000 to $30,000 in concessions in the past five years." [81]

In my opinion, however, the UAW "give-backs" are somewhat ballyhooed, especially compared with the real losses the GM bondholders, common stock owners, salaried retirees and dealers had to suffer. (I know the impact on my finances as a Ford retiree when Ford eliminated the health-care plan, and substituted it with an annual fixed amount– not more than peanuts.) Equally one-sided is the "gold watches" retired UAW workers continue to receive in the form of annual lump sum pension adjustments (2007, 2008, 2009, 2010) while salaried retirees have not received a penny of COLA in over ten years. These payments cost GM $200 million in mid-December 2010 and Ford $70 million. Retired salaried employees don't even get a bobble head doll! In a December 2008 article in

Workforce Management, auto analyst Craig Fitzgerald of Plante & Moran stated, "if GM had failed to make the payments, the company would have risked "world war" with the UAW." In addition, the VEBA Trust for hourly UAW retirees is "gold plated." All my retired Ford executive colleagues are up in arms over this unequal treatment. Yes, many hourly people lost their jobs (over 65,000 during the last five years), but they received very generous buy-outs (up to $140,000), which cost billions.

- Active UAW workers continue to receive their regular base pay. The 50% base wage reduction the UAW agreed to applies only to <u>new</u> workers, and they can't exceed 20% of the total workforce. Ford announced at the 2011 Detroit Auto Show that it will hire over 7,000 workers during the next two years, but they didn't specify how many would be new workers or recalled employees.

- UAW members continue to enjoy an outstanding medical plan which even includes Viagra type products, according to the UAW website. Paul Ingrassia stated in a November 23, 2010 article in the Wall Street Journal "active UAW workers...still pay only about 5% of their health-care costs." According to an April 28, 2009 article in "Real Clear Markets," GM spent $103 billion during the last 15 years funding its pension and retiree health-care obligations.

- Fortunately, Uncle Sam demanded drastic modification of the "Jobs Bank" because of public outcry. Further, there is a stricter attendance policy to reduce worker absenteeism. Nevertheless, UAW work rules continue to remain uncompetitive compared with transplants. Paul Ingrassia stated in his article cited above that "Ford's contract with the union, for example, allows workers nine unexcused absences in 18 months before they can be dismissed."

Some experts, however, believe that the UAW made concessions during the industry meltdown. Professor Harley Shaiken at the University of California (Berkeley) stated in a Bloomberg GM IPO show on November 17, 2010 "the UAW sacrificed tremendously." Another analyst on the show stated "the UAW has its hand in the GM cash register." To be fair and balanced, however, in an October 2010 agreement between GM and the UAW, the union agreed that 40% of the hourly workers at its idled Orion, Michigan plant would be paid Tier 2 wages, which are roughly 50% of the regular $28 per hour base pay. This will allow GM to profitably produce a subcompact car in the U.S.

However, there are dark clouds on the horizon; I believe the UAW's labor war mindset and entitlement mentality is still very much alive.

- In November 2009 Ford UAW members rejected contract modifications previously agreed to at GM and Chrysler.

UAW members, and some UAW officials will demand return of the "give-backs" negotiated during the last few years. Hopefully, the historic antagonism will not return. Demand for "give- backs" could intensify if Ford profits continue to increase. Messrs. Ford and Mulally recently received almost $100 million in shares which will fuel the fire in forthcoming negotiations.

• The UAW influence remains powerful in the auto industry. In its 2009 Annual Report, Ford stated that the existing agreements "may restrict our (Ford) ability to close plants and divest businesses during the term of the agreements." Moreover, many featherbedding work rules remain.

The first scrimmages toward the September 2011 negotiations have commenced. In September 2010, Ford announced that the sub-compact Kuga (similar to the Fiat 500) will not be build in its Louisville, Kentucky plant, as originally planned. Ford plans to continue production of the Kuga in Germany where labor cost reportedly are $10 per hour above U.S. levels. Auto analysts are speculating that the U.S. Kuga production "began to fall apart in November (2009) when UAW members rejected Ford's quest to match givebacks it gave to General Motors Company and Chrysler Group LLC." [82]

## Lincoln Brand

Ford announced in June 2010 that the 71 year-old Mercury brand would be discontinued. It was one of Mr. Mulally's gutsiest calls, and a stunner. It appears that Mr. Mulally is not a nostalgic person. No CEO before him had dared to face Mercury's invalid status.

Mercury sales declined from a roughly 2% market share in 2000 to 1.1% in 2006 (181,000 units), and to about 92,000 units in 2009 (0.9% share). Intense competition, primarily from imports, and a nondescript image affected Mercury sales. The elimination of Mercury is part of Mr. Mulally's focus on the Ford brand.

There are about 1,200 Lincoln franchises in the U.S. including 260 stand-alone Lincoln dealers. They will lose over 50% of their business and many will not operate profitability (Lincoln was acquired in 1922). Lincoln sold about 83,000 vehicles in the U.S. in 2009, and is a second-tier luxury brand (0.8% market share). This compares to 2.1% for Lexus, 1.8% for Mercedes and BMW's share of 1.9%. In late September 2010, Ford announced that it plans to eliminate 40% or 200 Lincoln dealers in major metropolitan markets, and require the remaining dealers to upgrade their facilities.

In my opinion, Lincoln is presently a weak nameplate. Accordingly, Lincoln's performance has been unsatisfactory in recent years with intense competition from Lexus, BMW,

Mercedes, Audi, and Cadillac (Hyundai in the future). Lincoln's confusing alphabet nameplates are not helping (MKS, MKZ, MKX, MKT). Lincoln sales per store are roughly one-tenth of average Lexus per store sales, and significantly below BMW and Mercedes-Benz sales per store.

Ford is launching an aggressive product blitz for Lincoln during the next four years, including seven all new or significantly refreshed vehicles. This includes Lincoln's first ever-compact car (Cadillac is also introducing a small car and BMW and Mercedes-Benz already sell small cars). Regaining the approximately one percentage point market share loss with Mercury's demise would be considered "Mission Accomplished."

Ford is now effectively a one-franchise brand because of Lincoln's weakness. This strategy is the opposite of former Ford CEO Jacques Nasser's early 2000 product strategy of "plenty as blackberries" (Shakespeare). Restoring Lincoln to its glory days will take several years, and billions of dollars. None of the top ten world automotive leaders are one-brand companies (VW has ten brands, GM has four, Chrysler five, etc.). If I had been asked about the Lincoln/Mercury strategy, I would have kept Mercury afloat for two more years until the Lincoln product pipeline is supercharged to the nth degree.

The jury is out if Ford Motor Company can improve Lincoln's brand identity to compete effectively against entrenched luxury car competitors. Lincoln also has an aging ownerbody. Will Ford succeed in creating a meaningful differentiation of Lincoln from the Ford brand? Can the investment be justified?

# Former Visteon Corporation Plants

In 2000, Ford spun-off the uncompetitive Visteon components operation with about 74,000 employees, 80 plants and roughly $20 billion in annual sales. Visteon derived almost 90% of its sales from Ford Motor Company.

In May 2005, to prevent a potential collapse of Visteon Corporation, Ford's most important supplier, Ford agreed to take back 24 plants and several engineering centers. The facilities employed 17,000 people including 15,000 UAW-represented workers.

Ford's objective was to expeditiously sell or close the remaining plants the company took back from Visteon. Primarily as a result of the auto industry decline, which significantly reduced volume, and the associated bankruptcy of many component suppliers, Ford's progress disposing of the plants has been relatively slow. Ford is continuing to sell or close the mostly uncompetitive plants, which are not part of the company's core business. It is uncertain and of some concern how the process will be impacted by 2011 UAW contract negotiations.

# CHAPTER 22

x x x

# THE FIFTH COLUMN IN AMERICA

## Washington's Job Saboteurs

As previously outlined, Mr. Mulally will have to continue attacking key imperatives to achieve a top ranking. However, as I am writing and rewriting this chapter, I am coming to the conclusion that there is really nothing more important to focus on than the saboteurs in Washington, and the ever-expanding government rules, which is stifling free enterprise and our personal freedom. The up to ten million Americans involved in the automobile industry (former Michigan Governor Jennifer Granholm's estimate) are confronted by a big problem—job killing fifth columnists in Washington—on our own shores. The two agencies, which are "messing around" with our lives are the EPA (Environmental Protection Agency) and the DOT (Department of Transportation) through its NHSTA agency (National Highway Traffic Safety Administration). We can thank the late President Richard Nixon (1969-1974) for creating the EPA and NHSTA in 1970—forty years ago (agencies never die).

Why am I so paranoid by these two alphabet agencies of which there are hundreds in the federal government? What is the smoking gun? Who are these rule-making dictators? What value-added wealth have they created for society? The last time I checked, we didn't live under a domineering Kaiser who told us what to do! (I lived under a dictatorship in Germany and know what it means. Within 52 days after Hitler gained power legally in 1933, the German people lost most of their freedom and Germany effectively became a one-party state.) Look what is happening in America. NRP, supported by taxpayers, is restricting freedom of expression. The December 22, 2010 headline in the Wall Street Journal had it right: "Government Bobbles the Web." In the same edition, Wall Street Journal columnist John Fund stated that the professor behind the new Internet rules has the objective "to get rid of the media capitalists." What will be next? Will it be flushing toilet rules, or a government light bulb police in 2014 to enforce use of the new bulbs? Now, according to a December 20, 2010 article in the Wall Street Journal, the FCC wants to take the "unprecedented step to expand government's reach into the Internet" (exactly what happened in Germany when Hitler took total control in the 1930s over the media and the radio network; we could only listen to the Deutschland Sender during the war).

Next, the EPA will restrict our freedom to drive our cars with their planned 62 mpg scheme. Ironically, the mission and vision statements of the two agencies sound like they are "throned on highest bliss." For example, the NHTSA's mission/vision is to: "Save lives, prevent injuries and re-duce economic costs due to road traffic crashes, through education, research, safety standards and enforcement activity, and global leader in motor vehicle and highway safety." The NHSTA's core values are a "commitment to serve customers."

The EPA's mission "is to protect human health and to safeguard the natural environment- air, water, and land – upon which life depends...the EPA has been working for a cleaner, healthier environment for the American peo-ple." According to the NHTSA website, the NHTSA sets and administers the CAFE (Corporate Average Fuel Economy) program, and the Environmental Protection Agency pro-vides the fuel economy data...and calculates the aver-age fuel economy for each manufacturer."

The EPA has 18,000 employees and a budget in excess of $10,000,000,000 annually. DOT, which was established in 1966, has ten agencies with a mind-boggling budget of almost $90,000,000,000 and roughly 86,000 employees. Can anybody imagine that! The NHTSA, which is part of DOT, has an annual budget of $900,000,000 (assuming an average annual DOT budget of "only" $45 billion over 40 years, this would mean that the hard-working U.S. taxpay-ers had to "dish-out" $1,800,000,000,000 to DOT since 1970 alone. The number should leave Americans speechless).

One of the most egregious news about the NHSTA was the revelation in early 2010 that they apparently slept with the U.S. auto industry's ruthless adversary–Toyota–who seems better at lobbying than American auto companies–another Toyota first! (Toyota spends roughly $5 million annually on Washington lobbying.) When we need the NHSTA to protect the public, they fail us. The Department of Transportation Secretary, Ray LaHood, told a Senate Subcommittee on Consumer Protection that there was no chummy relationship. However, he also stated that he was "not done with Toyota yet," that they are a little safety deaf."

The real story seems different. The Brookings Institute summarized it well: "Was the Car Safety Regulatory Agency Asleep at the Wheel? It appears that two former NHTSA employees run Toyota's "regulatory affairs" department. According to Bloomberg, former government regulators hired by Toyota helped to halt acceleration probes by NHTSA. Bloomberg reports at least four U.S. investigations into unintended acceleration by Toyota vehicles were halted with the help of former regulators who are current Toyota employees. Bloomberg contends that court documents evidence the relationship between Toyota and the former regulators. According to a Toyota Class Action attorney, the vice president of regulatory affairs in Toyota's Washington office (Mr. Tinto), and Christopher Santucci, joined Toyota directly from NHTSA. Bloomberg reports that

Mr. Tinto and Mr. Santucci helped persuade the National Highway Traffic Safety Administration to end NHTSA probes of Toyota vehicles, including those of 2002-2003 Toyota Camry's and Solaras. According to a February 10, 2010 New York Times article the "NHTSA failed to subpoena Toyota's records in 6 years it believed the automaker was withholding critical information...NHTSA opened 6 safety inquires on Toyota since 2003 and closed them all without significant action." According to a document released by Congress, Toyota boasted internally in mid- 2010 that it had saved $100 million by limiting a recall of floor mats in 2007.

So, what is the EPA/NHSTA coalition's latest plan? In May 2009, President Obama signed new stringent-fuel efficiency legislation, which was, admittedly, overdue. It raised mpg standards to a fleet average of 35.5 mpg by the 2016 model year (39.5 mpg for cars!). This is costing the industry $50 billion according to the Auto Industry Alliance. During the signing ceremony, four super-liberals, with a very poor job-creating history–Schwarzeneger (CA), Patrick (MA) Granholm (MI), and UAW leader Gettelfinger, flanked the president! (The companies affected by the new rules apparently were not invited.) The new legislation raised the fuel economy standards by eight mpg. The January 3, 2011 Automotive News website article stated the 35.5 target will require "some sophisticated technology: eight-speed automatic, variable valve timing, electric power steering, stop-start systems, turbochargers, direct injection, hybrid systems and diesels, primarily in light trucks. The technologies are migrating into smaller segments, and smaller engines are moving into larger vehicles."

Flush with the 35.5-mpg victory, and while automakers are struggling to meet the new mpg standards with empty coffers, the EPA/NHSTA alliance plus CARB (California hot heads) went immediately on an all-out attack to issue new plans to raise the fuel efficiency levels to an unimaginable unchartered territory of 62 mpg by 2025. This is definitely a bridge too far, and a jaw-dropping attack against car buyers. Who are the government leaders who have such power? These people are destroying the middle-class in the Heartland of America with their insane proposals.

The EPA and DOT, through NHSTA, jointly released a document consisting of hundreds of pages outlining the new attack on fuel economy and greenhouse gases. With Washington's "government knows best" mentality, the press release stated that the proposed standards are good for consumers and automakers. Washington estimated the cost of reaching up to 62 mpg at $51.5 billion over five years (probably $100 billion in the real world) and the cost to consumers between $2,800 and $3,500 per vehicle. This would push many average Americans into buying used cars instead of fuel-efficient new cars. Most "experts" with no real world auto industry experience prepare these government cost estimates and their so-called cost/benefit analysis is laughable. It is like the blind leading the blind. Keith Crain, editor-in-chief of Automotive News called it a "disastrous road" in a November 15, 2010 editorial. These saboteurs in Washington have been embolden by a 5:4 decision in 2007 by a Supreme Court ruling that the EPA has the power to regulate greenhouse gases (December 7, 2010 Wall Street Journal).

If these bureaucrats actually get away with the proposed new standards, we will all use donkeys or drive two-seat Smart cars, which the public has totally rejected or drive Nissan's new concept car with a single driver in front and a single passenger in the rear (December 6, 2010 issue of Automotive News). Alternatively, we'll be walking as Nancy Sinatra used to sing "These Boots Are Made for Walking." At least, it is safer than driving a tiny car. That's no bull.

However, it is the 62 mpg timing that is most disturbing. How can these EPA/ NHSTA bureaucrats not give a hoot what the economic consequences are? Incredibly, the EPA administrator, Lisa Jackson, called EPA's policies "common-sense" in an article in the December 2, 2010 edition of the Wall Street Journal. She also claims that there is "no evidence that environmental protection hinders economic growth." I consider these agencies anti-consumer and anti-business.

The EPA will issue a "final" ruling in July 2012. The new standards would commence in 2017. The announcement came only six months after the government issued new 35.5-mpg rules for the 2012-2016 period, which is a 40% increase from present standards. In other words, the train hadn't even left the station, and a barrage of new rules is being contemplated. Frankly, we prefer a period of "nothing burgers." The new mpg rules are on top of constantly new automotive regulations coming out of Washington including costly backup cameras, additional air bags, expensive new roll-over rules, and technologies that alert drivers before potential crashes.

The new rules should be called "industry murder by legislation." Benny Goodman described it perfectly in the 1940s song: "These Are Foolish Things." Moreover, they are inconsistent with a major op-ed by President Barrack Obama in the January 18, 2011 edition of the Wall Street Journal that "the goal of my administration has been to strike the right balance" regarding the regulatory system. Hopefully, his new philosophy is not the usual PR baloney because it is actions and not words that count. We should be cynical because it appears that the EPA is not coming on board; they are tone-deaf. The agency has already announced that it wouldn't have to make any rule making changes!! Mr. President, remember, we already have enough external enemies knocking on our door ready to destroy us such as China, Russia and Radical Islam. Look at the facts:

- Auto industry sales are at a 27-year low. The "patient" still has pneumonia, and there is still a crack in the foundation of the house. Implementing the 62 mpg rules is like putting the patient outside in minus 50-degree temperature. The government computer automatically adds the following words to all new rules: "within auto industry reach." According to June 8, 2006 edition of the Detroit News, "There's little doubt that the global economy has turned a blowtorch on Detroit," said Harley Shaiken labor professor at the University of California-Berkeley. "At stake is nothing less than the future American manufacturing."

- The "Big Three" are just emerging from the "Dark Ages." Through Uncle Sam, GM and Chrysler are experiencing light at the end of the tunnel thanks to their successful wealth-destroying bankruptcy. However, none of the three U.S. auto companies' balance sheets are chock-full. With its unlimited resources and never-ending quest to destroy the U.S. "Big Three," Toyota has already announced that it can meet the proposed 62 mpg fuel economy levels.

- Asian competitors are still eating our lunch and have solid financial resources to meet the mpg rules. Who will provide the $100 billion required to meet the new rules? There won't be another bailout. The 62 mpg rule is in addition to billions required for air, water and solid waste pollution abatements at auto plants.

- The U.S. auto industry has "just one design cycle to make significant changes that will require costly steel substitutes including aluminum, new steel alloys and magnesium" (December 27, 2010 Automotive News website).

- The economy is in shambles, and we have an unemployment rate in the 9% range, 26 million people are looking for jobs, and the U.S. experienced the loss of over 500,000 auto jobs in recent years. How many more costly blows can the industry sustain? (Billy Joel's "Allentown" had, unfortunately, the correct lyrics: "... and they're closing all the factories down.") The EPA/NHSTA proposal is almost like burning down a house with millions of people in it who depend on the automobile industry for a living, thus weakening the home front. The Auto Industry Alliance estimates a loss of 220,000 jobs due to a projected 25% decline in car sales as a result of a projected $6,400 increase in car costs.

- According to a CNN report (August 7, 2007), "41% (of people) live from paycheck to paycheck." Moreover, the U.S. lost over six million jobs since 2008, and we continue to experience slow economic growth. In addition, 45 million people live in poverty, 30 million households don't even have a bank account, and over 53 million are on Medicaid at a cost of over $350 billion. Concurrently, there are 44 million people on food stamps (one in seven Americans), 50 million are without health insurance, we have $14 trillion of mortgage debt, we lost 7 million homes to foreclosure, 1.5 million people filed for bankruptcy in 2010, and the national unemployment rate among African-Americans is 15%. In the meantime, the Washington barons live in luxury in the suburbs of the capitol.

• We are in the middle of the storm in Michigan. The official unemployment rate in Detroit is 30%, although the Detroit News claims it is actually 50%! There are 35,000 vacant homes in Detroit. The Center for Automotive Research stated that the job-killing rules would depress sales and employment in the industry by increasing the cost of vehicles. Contrary to Uncle Sam's 62 mpg cost estimates, the real word estimates forecast is a cost of $1,800 for small cars, $4,500-$6,000 for mid-size cars and $8,000 for the "All-American" pickups, according to Autoweek.com. (This could encourage even more auto thefts, which is already a $7 billion business.) The Heritage Foundation calls the new rules "bad news for consumers." How will the displaced auto workers find new jobs? How many more American compatriots lose their middle-class jobs as a result of the 62 mpg rules? Maybe I should send these bureaucrats a copy of the classic 1952 Western film "High Noon" with the haunting instrumental "Do Not Forsake Me."

• U.S. auto companies are struggling with the new 35.5-mpg, which they supported. Thus, before the paint is dry, the EPA/NHSTA self-governing hotheads will force the industry to come up with very costly and unproven technology, assuming it can even be developed in such a short period. Auto experts claim "all the low-hanging fruit for fuel efficiency...has been harvested. From now on, it's going to cost more moolah." (Automotive News website December 15, 2010).

• The supplier industry is still largely in shambles (54 bankruptcies according to the President's report). Maybe the EPA/NHSTA/CARB, etc. boys can ask the U.S. Treasury to release the $110 billion in unusable $100 bills they had to store because of a printing error. (Nobody will be fired over this humiliation.)

• We don't have enough engineering talent since America only graduates about 78,000 engineers annually of which 50% are from overseas. GM and Chrysler already have a difficult time to hire the thousands of new engineers they need. Who would want to work in the cyclical auto industry when there are more attractive engineering opportunities available in other industries? Already, the December 6, 2010 headline in Automotive News said it all "Engineers wanted." This, is, of course, not an issue the car "czars" in Washington worry about. Delphi Automotive, in December 13, 2010 Automotive News website interview stated that finding "both power electronics and automotive applications is rare."

• What will a family of six drive or the millions of small businesses who need a larger vehicle? Have these people in Washington ever built a 62 mpg prototype?

(Paper exercises don't count.) They will literally want us to go back to the horse and buggy age with its unpleasant smelly side effects.

• Consumers can't afford to pay higher car prices, which already include thousands of dollars in mandated government vehicle requirements. (The Bloomberg poll conducted December 4-7, 2010 reported that 51% of the respondents stated that they are "worse off," and 66% claimed that the U.S. is headed on the "wrong track.") Private household income has been flat while government wages are going through the roof. In addition, the EPA is proposing tough new ozone rules by 2020, which, according to the EPA will cost at least $90,000,000,000 annually and will sharply increase electricity prices. Cheered on by environmentalists, the Sierra Club, the EPA demonstrated its dictatorial power in January 2011 by retroactively revoking a coal-mining project permit previously granted. It was an unprecedented act. It is one of the few industries that America has a competitive advantage. We must curtail their ever-increasing power.

• Americans love to drive their cars. For example, "urban" annual vehicle miles traveled increased from161 million miles in 1980 to 476 million miles in 2008 (latest data available). Secondly, vehicles per household increased from 1.16 in 1969 to 1.92 in 2009, according to the NHSTA.

Vehicles per worker increased from 0.96 to 1.52 during the same period.

- The average vehicle age increased by over 50%, which is probably related to lack of growth in real household income. Even during boom industry sales, consumer expenditures for vehicles decreased from 7.6% in 2005 to 5.5% in 2008.

- The proposed rules discriminate against the poor, the elder, and against African-Americans. Of the roughly 121 million "consumer units" in America (it is a government term what used to be called households), about 50 million are in the lowest 20% quintiles and 20% in the second lowest quintile. Their "net outlays of vehicle purchases" is $1,234 and $1,672, respectively, compared with an average of $2,755 for all "consumer units." For African-Americans, the amount was $1,969, and only $1,604 for retirees. Amazingly, and unfathomably, these lower-income consumers will be driven in ever-larger numbers into used cars with lower fuel economy. These cars also have a higher level of emissions based on EPA's own computer model MOBILE!! The vehicles driven by these Americans already average 10 years or up to four years older than the vehicle driven by the highest quintile income bracket according to BEA data, and cited in a study by Anna Yurko of the University of Texas. Hey, big thinkers at the EPA/NHSTA, what were you thinking of when they devised the latest "government knows best" miracle plan? Did they forget the impact on struggling Americans?

The EPA leaders obviously never heard of the great American spiritual "Let's Break Bread Together." Fearlessly, they are taking a leap in the dark with their socialist-inspired ideas because neither the auto companies nor the authors of the proposed 62 mpg rules know what this will do to an industry employing ten million Americans. Was this the vision of the Founders?

Folks, we are drifting frighteningly into George Orwell's "Nineteen Eighty Four" (published in 1949). The Orwellian thesis included a warning of a future world where the state exerts complete control over our life. It is also similar to Austrian economist Friedrich Hayek's early 1940s book "The Road to Serfdom" in which he warned of government control of the economy, which eventually leads to encroachment of our individual freedom. People, the apocalypse has arrived in America! Orwell probably wouldn't even roll over in his grave after hearing the news; he predicted it. In Russia (1917) and France (1789), the people revolted; in America the bureaucrats are seizing control! Can anybody stop this out-of-control express train?

## America, Wake Up

Yes, we should all be angry about the power grab in Washington, and we are not "in good hands" with them. In my opinion, the top Washington bureaucrats at the EPA and the Department of Transportation do not have the traditional American "frame-of-mind" unlike our brave military, veterans, CIA and FBI agents, TSA employees, boarder guards, honorable Diplomats and even IRS employees. These auto "czars" are middle-class job destroyers and I have zero respect and nothing but contempt for the "High Priests." It is my feeling that they don't represent American traditions, goals, interests and values. With their government overreach, they are leading us ever closer to European style socialism. They are not positive provocateurs; they are job-killing saboteurs. (I am neither a Palin supporter nor a registered Republican. I am only registered **FOR** America.).

While the labor market remains weak, another shocker arrived on December 23, 2010. The AP dispatch had the following headline: "EPA Moving Unilaterally to Limit Greenhouse Gases." The January 3, 2011 headline in the Wall Street Journal highlighted "the EPA War on Texas." As usual, the EPA release contained the soothing buzz words: "measured and careful." Reader comments after the AP story on the subject included the following (I excluded the more inflammatory words): "They are traitors to this country," "This needs to be stopped NOW," "President Obama...NOT the Tsar," "FASCIST manifesto. We know better than you the consumers or the manufacturer and you must do as we say." Moreover, a December 30, 2010 editorial in Investor's Business Daily (IBD) had the following headline "EPA Rules Will Trump Your Rights." The IBD editorial also talked about "job-killing regulations" and cited a 2009 article in the New York Times which advocated to "ram it (cap-and-trade) down our throats" if Congress doesn't pass cap-and-trade legislation!! The most insane EPA rule ever is the late January 2011 announcement to force our hard-working dairy farmers to have in place costly and complex milk spill containment facilities. (The U.S. has 65,000 dairy farms with 9 million cows or 140 per farmer.) Having spent many summers on my relatives' dairy farm, I know it is a tough life (seven days per week) because cows must be milked twice a day. It's obvious we have too many EPA bureaucrats to think of such an idea.

Other agencies are working diligently to restrict our freedom. The NLRB bureaucrats are now attempting to impede the historic secret election process to help union bosses to achieve organizing victories (union membership declined by 600,000 in 2010).

With the lust for power, and control over our daily life, we have an employment "boom industry" in Washington. These lords live in Shangri-la because there is no recession in our capitol, with federal government employment increasing from 1.8 million in fiscal 2007 to 2.2 million in 2010– employment keeps multiplying like rabbits. (Federal, state and local employment increased from roughly 6 million in 1946 to about 23 million today.) Will there ever be an end to this plethoric bureaucracy? Austerity is a word they don't know. Nobody ever gets fired for incompetence or low productivity–only about 8,000-10,000 lost their job in a typical year because powerful government unions (7.6 million members), who are bankrupting federal, state and municipal coffers protect them.

To illustrate that Washington is not experiencing a dark and dangerous period and these bureaucrats live "the American story" at taxpayer expense, the following shows federal compensation trends:

- Between 1980-1991, federal employee compensation rose by $5 for each $1 of private sector compensation according to "the Public Purpose" website.

- In 1991, federal employees received on average $46,789 compared with $31,800 for the private sector.

- In 2000, average federal compensation was 66% above the private sector according to the libertarian Cato Institute.

- In 2010, "Fox & Friends" reported federal employee compensation of $123,049, or twice the private sector level. Thousands of these EPA/NHSTA/DOT, etc. employees take home six-figure salaries. Bloomberg reported on December 14, 2010 that the Washington suburbs are the richest areas in the entire country!!! Further, the metro Washington, D.C. area has the lowest unemployment rate in America. We are paying with our taxes for their lifestyles. Moreover, they have lifetime assured income as Benjamin Franklin once said: "In this world, nothing is certain, except death and taxes." Today, we can add: ever, ever increasing EPA/NHSTA rules, rules, rules.

Compared with the private sector, government employees (federal, state, local) live in a world the rest of us can only dream about:

• Great base pay

• Annual pay increases

• Excellent medical benefits

• More paid vacation

• More paid holidays

• More paid personal days off

• More paid sick leave

• Dream-like pensions

• Paid retiree health-care

• Far greater job security

Clearly, these bureaucrats have taxpayer "Candy Girls." We need to moderate this gravy train of sweet deals. According to a mid-December Wall Street Journal/NBC News Poll, 83% of respondent demanded a freeze on federal government employees. The January 4, 2010 edition of Automotive News, when discussing the upheaval in the U.S. auto industry stated, "In a cataclysmic year, the anguish was etched on the faces of the people who ran the businesses and employees who bore the brunt of the pain." This is of no concern to the Washington bureaucrats working in a Garden of Eden. Thomas Jefferson reportedly said, "a little rebellion now and then is a good thing." This time has arrived against the EPA/NHSTA/DOT/DOE/CARB dictators or we will all be singing Bob Hope's closing lyrics "Thanks For the Memory" of a bygone democracy.

To illustrate the insensitivity in Washington about the rest of America, three years ago, the Department of Human Services in Washington told its 67,000 employees to buy Asian cars. No government in Japan Inc. and Korea Inc. would ever talk-down the fruits of labor of the people who pay their grandiose compensation packages.

I am not a wimp anymore hiding behind my "silent majority" curtain. I am following, in a minor way, in my German grandfather's footsteps; he had moral principles. He worked for the Reichsbahn (railroad), and was fired by a local Gauleiter (mini Hitlers at a local level) for refusing to join the Hitler's Nazi Party. He paid a high price for his beliefs; nobody would hire him, and he lived in poverty while his six children had gone off to war. After World War II, at age 63, he was able to get his old job back.

## The Ballot Box Still Works

Thanks to the power of the ballot box, there is hope for the future. We finally raised our heads against these bureaucrats who act contrary to the vision that shaped the United States of America. As the Pacific Research Institute (PRI) stated it in a December 3, 2010 letter to subscribers, "Americans are fed up with the growth and overreach of government." The PRI also noted that this was a "historic electoral sea change." Read our lips, we don't like what's happening. Send them on a perpetual honeymoon. Folks, and dear Americans, shortly after the November 2010 election, which was heard "round the world," the "change" boys and girls in the nation's capitol apparently got the message loud and clear and even the former blue states in Michigan, Ohio, Indiana, Wisconsin and Pennsylvania had enough of their dangerous experimentation, and want more common sense, honesty and transparency in rule making. We don't live in Cuba, Venezuela or China—we are free Americans. We still have the right to vote in free elections, and can throw out the bums if their entire agenda is more government solutions. However, these EPA bureaucrats keep charging ahead. Television and newspaper reports in late December 2010 reported that the EPA will "speed up new greenhouse gas rules."

Their entire 62 mpg rule making process was deeply flawed, and didn't take into consideration the "societal impact" which hopefully will now be assessed, including such issues as greater traffic death with Smart-like cars we have to drive, vehicle performance, towing capability, comfort, etc. We can't let Washington put us in a straight-jacket! These EPA/NHSTA/DOE/CARB, etc. leaders had their 15 minutes of fame. Maybe Time magazine should award them a millennium "goody-goody award" to get them off the stage. As The Cordettes' hit song says: "Mr. Sandman, Bring Us Our Dream." <u>God save America from Washington</u>.

# CHAPTER 23

✖ ✖ ✖

## THE CAT WITH NINE LIVES

Chrysler Corporation is still in surgery, with an uncertain prognosis, even with Fiat as a partner. U.S taxpayers granted Fiat 25% equity without cash contribution. In mid-April 2011, Fiat increased its stake in Chrysler to 30%. Fiat may eventually control 51% of Chrysler, if certain financial and technology goals are met. The U.S. government injected approximately $7 billion in loans into the company. The Chapter 11 process wiped out billions of Chrysler's debt.

Angus Mackenzie of Motor Trend observed in the January 2008 edition that Chrysler Corporation is "America's perennial to-the-brink-and-back automaker." In 2008 alone, Chrysler eliminated 12,000 salaried positions, and between 2006 and June 2009, the company's workforce declined from roughly 82,284 to 47,188 employees (December 6, 2010 Automotive News).

The April 1996 American Automobile Centennial edition (1896–1996) of Automotive News stated that "crisis management isn't new at Chrysler; it began in 1960."

Moreover, in the 1980s Lee Iacocca had to save Chrysler twice from bankruptcy. The first bailout occurred in 1979. Chrysler is a company which keeps "muddling through;" many experts questioned if the company should have been bailed out in 2009.

- Absence of exciting, and innovative products, especially small cars. Chrysler lacked the funding prior to Chapter 11 filing to develop new products. Moreover, five brands with a market share under 10% appear excessive.

- Major image problem relating to poor product quality. Chrysler consistently ranks low in consumer quality surveys. Many of Chrysler's vehicles are not fuel-efficient (Chrysler does not have any entries in EPA top ten fuel-efficient list). It was ranked last in Consumer Reports 2011 Reliability Survey.

- Chrysler's market share is declining–9% in 2009 compared with a 13% historical share, but recovered to 9.4% in 2010. Chrysler's 2010 gains are largely driven by very high rebates the company is offering, and very large fleet sales. Retail sales remain poor, possibly because Chrysler's consumer base is blue-collar centered.

- The Chrysler dealer organization is still in turmoil.

However, as John Rosevear of "Motley Fool" stated on November 12, 2010, "Chrysler: not dead yet...it is showing signs of recovery." Moreover, the six new vehicles introduced at the November 2010 L.A. Auto Show were well received by auto analysts. In addition, Joann Muller of Forbes (January 17, 2011 website) stated "Against All Odds, Chrysler Goes From Third World to World Class." The highly respected David E. Davis, Jr. of Car and Driver magazine stated in a May 2011 article "Chrysler may just rise from its grave one more time."

# CHAPTER 24

✠ ✠ ✠

## THE SLEEPING GIANT IS AWAKENING

### Introduction

General Motors was founded in 1908, and was under the leadership of the legendary Alfred P. Sloan (1923–1946). For 76 years, GM was the largest auto company in the world, but in 2007, Toyota toppled GM. As late as 2002, GM outsold Toyota by over 2.4 million units. For the cold-blooded Japanese, this was the culmination of their openly announced goal to be number one in the world after dethroning Ford from the second world position in 2003. The official Toyota slogan was "We Can and We Will." In plain English, it means that we will be the top automotive company in the world. For "Japan Inc.," it was a glorious moment because Toyota is the most important Japanese icon. For an American icon, this was a devastating defeat, and the beginning of the twilight of supremacy. It closely parallels America's fading prominence and power, which reached new heights in the 1940s and 1950s.

During the first sixty years of the 20th century, the U.S. had a carte blanche in the world, and was omnipotent. That was also the mindset of U.S. auto companies, which controlled over 75% of world vehicle production in 1950 and still almost 50% by 1960.

At its peak in the late 1970s, GM employed 853,000 people including 618,000 in the United States. By 1990, GM still employed over 750,000 people. By 2010, employment had declined to 202,000, with 500,000 retirees. UAW-represented employee levels declined from 140,000 in 1999 to 49,000 in 2010. The following table shows the evolution of GM's U.S. market share and net income:

| YEAR | U.S. SHARE | Net Income (Millions) |
|------|-----------|------------------------|
| 1920 | 37% | $37 |
| 1930 | 41 | 151 |
| 1940 | 44 | 195 |
| 1950 | 46 | 834 |
| 1960 | 48 | 959 |
| 1970 | 45 | 609 |
| 1980 | 41 | (763) |
| 1990 | 35 | (1,986) |
| 1995 | 33 | 6,881 |
| 2000 | 28 | 4,452 |
| 2005 | 26 | (10,567) |
| 2010 | 19 | 4,668 |

Source: Automotive News Data Center; Automotive News "American Automobile Centennial" Edition; R.L. Polk; GM 10-K Reports

James Quinn of "TheBurningPlatform.com," stated that GM's peak U.S. market share was 54% in 1954. GM's share has declined consistently since 1960. It was 35% in 1990, 28% in 2000, 26% in 2005 and 19% in 2010. Worldwide, GM's share dropped from 13.2% to 11.4%, according to the GM IPO filing.

Each auto company defines vehicle segments differently. Therefore, GM's data is not comparable to Ford's segment shares. GM remains a strong competitor in the U.S. midsize segment with a 19.3% share although a decrease from 25.9% in 2007. The company's small car segment share declined from 14.6% in 2007 to 9.5% in 2010.

GM entered a new phase with the June 1, 2009 Chapter 11 filing; its stock traded at less than $1 at the time of bankruptcy (Chrysler filed on April 30, 2009). James B. Stewart, in a June 3, 2009 Wall Street Journal article cited famous author Tom Peters who said the following about GM: the custodians of GM simply gave up trying to build the best cars in the world. To accommodate a host of competing interests, from shareholders to bondholders to labor, they repeatedly compromised on excellence. Once sacrificed, that reputation has proved impossible to recapture." Ron Bloom, a senior Treasury Department advisor, who was closely involved in the GM bailout negotiations, stated on Bloomberg's November 18, 2010 "Inside Track" program that "the U.S. government intervention saved one million jobs." The alternative was chapter 7 (liquidation). The highly respected Center for Automotive Research, a think tank, released a study stating government assistance for GM and Chrysler saved more than 1.4 million jobs in 2009 and another 314,400 in 2010 (Automotive News November 17, 2010 website).

GM CEO Dan Akerson in a December 10, 2010 speech in Washington stated, "Besides cost structures, one of the challenges in turning GM around has been a corporate culture resistant to change." The bankruptcy filing of the two American icons was humiliating for everybody associated with these corporations, as well for the United States. There was Schadenfreude in Europe and Japan; it was proof to them that our economic system doesn't work anymore. They had no problems "picking up the crumbs" from this paradigm.

## General Motors' Restructuring Plans

In April 2009, GM announced a revised "Viability Plan" to accelerate its reengineering efforts. It was a replacement of the February 2009 plan, but was more aggressive. In January 2008, GM also announced another restructuring plan, which would reduce labor costs by $5 billion by 2011, and structural costs to 23% of revenue by 2010 compared with 34% in 2005. The 2008 plan, it turn, is a continuation of the historic March 2006 agreement with the UAW to eliminate 30,000 hourly employees and close six assembly plants. Accordingly, there was no such thing as "All Quiet on the Western Front" (Remargue's famous 1929 masterpiece) at GM. Such constant upheavals often result in serious employee morale problems.

In late December 2008, under the Bush Administration, the U.S. government granted GM and Chrysler a $17.4 billion loan. Both companies had to prove to the government by the end of the first quarter 2009 that they can become viable entities again.  Mr. Mulally represented Ford Motor Company at the humiliating Congressional meetings. Ford supported the bailout of its competitors, not all for altruistic reasons. It might have destroyed Ford's supplier base if GM and Chrysler had gone out of business.

Fritz Henderson, who had succeeded the dismissed CEO Rick Wagoner, spearheaded GM's reinvention. (Rick Wagoner was CEO of GM Brazil during my tenure in Brazil and did an excellent job.) Mr. Henderson was subsequently fired and succeeded by Edward Whitacre, who left after only one year on the job!

GM summarized the latest restructuring of its U.S. operations as follows:

- "A focus on four core brands in the U.S.- Chevrolet, Cadillac, Buick and GMC.

- A more aggressive restructuring of GM's U.S. dealer organization to better focus dealer resources for improved sales and customer service. (A typical dealership averages approximately $30 million in annual sales, with a before-tax profit margin of less than 2%.) [83]

- Improved U.S. capacity utilization through accelerated idling and closures of powertrain, stamping, and assembly plants.

- Lower structural costs, which GM North America (GMNA) projects will enable it to breakeven (on an adjusted EBIT basis) at a U.S. total industry volume of approximately 10 million vehicles, based on the pricing and share assumptions in the plan. This rate is substantially below the 15 to 17 million annual vehicle sales rates recorded from 1995 through 2007." [84]

GM also announced the phase-out or sale of Hummer, Saab, Saturn and Pontiac. A 50% reduction of its U.S. dealerbody was also announced.

The "Viability Plan" also included the following changes:

- "Manufacturing: Consistent with the mandate to accelerate restructuring, we plan to reduce the total number of assembly, powertrain, and stamping plants in the U.S. from 47 in 2008 to 34 by the end of 2010, a reduction of 28 percent, and to 31 by 2012. This would reflect the acceleration of six plant idling/closures from the February 17 plan, and one additional plant idling. Throughout this transition, GM will continue to implement its flexible global manufacturing strategy (GMS), which allows multiple body styles and architectures to be built in one plant. This enables GM to use its capital more efficiently, increase capacity utilization, and respond more quickly to market shifts.

- Employment: U.S. hourly employment levels are projected to be reduced from about 61,000 in 2008 to 40,000 in 2010, a 34 percent reduction, and level off at about 38,000 starting in 2011. This further planned reduction of an additional 7,000 to 8,000 employees from the February 17 Plan is primarily the result of the previously discussed operational efficiencies, nameplate reductions, and plant closings. GM also anticipates a further decline in salaried and executive employment as it continues to assess its structure and execute the Viability Plan.

- Labor costs: The Viability Plan assumes a reduction of U.S. hourly labor costs from $7.6 billion in 2008 to $5 billion in 2010, a 34 percent reduction. GM will continue to work with its UAW partners to accomplish this through a reduction in total U.S. hourly employment as well as through modifications in the collective bargaining agreement." [85]

GM projected that the actions outlined above would reduce its structural costs by 25% –from $31 billion in 2008 to $23 billion in 2010. Auto analysts looked with some skepticism if this is just another one of the many GM plans the company announced since the 2000's. In assessing GM's eye-popping "Viability Plan," it appears that it contains virtually all the elements of "One Ford." The difference is that Ford Motor Company has successfully executed the promised actions while GM is in its initial phase.

GM's "New Business Model," as outlined in the November 2010 IPO video appears to be a blueprint of the successful "One Ford" plan. Following is a summary of GM's strategy:

• World's best vehicles

• Fewer brands, global architecture

• Reduced inventories

• Lower incentives/higher prices

• Improved brand equity

• Higher residuals

• Higher profitability and ROA

• Reinvest in vehicles

The IPO presentation by the GM CFO also stated that the company has reduced its breakeven from a 15.5 million industry, and a 25% market share in 2007 to 10.5-11 million industry, and a18-19% share in 2010!

Similar to Ford Motor Company's strategy, GM is changing its marketing approach to achieve higher residuals, offering lower incentives, and managing inventory levels. GM claimed its November 2010 IPO video that its three new vehicles–Buick LaCrosse, Chevy Equinox, and Cadillac SRX recorded major increases in segment shares, significantly higher transaction prices and substantial increases in residual values.

General Motors' 517 pages Preliminary Prospectus included the following GM competitive strengths to "design, build and sell the world's best vehicles:"

- Global presence, scale and dealer network.

- Markets share in emerging markets, such as China and Brazil.

- Portfolio of high-quality vehicles.

- Commitment to new technology.

- Competitive cost structure in GM's North American Operations.

- Competitive global cost structure.

- Strong balance sheet and liquidity.

• Strong leadership team with focused direction.

☐ More direct lines of communication

☐ Quicker decision making; and

☐ Direct responsibility for individuals in various areas of GM's business.

The competitive strengths outlined above are lofty objectives; to turn them into reality is another story. Moreover, these goals probably apply to each of the top five world automotive companies; many already achieved these targets.

Following is GM's current mission statement: "GM is a multinational corporation engaged in socially responsible operations worldwide. It is dedicated to provide products and services of such quality that our customers will receive superior value while our employees and business partners will share in our success and our stockholders will receive a sustained superior return on their investment."

There is no mention of financial services because GM had sold its GMAC operation a few years ago to buy-out specialist Cerberus. This was one of GM's major mistakes because auto companies have to have a captive finance subsidiary. GM is now re-entering the auto financing business with the recent acquisition of a sub-prime company.

# CHAPTER 25

# WHO HAS THE CARD UP ONE'S SLEEVE? (FORD VS. GENERAL MOTORS)

Ford's highly successful restructuring since 2006, concurrent with GM's slow reengineering efforts, and the turmoil associated with GM's June 1, 2009 Chapter 11 filing, has changed the landscape in Detroit. Today, the lead singer of the band is Ford Motor Company. Ford is profitable and gaining market share.

Following is a brief comparative assessment of the two companies. Such an analysis is very fluid as each company constantly attempts to strengthen its competitive position.

## Ford Motor Company Advantages

Ford has established a fully integrated global product development organization. It is developing truly global vehicles, with significant commonality between regions. Products such as the highly competitive 2011 Ford Fiesta, and 2012 Ford Focus are the direct result of the new global structure. As blogger Dennis Mull stated it succinctly on the December 20, 2010 Automotive News website, "Ford leads in technology, safety, mpg and value." Moreover, according to Ford's top sales analyst, George Pipas, Ford is making major inroads with the Fiesta in the all-important 18-24 age groups.

## General Motors Situation

GM claims that it is aggressively moving towards a global structure. However, the uncertainty regarding the future of its major European group (sell or maintain) delayed the global integration process. GM has introduced several highly competitive products such as the compact Chevy Cruze, Chevy Equinox, Chevy Traverse, the Buick Regal, Buick LaCrosse, and Cadillac CTS. In addition, the company announced that it is planning to introduce 20 new vehicles during the next two years. It is focusing on four core brands–Chevrolet, Buick, Cadillac and GMC. Pontiac, Saab, Hummer and Saturn were sold or eliminated. Some auto analysts claim four GM brands are still too many.

❃ ❃ ❃

## Ford Motor Company Advantages

Ford has been demonstrating momentum in the U.S. since 2009. Its market share improved in 2009 for the first time since 1995. The share gains continued in 2010 (up over two points since 2008). Incentives and inventory levels are tightly managed to assure solid resale values.

## General Motors Situation

GM's U.S. 2009 and 2010 market share declines are primarily attributed to the elimination of four brands. The remaining core brands are selling well. GM, however, has lost market share for about 35 years.

⌘ ⌘ ⌘

## Ford Motor Company Advantages

Ford is profitable in all global regions because of its North American restructuring, and the significant and costly European reengineering. In the late 1990s Ford of Europe, which was established in 1967, initiated a major restructuring plan called "Transformation Strategy." It involved closing of facilities, and an overall employee reduction of at least 8,000 people. It appears that by 2005, the restructuring was largely completed. The total cost is difficult to assess because it was sometimes classified in "Automotive Operations" (U.S., Europe, etc.). However, it easily exceeded $3 billion.

Today, Ford of Europe employs approximately 66,000 people, has 22 manufacturing facilities, and average annual 2006-2009 sales of about $51 billion, which would place it among the top 135 on Fortune's "Global 500" list.

## General Motors Situation

GM is achieving profits again in North America. However, its struggling European operations continue to lose money ($1.8 billion pretax in 2010). GM announced an investment of about $4.4 billion in Europe. GM's Preliminary Prospectus stated that the company's European "Restructuring Plan includes an agreement to reduce European manufacturing capacity by 20% and reduce labor costs by $323 million per year."

GM's European market share has declined from about 10.2% in 2001 to 8.8% in 2010.[86] Ford's European market share declined to 8.0% in 2010 compared with 8.8% in 2009, primarily reflecting the escalation of very high competitive discounts, which Ford has refused to join because of its future impact on resale value and the affect in its bottom line. Ford of Europe is chasing profits not volume.

❊ ❊ ❊

## Ford Motor Company Advantages

Ford had a three-year restructuring head start compared with GM in the U.S. Also, Ford has more operating momentum than GM, and a clear vision of its mission. In a Reuters November 8, 2010 article in Automotive News entitled "GM's Quiet Partner: Uncle Sam," Dennis Virag, President of the Automotive Consulting Group is quoted as saying: "GM doesn't have the kind of clear leadership that Alan Mulally brought to the Ford organization...they (GM) are making progress, but it's at a snail pace." Web editor of Mad Money, Tom Brennan, stated on November 12, 2010 that Jim Cramer believes that "Ford is a better company (than GM), hands down."

## General Motors Situation

GM's June 1, 2009 bankruptcy filing caused chaos within GM. Even prior to filing Chapter 11, GM was slow to make changes such as consolidating its eight nameplates. It did, however, close 12 plants. Under Mr. Whitacre, the bureaucracy was shaken-up including replacement of many of the top executives. Mr. Whitacre left after about one year on the job. It is too early to judge the new CEO's job performance.

## Ford Motor Company Advantages

Ford has a stable and thoroughly proven top management team in place. It is a group that appears to act in unison. Except for Mr. Mulally, who had 37 years of manufacturing experience at Boeing before joining Ford, every other member of the top thirty Ford senior executives has many years of automotive experience.

## General Motors Situation

GM has been playing CEO musical chairs with four CEO's in two years. (Each time a new CEO comes on board, it uproots the culture and employees worry about the next change.) The latest CEO, Daniel Akerson, is a buy-out specialist, with no prior industrial experience, and only one year on GM's Board of Directors. GM's CFO is new, and also has no auto industry experience. Editor-in-Chief of Automotive News, Keith Crain, summed it up as follows: "GM is starting to sound like Peyton Place."[87] At a November 17, 2010 Bloomberg GM IPO special program, analysts stated that the frequent CEO changes "freeze employees in the track," and that somebody "needs to stick around." Nevertheless, effective April 1, 2011 the merry-go-round continues with the resignation of the CFO after 14 months in his position. The GM Treasurer who has been at GM for only one year replaced him.

Chevrolet had four top marketing leaders in two years, with several advertising agency changes. As stated in GM's IPO prospectus, the "new executive management team (has) to quickly learn the automotive industry." Moreover, of the 12 members of GM's Board of Directors shown on page 191 of GM's Preliminary IPO Prospectus, not one member has automotive experience except Stephen J. Girsky who was previously a well-respected auto analyst. Further, five are retired CEO's of major companies.

⌘ ⌘ ⌘

## Ford Motor Company Advantages

Ford's finance arm, Ford Motor Credit Company that is part of a $700 billion U.S. market, is a key strategic asset, and a major profit contributor to the company (based on average 2005–2009 revenues, Ford Credit would rank among the top 150 largest U.S. companies on Fortune's "500" list).

## General Motors Situation

GM sold 51% of its GMAC's captive finance unit to Cerberus Capital Management in November 2006 to raise funds for it's restructuring. (The U.S. government had to inject $17 billion into GMAC in mid-2009 to save the company from collapse. U.S. taxpayers received a 74% stake in GMAC; GM's and Cerberus' ownership was reduced.)

GMAC has been renamed Ally Bank. GM now has an arm's-length relationship with GMAC, and must rely on this company to finance retail consumer vehicle loans, and dealer floor planning. GM has stated that its relationship with Ally is risky. GM recently acquired a major sub-prime company, AmeriCredit Corporation for $3.5 billion.

# CHAPTER 26

❡ ❡ ❡

# THE "OLD MAN" STILL HAS MUSCLES (GENERAL MOTORS VS. FORD)

This section outlines the current, but constantly changing major General Motors' competitive advantages compared with Ford Motor Company.

## General Motors Advantages

GM's Chapter 11 filing on June 1, 2009 wiped out common shareholders as GM's stock was delisted from the NYSE (in 1999, GM recorded $9 billion in pretax profits, and in 2000, GM's shares reached a record around $94 per share). The bankruptcy substantially improved GM's precarious financial situation. Debt was reduced from $30 billion to $8 billion, and the U.S. government injected $50 billion into GM and received a 61% ownership of the "new" GM. The Canadian and Ontario governments received a 12% stake for a $10 billion investment.

General Motors' "wink and nod" bankruptcy and subsequent November 2010 IPO raised $ $23 billion and reduced the government's ownership to about 27%. GM has very little debt thanks to its un-American bankruptcy plus about $13 billion in 2008 taxpayer funds through the much-maligned Troubled Asset Relief Fund (TARP). GM also received $45 billion in tax loss carry forwards on future profits which is good for up to 20 years from the U.S. funded TARP financing!! It is understandable that the GM CFO touted this taxpayer gift and smirked when he stated in the IPO video that the GM's operating income will flow straight to the bottom line because of GM's little debt and loss carry forwards. With friends like that in Washington, which are deep into corporate welfarism, it probably would make the old Soviet Union commies and commissars blush with envy. The U.S. government makes it much easier to get "free" money if you fail. At Ford, as the old Smith Barney tagline used to say: "We Make Money the Old Fashion Way."

George W. Bush's "Decision Points" memoir devoted only a few paragraphs to the auto crisis, which commenced on his watch. On page 468, he blames the auto industry's woes on "decades of poor management that saddled automakers with enormous health-care and pension costs. They had been slow to recognize changes in the market. As a result, they had been outcompeted by foreign manufacturers in the product and price."

GM earned $4.7 billion in 2010 compared with a $23.5 billion loss in 2009. GM's 2010 automotive cash flow was

$6.6 billion compared with Ford's $4.4 billion. GM had a strong cash and cash equivalent position of $ 28 billion at the end of 2010. The company's Automotive debt as of December 31, 2010 was $11 billion without significant repayments until 2015 ($3 billion). However, GM has worldwide under funded pensions of $21.9 billion as of December 31, 2010 compared with Ford's $11.5 billion. In addition, GM had $9.3 billion in postretirement benefit liabilities at the end of 2010.

## Ford Motor Company Situation

Ford had $19.1 billion in Automotive debt as of December 31, 2010, or significantly above GM levels. The company has paid off its hourly VEBA Trust health care obligations, which GM still has to accomplish. Ford's 2010 interest expenses totaled roughly $1.8 billion, equivalent to $340 per vehicle sold. GM's 2010 interest cost was $130 per vehicle, based on $1.1 billion in interest expenses.

❄ ❄ ❄

## General Motors Advantages

General Motors has a comprehensive and competitive vehicle line-up. GM remains the largest U.S. vehicle producer with four brands and is a leader in the booming Chinese and Brazilian market. GM's annual capital and engineering budget totals $13 billion, far above Ford Motor Company levels. There is a new urgency at GM to accelerate its recovery. The company is launching 19 vehicles between 2010-2012. In addition, GM announced that between 2011-2013, it plans to launch 94 vehicles worldwide including 25 in America. Further, GM's new cars have been well received including the Buick LaCrosse and Regal, Chevy Equinox and Cruze, Cadillac CTS Wagon and SRX models.

Similar to Ford, GM should achieve significant cost reductions with its aggressive platform and parts commonization strategy. GM's IPO claims that the company is moving from 17% common global platforms in 2010 to over 50% of its vehicles by 2014.

## Ford Motor Company Situation

Ford has launched highly competitive global passenger cars. However, when the market returns to a 14-15 million-unit range, it will be challenging for Ford to compete with one and one-half brands (I consider the Lincoln franchise quite weak) compared with four solid GM brands. Ford has no facing competitor with Buick, and the Ford truck brand must compete against GMC and Chevrolet. Lincoln's entry into the small car segment will not generate significant sales gains. Small-car buyers are not typical Lincoln showroom visitors. Mercedes and BMW, however, successfully expanded their product range into small cars with Audi, Cadillac, and other luxury producers to follow.

Many auto analysts consider Ford's product portfolio superior to GM's. Ford has narrowed GM's eighty yearlong market share lead in the U.S. to an historic low of a couple of percentage points and is now at GM's heels. The Detroit Free Press reported in a September 2009 article "Ford sales will top GM by 2012, economist says." [88] In the July 2009 Merrill Lynch's "car wars" study, the author claims that Ford management is making all of the right moves" and that "Ford's share of the U.S. market could rise 3 percentage points over the next four years to about 18 percent, overtaking GM." [89] I am not convinced that it will happen.

## General Motors Advantages

GM remains a major world player with total sales of 8.4 million units in 2010, a significant increase compared with 2009. GM has a significant lead over Ford in the rapidly growing emerging markets. For example, in China, GM sales totaled 1 million units in 2007, followed in 2009 with 1.8 million units, and 2010 sales of 2.4 million vehicles. (Ford sold almost 600,000 vehicles in China in 2010, up 40% from 2009.) GM stated in its IPO video that it increased its market share in China from 3% in 2000 to 13% in 2010. Moreover, GM claims leadership in the fast growing, but highly volatile BRIC countries (Brazil, Russia, India and China). Increasingly, this seems to be the cornerstone of GM's worldwide strategy. GM claims that it has an average 13% market share in the BRIC markets compared with 11% for VW AG, 4% for Toyota and Ford's 3%. (In 2010, these four countries led the world in GDP growth–China with 10.5%, followed by India with 9.7%, Brazil 7.5% and Russia with 4%.) GM has entered into ten joint ventures in China, including an alliance with SAIC which is the largest Chinese-owned auto company. There appears to be, however, a power struggle between the assertive Chinese partner and GM. GM had to cede majority control to SAIC in 2009, with SAIC taking full advantage of GM's weak position at that time. SAIC purchased about $500 million of GM stock at the November 17, 2010 GM IPO. It is a harbinger of SAIC's future involvement with GM. I could even conceive a takeover of GM within ten years.

GM is establishing a $250 million R&D center in Shanghai. [90] It is also building a $225 million proving ground (2008 Automotive News' "Guide to China's Auto Market"). GM plans to use its Chinese base to launch a major export drive. Automotive News' October 21, 2010 website stated, "GM's China venture starts Chevrolet exports to South America." A joint venture in India with SAIC has also been announced.

In an article in the November 4, 2010 issue of The Wall Street Journal, GM and SAIC agreed to "deepen their technical cooperation and further integrate SAIC into GM's global product development." This will further strengthen SAIC in its drive for a leading role in the world automotive industry, at the expense of Western companies. Automotive News reported on April 14, 2006 that SAIC plans to produce its own brand of cars for China and for export. The U.K. Globe and Mail stated on April 9, 2009 that SAIC launched production of "its first own brand car; the eventual target is two million units.

As world-renowned Tom Peters stated in his book: "The Little BIG Things," "Get China on Your Mind! Get India on Your Mind!" Accordingly, the attachment provides a brief summary of China's economy and its auto industry–the new automotive battleground. China will have a profound affect on the West–politically, economically, and militarily.

In a provocative look into the future, Charles Child of Automotive News, in a January 3, 2000 article offered the following prognosis for 2100: "Asia Rules the Next Century." [91] Approximately 150 years ago, the Americans were strongly influenced by the westward movement. "Go West, Young Man" was the battle cry. Today, it is "Go East" to China!

## Ford Motor Company Situation

Ford has acknowledged its weaknesses in the rapidly growing Asian and South American markets with a car-hungry middle-class (400 million in China and 300 million in India). Ford Motor Company has launched major expansion drives, as described previously and is adding thousands of employees in China and India. "Ford intends to raise annual production capacity from 450,000 vehicles to 600,000 vehicles in China and double to 200,000-250,000 units in India from 2010." [92] (By 2015 VW plans to invest $14.5 billion in China, and between 2010-2014 invest $3.5

billion in Brazil.) In Thailand, Ford announced a $450 million investment in June 2010, followed by another $350 million during the third quarter 2010, in conjunction with Mazda.

X X X

## General Motors Advantages

Together with Suzuki, a Korean bank, and its Chinese partner SAIC, GM owns a majority share of Korea's Daewoo, which is a major strategic advantage compared with all Western competitors, and a significant leg up compared with Ford's low-cost sourcing efforts. Daewoo, which was South Korea's third-largest automotive company, filed for bankruptcy in 1999. Ford was selected as the lead bidder after the company made a $6 billion offer to purchase the Daewoo, subject to due diligence. After thoroughly reviewing Daewoo domestic facilities, and its extensive worldwide operations, Ford decided not to proceed with the acquisition. GM, together with its partners, bought the bankrupt company in 2001 for peanuts. The new owners invested $400 million in Daewoo. This decision was a major GM coup d'etat in Asia. Today, it is GM's low-cost Asian source producing 1.8 million units in 2010 (includes unassembled cars), and exporting hundreds of thousands of vehicles around the world including about 200,000 units annually to Europe under the Chevrolet brand. According to the December 13, 2010 edition of Automotive News, GM Daewoo:

• Exports more than 90% of the company's production

• Accounts for 22% of GM worldwide sales

• Expects sales to increase 64% during the next 5 years, or to 3 million units by 2015, with one million Chevrolet sales Europe by 2016.

## Ford Motor Company Situation

Ford does not have a low-cost export source at this time. However, China could be the potential future base to export inexpensive vehicles, as well as the new Romanian facility, which was previously owned by Daewoo until it entered into bankruptcy. It appears that Ford is in discussions with its Chinese partner, Changan, to expand their partnership into India.

## Analysts' View of GM Today

Headlines are increasingly claiming, "GM is back." The March 1, 2010 issue of Barron reflects the theme: "The auto maker, long synonymous with bloat and misman-agement, has undergone an impressive turnaround since it emerged from a brief stay in bankruptcy last year. GM still is no Honda or BMW, but it's probably in its best shape since its heyday in the 1960s." [93] The headline in the No-vember 1, 2010 issue of Fortune magazine's "Briefing" sec-tion stated: "GM: Morning Again In Detroit."

A Motley Fool.com article on October 14, 2010 by John Rosevear stated: "GM is not the same company it was two years ago, or five years ago, or 10 years ago. A new management team that seems to have a realistic grasp of the challenges facing the company, and the skills to do something about them is running it. Ford's spectacular turnaround has given GM's rank and file a shining, local, easy-to-understand example of what's possible… there are signs that, after all these years, things might just be coming together … seismic changes are happening at this company."

Jim Cramer of CNBC's "Mad Money," recommended GM's new shares on November 17, 2010 (IPO day) claim-ing it is "a ticket to emerging markets" and that it is not "your father's GM." He stated that it is a "leaner, meaner" company. On his January 12, 2011 program from Ford's

F-150 plant in Dearborn, Michigan he stated, "GM's turn-around is going to happen." (Over 90% of GM dealers are already profitable.)

## GM's November 2010 IPO

On November 18, 2010, General Motors "stormed out of bankruptcy" (CNBC headline), with a lot of hoopla and celebrations and hi-fives on the NYSE trading floor because of the successful IPO. I was afraid that at any moment the pretty University of Michigan cheerleaders would start dancing in the isles of the NYSE, with their pompons swinging and with GM "victory" flags! Even the "matter-of-fact" Automotive News stated on its November 19, 2010 website that "Ackerson was granted rock star status all day yesterday on the exchange." (Rock star for what achievements?  He had nothing to do with GM's great new vehicles which Bob Lutz and Rick Wagoner developed, nor the restructuring of GM. I assume that he is a rock star for doing his CEO job on the IPO road show.)

My perception of GM is a little different, and I was not fooled by the hullabaloo I witnessed. The entire IPO day seemed like a "Second Coming." However, GM returned to the NYSE from its profligate and ignominious bankruptcy, which eliminated 92% of its debt, and in the process, destroyed or seriously harmed many common stocks and bond holders. As James Stewart stated in the November 20-21, 2010 issue of the Wall Street Journal, "GM has a long history burning its shareholders." In response to an article in the December 29, 2010 edition of the Wall Street Journal, about banks being bullish about GM, a reader responded as follows: I salvaged $1,400 in 2008 from a $10,000 General Motors bond I bought in 2005. Now that's bull." In addition, GM's bankruptcy ruined many GM dealers with thousands of employees. They even stiffed their former partner Toyota. In a lawsuit filed in late November 2010 by Nummi (GM's and Toyota's California joint venture), the company is seeking $185 million from GM's bankruptcy estate to pay for its share of the plant closing.

Moreover, I didn't like all the frenzy and self-congratulations. Even the President of the United States of America got into the act which Automotive News called "a little trash talking from President Barack Obama." It would have been fair if he had mentioned that Ford, unlike GM, didn't raise a white flag of surrender when it was on the verge of bankruptcy. Instead, Mr. Mulally chose the honorable "American Way of Life" as Ford's philosophy.

The IPO day hoopla seemed inappropriate because it was a celebration of a pyrrhic victory. The November 19, 2010 Wall Street Journal had the correct headline "Wall Street payday for New GM." I would have added a subtitle like: "A great day for GM senior executives" who had received tens of thousands of options in 2010. Reportedly, CEO Akerson alone received $5.3 million in stock options over three years starting in 2011. In addition, there was a generous payday to the 35 banks who acted as underwriters. (I consider it totally inappropriate for GM executives to receive stock options while we, the taxpayers, are waiting to receive 100% of the $50 billion we "invested" in

GM.) Lastly the big winner was the UAW VEBA Trust, which received $3 billion from the sale of shares, but still owns about 11% of GM stock including warrants. (The UAW Trust also owns about 64% of Chrysler stock.)

The IPO raised over $23 billion from the sale of common and preferred stock–a world record! Our share (taxpayers) of GM decreased from 61% to about 27%. GM's Chinese partner, SAIC, and Saudi Arabia billionaire Prince Alwaleed Bin Talal each purchased a $500 million stake in GM's IPO. (GM didn't wait long to start spending its newfound wealth by announcing that it will again sponsor high price golf tournaments and venture into costly car racing in 2012. It also awarded its new CEO a $9 million compensation package in 2010 according to Ward's January 4, 2011 website.)

The company still faces transcendental challenges:

- Over $20 billion in unfunded pension obligations.

- Continuing major problems in Europe with declining market share, heavy financial losses, and complex and costly restructurings.

- Falling prices in China.

- A new and unproven senior management, which GM acknowledged in its IPO.

- Most importantly, an untested ability to keep product hits coming.

Nevertheless, Mr. Akerson stated on CNBC's "Squawk Box" on November 18, 2010 that "the company (GM) is fundamentally in great shape" (most previous GM leaders used similar old clichés as GM slowly slipped into bankruptcy). Even CNBC's top auto analyst Phil LeBeau stated on the same show that GM in now a "far different company."

Lastly, one of the most confusing remarks by the GM CEO was his statement that "GM's financial health is now on par with Ford...now, we are both viable, strong competitors with a level playing field" (November 19, 2010 Wall Street Journal, page B9). Wow, you've got to be kidding. If anybody should be talking about "level playing field," it should be Ford Motor Company, which didn't receive GM's un-American free ride. On its November 22, 2010 website, the Automotive News executive editor Edward Lapham claims that the bailout of GM and Chrysler "saved nearly two million jobs." If his calculations are correct, then Mr. Mulally and his "One Ford" team saved over 1.1 million livelihoods without a bailout.

# CHAPTER 27

✵ ✵ ✵

# THE $64,000 QUESTION

## Introduction

In our American-style capitalist system with unbridled, and unstructured laissez-faire, no company has a right to exist. Similar to most great civilizations, many companies rise, achieve glory, and collapse subsequently. The grave-yard of once highly successful companies, often led by self-important leaders, is a "Who is Who" in America:

• Bearing Point

• Lehman Brothers

• Bear Stearns

• Washington Mutual

• Countrywide Financial

• Blockbuster

• Enron

• WorldCom

- Circuit City

- Bethlehem Steel

- Eastern Airlines

- Studebaker

Without government support during the 2008 financial crisis, other major institutions would have probably entered bankruptcy or had to be acquired like Bear Stearns and Merrill Lynch. The companies in greatest danger included giants Citigroup, Bank of America, AIG, Fannie Mae and Freddie Mac.

In addition to Toyota, other companies that seem to have lost some of their former luster and belief in invincibility, include: Hewlett-Packard (CEO turmoil and technology issues), Goldman Sachs (ethical issues). DuPont (lost focus), AIG (speculator), Citigroup (reckless tactics), Merrill Lynch (CDO debacle), Johnson & Johnson (serious quality issues), Motorola (outdated products; it split into two entities), Nokia (lost innovative edge), Kodak (transformation still not succeeding), Fannie Mae and Freddie Mac (controlled by Washington). While the reasons for corporate failures vary from company to company, they often include some of the following: losing a sense of urgency, shifting priorities to noncore ventures, ignoring changing consumer patterns, exodus of key executives for "greener pasture," infighting to jockey for the top job, becoming insulated from success, believing your own press clippings, and being too occupied with outside interests or requirements.

Unlike General Motors and Chrysler Corporation, who filed for Chapter 11, Ford Motor Company didn't take the easy way to solve its numerous problems. It is aggressively restructuring without a bailout.

## Ata Boys for Mr. Mulally

Under Mr. Mulally's leadership, sense of urgency, spirit of unity, and a company in sync, Ford Motor Company has moved from the weakest of the "Big Three" to the top of the class. It is truly history in the making because a seismic and paradigm shift is taking place. Ford is the new "Wunderkind" of the worldwide automotive industry. Mr. Mulally reminds me of the classic 19th century American hymn "Bringing in the Sheaves." His efforts since 2006 are head and shoulder above all previous Ford restructurings in history.

- Production capacity has been reduced by 40%, and the break-even level has declined by about 45%–from 3.5 million units in 2007–2008 to 1.8 million units.

- Hourly manpower reduced by 40%, and salaried employees headcount lowered by 50% (total workforce reduction of 120,000 since 2006).

- Product quality improved dramatically, which significantly reduced warranty repair costs (from $4 billion in 2005 to $2.5 billion in 2009).

- The historically poor supplier relationship has improved dramatically.

- Achieved 2010-industry safety leadership with the most "Top Safety Picks" from the Insurance Institute for Highway Safety.

• Strengthened the balance sheet and achieved outstanding profits during a time when tumbleweeds were blown in the U.S. auto industry. Most astonishingly, and a signature moment in his Ford career, Mr. Mulally–the over-achiever–and the Ford team achieved a net cash position at the end of 2010. This compares with a negative net cash position of almost $11 billion on December 31, 2008. The miracle was accomplished during a thirty-year low in U.S. auto industry sales! Mr. Mulally's forte clearly is to think outside of the box.

• Dramatically improved operating-related cash flows, which totaled $4.4 billion in 2010 compared with negative cash flows of $19.6 billion in 2008 and $0.8 billion in 2009.

• Improved the product development process by reducing the time to develop a new vehicle by 8 to 14 months.

• Replaced or refreshed 45% of its U.S. lineup during the last two years–more than any other company. Further, Ford plans to replace or refresh up to 90% of its lineup in the Americas, Europe, and Asia Pacific by 2012. [94]

• Reducing the number of platforms for its vehicles to 12 by 2013 from 25 in 2009. This will result in major cost efficiencies. In addition, Ford is significantly expanding parts commonality, which is leading to lower development costs, and substantial economies of scale.

In addition, Mr. Mulally has changed the culture at Ford Motor Company, which used to be one of the company's unchanging negative hallmarks. High-level former colleagues told me that the new "Mulally culture" is now embedded at Ford, and the company won't return to the old ways. They also stated that any executive who puts roadblocks on the free flow of information gambles with his or her career.

Employee morale is sky high and all stakeholders are "as happy as a clam" which is consistent with an article in the December 2010 issue of SmartMoney: "Upbeat workers, Upbeat Investors." For example, according to 2000-2009 Ford Motor Company's "Sustainability Reports," overall employee satisfaction increased from a low of 58% in 2003 to a high of 68% in 2009. Moreover, the "employee lost time rate" (per 100 employees) decreased from a high of 4.0 in 2000 to a low of 0.6% in 2009 (numbers are skewed by inclusion of salaried employees who are rarely absent). However, the lost time rate is significantly higher in the Americas than in Ford's Asia Pacific/Africa region. For example, in 2009 the latter's rate was 0.2% compared with 0.9% in the Americas.

Lastly, Mr. Mulally and the "One Ford" team has been a creator of wealth. From its low of $1.01 per common stock in November 2008, Ford's shares increased to over $18 in early 2011. The market value of Ford Motor Company increased from a 2008 low of less than $5 billion to about

$60 billion in January 2011. Lastly, when Mr. Mulally joined Ford in September 2006, the company's third quarter 2006 Automotive operating loss was $7.8 billion. In 2010, Ford had a profit of $6.6 billion, which was the highest in ten years. (GM's 2010 net profits totaled $4.7 billion.) Ford also regained the number two sales in the U.S. position in 2010, outselling Toyota by over 200,000 units. (Toyota increased its incentive spending by one-third while Ford reduced its spending according to Edmunds.com.) On the January 12, 2011 CNBC "Street Sign" program, Jim Cramer stated, "Ford is in growth phase." (According to the July 23, 2010 posting on "24/7 Wall Street." Mr. Mulally reportedly received five million options, which were worth roughly $9 million in February 2011 for his outstanding achievements.)

However, are these temporary achievements, and will Ford repeat its historic mistakes of the late 1980's and late 1990s? The next section reviews some of the potential concerns.

## The $64,000 Question

Ford Motor Company has a history of going from minting money to almost losing it all. Will the present euphoria eventually lead again to the costly mistakes Ford made in the past, and will it be Déjà Vu all over again and lead to instability? The next two years will be the key litmus test.

• Instead of the old adage "stick to your knitting," will the company start ignoring the core business again by expanding into unrelated activities and going on frenzied "Black Friday" type acquisition binges and recycling the ruinous decisions of the late 1980s and late 1990s? Micheline Maynard, a former New York Times reporter stated during the November 10, 2010 CNBC special "Ford: Rebuilding An American Icon," that during the giddy times when Ford literally is awash with cash, "confidence overtakes them during booms and bust... leadership takes off the eye of the ball."

• Ford Motor Company went on acquisition sprees by buying high, and selling low which cost in excess of $20 billion. None of the acquired companies are in Ford's stable today! (Ford experienced sales declines in the late 1930s, late 1950s, early 1970s and early 1980s, but they were primarily related to the U.S. economic environment.) Corporate America is teaming with companies trying to move beyond their core roots. Sears acquired Dean Witter and Caldwell Banker in 1981, Orchard Supply

Hardware (1996) and Delver (a social search engine). Kmart purchased the Sports Authority, Builders Square, and Waldenbooks. This was at a time when a company called Wal-Mart was emerging as a real threat.

- Returning to its historic inconsistent product quality. Today, Ford Motor Company is a quality leader.

- Not resisting the temptation to quickly improve market share by resorting to heavy discounting or large sales to daily rental car companies. This negatively affects resale value (Toyota's and Honda's fleet sales as a percentage of total sales are less than 10% compared with 35% for Ford Motor Company and 40% for Chrysler Corporation). [95]

- Entering into uncompetitive labor agreements in a labor-intensive industry. As Steven Rattner stated in his 2010 book "Overhaul," the UAW still remains problematic. They helped sink the "Big Three" to the bottom of Lake Michigan.

- Inability to return Lincoln to a viable franchise. This leaves Ford effectively as a one-franchise company. None of the top ten world automotive companies are one-brand entities.

- Commencing internal rivalries and turf wars again with the unsettling struggle for leadership when Mr. Mulally nears retirement?

- Celebrating too early with "Mission Accomplished" banners. Moreover, executives should be cautions about believing their own PR. In the March 21, 1983 issue of Time magazine, Mr. Iacocca was on the cover with the following caption: "Detroit's Comeback Kid." [96] On April 1, 1985, Mr. Iacocca was on the Time cover again: "America Loves Listening to Lee."[96] In March 1992, Mr. Iacocca retired after Chrysler had three relatively poor years. However, Mr. Iacocca was the savior of Chrysler Corporation and did an excellent job at Ford.

Other potential early warning signals, similar to NORAD, include:

• Becoming complacent again and not looking over the right shoulder after achieving the basic tenets of "One Ford." No more 24/7's as the work attitude changes. In the meantime, new wolfhounds are ready to attack and build cheaper and better mousetraps (China and Korea). As Robert S. McNamara, a former Ford CEO and Secretary of Defense stated in the documentary film "Fog of War," "you can't change the fallible human nature" (October 29, 2010 Wall Street Journal.) (Even countries like Germany and Japan made the same mistakes after reaching the top of the economic mountain.)

• Stakeholders, especially labor unions, again demand unrealistic pieces of the pie, and the vicious cycle of uncompetitiveness returns (my greatest fear).

• Entering again into multi-billion dollar share buy-backs to artificially increase EPS when there should be more focus on R&D (Ford's 2010 Research & Development expenditures totaled $3.9 billion compared with Toyota's $8 billion).

Other potential storm warning signals could include the following, although they are not part of Ford Motor Company's repertoire:

• Building an expensive new World Headquarters (big CEO "ego" trip).

• Spend $10 million to refurbish a CEO office.

• Purchasing costly condominiums for visiting executives in Washington or New York with high-priced antique furniture, and $7,000 shower curtains.

• Buying the latest corporate jets.

• Dramatically increase corporate staffs instead of focusing on line operations.

## The Korean Threat

The most serious threat facing the "Big Three" is from South Korea. It is unusual that the world's most powerful country should have to be concerned about a tiny country. Generally, the U.S. focuses on economic giants such as China, Japan, the European Union, and soon India. South Korea has an area of 39,000 square miles compared with America's 3.6 million. Korea's population totals about 50 million versus 310 million in the United States; Korea's labor force is one-sixth of the United States, and its GDP is one-tenth of the U.S. ($1.4 trillion versus $14 trillion). However, South Korea has many of the same characteristics as Japan–highly educated (world ranking in science, mathematics and problem solving), and hard working people. Most importantly, there is a government-business relationship, which is the envy of the West (Korea's survival depends on its export machine–automobiles, semiconductors, electronics, shipbuilding, overseas construction). This gives South Korean companies a significant competitive advantage (currency manipulation, closed markets, especially to automobile imports which finally changed in 2011).

The "Big Three" ignored Japan's auto invasion until it was too late. Therefore, will they again overlook emerging competition from South Korea, China and India as they did in the 1960s when Japan started its U.S. invasion? The next extraordinary threat, and my deepest Angst is Hyundai/Kia, which is rapidly joining and even dethroning the

"Big Boys." The company is only 45 years old, and didn't even enter the U.S. market until 1986. Kia, in which Hyundai acquired a 34.6% controlling stake in 1998, and is consolidated in the company's financial results, entered the U.S. in 1994.

Until the early 2000s, Hyundai (means modern in Korean) had a reputation for low-priced but poor quality cars, and nobody in the auto industry took the company seriously. Hyundai became the joke on late night television shows. This humiliation led the company to heavily invest in quality. Today, Hyundai ranks consistently in the top echelon in quality surveys. In 2009 alone, Hyundai received 19 top awards around the world for vehicle quality, "top picks," etc. Over 8,000 people work in Hyundai's R&D according to the company's Annual Report. Hyundai's boilerplate mission statement is as follow: "To create exceptional automotive value for our customers by harmoniously blending safety, quality and efficiency. With our diverse team, we will provide responsible stewardship to our community and environment while achieving stability and security now and for future generations." Hyundai's innocent sounding mission statement doesn't tell the real story. In its 2009 Annual Report, the company stated its fundamental objective: "Tomorrow's global leader, not merely a dream." The January 3, 2011 issue of Automotive News claims that the "Japanese rivals (of Hyundai) began to shudder."

The headline in the January 29, 2010 edition of Fortune magazine summarized everybody's fear about Hyundai: "The toughest car company of them all." Even Toyota, in its fiscal 2010 Annual Report stated, "Hyundai has shown remarkable growth." The company has well-seasoned management, and is the fastest growing major auto company in the world. It is building plants in the U.S., Europe, Russia, Brazil, etc. (Korea's Daewoo was even more aggressive; it literally built plants on the moon, but eventually went bust due to over expansion, and filed for bankruptcy in 1999.)

In 1991, Hyundai Motor Company produced 1.1 million units, and was ranked number twelve worldwide (GM was number one and Ford number two; today, Ford is number five). By 2001, the company produced 2.5 million units, and advanced to number seven. In 2008, Hyundai worldwide production increased to 4.2 million units (number five position). In 2010, the company produced 5.7 million units despite the auto meltdown and moved up to fourth place in the auto world! (Hyundai is targeting 6.3 million units in 2011, coming ever closer to VW's 2011 forecast of 7.5 million units.) Hyundai has already reached unlikely heights for a corporation from the smallest country among all major industrialized nations. As the Wall Street Journal stated in an extensive January 8-9, 2011 article, "in the space of two decades, Hyundai has transformed itself from a pitiable also-ran Asian car maker to a powerhouse."

In the U.S., Hyundai increased its market share from 2.3% in 2000 to 7.7% in 2010 while GM and Ford lost a combined 17 percentage points during the same period (from 52.4% to 35.6%) according to Automotive News data. In 1990, Hyundai's U.S. sales totaled 117,000 units; in 2010, they reached almost 900,000 units. In Europe, Hyundai has dethroned Toyota.

Hyundai sales increased from 18 trillion won in 2000 ($14.5 billion) to 92 trillion won in 2009 ($78 billion). Net income increased from 0.7 trillion ($530 million) in 2000, to 4.1 trillion in 2009 ($3.5 billion). Assets increased from $14.7 billion in 2000 to $87.6 billion in 2009 with a 14% ROE in 2009. Stockholder equity totaled $24.8 billion (Ford had a $6.5 billion negative stockholder equity in 2009). In Korea, Hyundai received a credit rating of AA+ (not comparable to U.S. ratings). In 2009, Hyundai's net interest expenses totaled $0.8 billion compared with Ford's $1.5 billion. Provisions for accrued warranties totaled $0.8 billion in 2009 ($1.2 billion in 2008) versus $1.6 billion at Ford Motor Company in 2009.

Hyundai is exhibiting Toyota's early momentum, and is utilizing its product strategy.

• Outstanding management. The prestigious Automotive News 2010 CEO for Asia named the Hyundai/Kia CEO, Chung Mong-Koo. (He is the Mulally of the Orient, but he plays with an ace card Mr. Mulally can never match– a pro-business government.)

- Achieving platinum standard with absolutely top-notch products (quality, style, cost, etc.). The Sonata was voted one of the top ten 2011 cars by Car and Driver magazine. The highly respected Wall Street Journal auto critic, Dan Neil, stated in his February 26-27, 2011 review that "Hyundai Takes a Bold Stand in the Compact Race." Mr. Neil concluded "only the Ford Focus (2012) keeps Hyundai (Elantra) out of clear first place." (This is the segment the Toyota Corolla and Honda Civic compete in.)

- Hyundai's R&D chief told Automotive News (December 13, 2010 edition) that his company is "targeting 50 mpg by 2015." Huyundai/Kia received nine 2011 IIHS top safety picks in tie with VWAG followed by Ford, GM and Toyota with eight (Honda and Nissan received two awards).

- Hyundai is moving up-market; the mid-sized Hyundai Genesis recently beat the Ford Taurus and Toyota Avalon in a comparison test. [97] It was named "2009 North American Car of the Year." Automobile magazine, in its February 2011 addition, described the Hyundai Sonata "as unquestioned leader in the (mid-size) segment" (includes Taurus, Camry, Accord). Recently, Hyundai entered the luxury segment with the $60,000 Hyundai Equus. The company is challenging the long-established titans of luxury–BMW, Mercedes, Audi and Lexus. In its November 2010 edition, Automobile magazine stated that the Equus "fits the upper-luxury mold to a mold to a tee: fast, quiet, capable." Road & Track stated that Hyundai "should have no problems finding buyers for its new luxury flagship." A Car & Driver magazine comparative evaluation (February 2011) ranked the Equus ahead of the $30,000 more expensive Lexus LS 460!!

- Superb marketing. Hyundai was "the first to offer five-year warranties on their cars and to offer 10-year warranties on powertrains" according to the Financial Times.com website (December 15, 2010).

- Highly attractive labor costs in Korea compared with the West.

- An incredible workplace culture with 2,390 average hours worked per year in Korea (1,777 in the U.S., 1,828 in Japan and 1,362 in Germany). Work is an obsession in Korea (even civil servants are forced to take vacation days!).

- The Korean government manipulates the won, which gives Korean exporters a cost advantage. (The won has slipped under the radar screen because of our historic focus on the yen and the yuan.) In its October 15, 2010 edition, the Wall Street Journal stated the following: "Having a pricing advantage is especially important to South Korea because exports account for 43% of its economy." This, of course, is the same strategy the original master manipulator–Japan–utilized to make mincemeat of U.S. auto companies through aggressive pricing. (We don't have any bare-knuckle negotiators to fight the Asian manipulators.) Ironically, the October 15, 2010 Wall Street Journal headline said: "Japan, Korea Tussle Over Won." (Meanwhile, the U.S. keeps defending this ruthless economic foe. We still have 28,000 troops in South Korea defending our "friends." During the last 60 years, the United States of America has spent hundreds of billions of dollars defending this country. South Korea is only paying about 40% of the "upkeep.")

- The Korean auto market is effectively closed to imports through tariff and non-tariff barriers. The Wall Street Journal stated that on December 6, 2010 that over 95% of domestic Korean auto sales are locally produced– unheard among all major world automotive markets in a 1.2 million units industry. Korea exports over 500,000 vehicles to the U.S. annually (2008 car exports to the U.S. totaled about $7.5 billion). We export only 5,000 cars. (The usual excuse of shoddy U.S. cars is baloney because Ford and many of GM cars are absolutely world class and sell well in sophisticated Europe and the growing Chinese markets.) Korea is practicing one-way trade. Is this the reward for an Ally, which has protected South Korea for 60 years at billions and billions in U.S. taxpayer funds?

- Lastly, Hyundai has exceptional financial resources. First, Hyundai is a member of the powerful family-controlled "Chaebol" (means monopoly in Korean). Chaebol are somewhat similar to the Japanese Keiretsu affiliated companies. The Hyundai Chaebol family group is ranked second behind the Samsung Chaebol. Hyundai is involved in autos, steel, heavy industries, construction and insurance with assets of 204 trillion won (about $181 billion).

The only positive news for Western auto companies is that Hyundai Motors' success appears to be leading to imperial delusions. This belief in invincibility and "good times forever" led Ford Motor Company to its late 1980s and late 1990s "Black Friday" type shopping sprees. It almost resulted in its "Untergang" (ballywrack). According to a November 30, 2010 article in the Wall Street Journal, Hyundai Motor Company reportedly made a $4 billion bid for Hyundai Engineering & Construction Company–far outside its core business.

Moreover, "watch ya back," because lurking around the corner within less than ten years will be low-cost Chinese imports. Again, the manipulated yuan will give these new entries a significant competitive advantage over Western companies.

## Ford's Next Phase

Ford Motor Company's reinvention is an "American Story" with resonates in America. Since the rightsizing of Ford is essentially completed, and the product revolution is underway, nobody is asking "what have you done for me lately." However, with the relentless competition in the automotive industry, the upward curve must continue. The paramount challenge now has to shift from a defensive to an offensive strategy, in other words, into an attack mode for growth. In 2005, Ford had record sales of $174 billion; in 2009 they declined to $116 billion, and they totaled almost $129 billion in 2010. Since the hectic days of growing Ford through acquisitions are history, the growth has to be generated internally with great products.

In 2007, global sales reached record 70 million units. As a result of the meltdown in the West, sales declined to 65 million in 2009, however rebounded to roughly 73 million in 2010. Ford Motor Company's top sales analyst, George Pipas, is forecasting 2011 global auto sales at 75-85 million units. J.D. Powers & Associates are projecting 2020 global sales at 118 million units according to a December 15, 2010 report in Automotive News. Accordingly, Ford's key competitors are aggressively expanding, and the company must be the bellwether. Will complacency start the cycle of destruction all over again?

Toyota is still rapidly increasing worldwide capacity despite its present product quality upheavals. Toyota mission statement is: "to sustain profitable growth by providing the best customer experience and dealer support." Bloomberg reported on January 4, 2011 that Toyota's U.S. V.P. of Sales projects Prius to be the top seller in the U.S. by 2020 followed by the Camry! (This illustrates Toyota's mindset.)

Daimler AG's mission statement has four-key points: "Leading products and brands, pioneering technologies and business models, new markets and networks, and continuous efficiency improvements with a culture of high performance." [98]

VW AG's announced is as follows: "Our long-term goal is defined in our Strategy 2018: to turn the Volkswagen Group into the World's leading automaker—economically and ecologically." [99] VW is becoming quite cocky about its "2018" goal. According to an October 27, 2010 Automotive News Europe report the VW CEO stated, "the Volkswagen Group continues to have its sights firmly set on capturing pole position in the automotive industry." In its quest for world domination, similar to Toyota's strategy, VW AG might fall into the same trap as Toyota's recent quality problems. J.D. Powers & Associates surveys, according to an article in the October 18, 2010 edition of Fortune, ranks VW cars "near the bottom of initial quality and three-year dependability."

Following is Honda's mission statement: "maintaining a global viewpoint, we are dedicated to supplying products of the highest quality, yet at a reasonable price for worldwide customer satisfaction." Lastly, Nissan "provides unique and innovative automotive products and services that deliver superior measurable values to all stakeholders in alliance with Renault." [100]

# CHAPTER 28

❌ ❌ ❌

# THE FORD RENEWAL SERIATIM

## Step by Step

Mr. Mulally stated in a May 25, 2009 article in Fortune magazine by Alex Taylor III that he uses "a disciplined business review process that continuously assesses the business environment, updates our strategy and plan ... and relentlessly drives execution and performance individually and as a team." [101] Indecision and procrastination are not in Mr. Mulally's lexicon. The mid-2010 announcement to discontinue the seventy one year old Mercury line is an example. Systematically, Mr. Mulally attacked the serious issues Ford Motor Company was awash in mid-2006. Magically, he can report to Ford stakeholders with pride and satisfaction, after less than five years on the job, that the home team won a big victory in its battle for survival. Ford has entered a new era; it accomplished the feat despite a playing field, which was not leveled versus its bankrupt Detroit rivals.

Ford Motor Company avoided potential bankruptcy through one of the most successful restructurings in U.S.

corporate history. It was achieved in nanoseconds, which makes Ford's revival even more astounding. Ford's approach is a case study how to reinvent a giant company. Under Mr. Mulally, all elements of the company are being transformed—from Ford's culture, balance sheet, cost and product competitiveness, manufacturing facilities, capacity utilization, technology, union, supplier and dealer relationships.

Following is a brief outline of Ford's restructuring sequence. It appears that Mr. Mulally followed the advice of the famous 6th century BC Chinese mystic Lao-Tzu: "the journey of a thousand leagues begins with a single step."

- Thoroughly assess the fundamental problems the company is facing.

- Determine the new mission of the company.

- Identify strategic assets, and an exit strategy for noncore assets.

- Develop a recovery plan with a "compelling vision that delivers profitable growth for all" (Mr. Mulally's words). The plan must have a consistent vision. Mr. Mulally's basic building blocks outlined in Chapters 17 and 18 have not changed since 2006. In addition, the plan must lead to sustainable competitive advantages.

- Gain Board of Directors approval.

- Secure adequate financing

• Promptly implement the approved plan.

• Develop an on-going Business Plan review process. Mr. Mulally meets with his senior team every Thursday to review program status in great detail.

• Communicate the restructuring plan to all stakeholders–employees, union, dealers, suppliers, customers, bankers and investors. The new CEO of Bank of America, Brian Moynihan, apparently did not promptly communicate his bank's new vision to the world, according to a September 14, 2010 headline in the Wall Street Journal: "BOFA Chief Shares His Vision, Finally." [102] Similarly, the headline in the November 23, 2010 edition of the Wall Street Journal blared, "H-P Chief Surfaces, Mum on Strategy."

• Foster stable management (GM has had four CEO's in 2009-2010, and four heads of Marketing in the all-important Chevrolet Division). Any senior executive who is not a team player must be replaced. Only one team can implement the survival plan.

• Keep focus on key competitors, especially rapidly emerging threats.

• Actively utilize the never-ending continuous improvement strategy.

• Constantly analyze progress compared with plan objectives.

The "One Ford" stepping stones described previously are similar to the process outlined in "The Challenge of Organizational Change" by Rosabeth Moss Kanter, Barry A. Stein and Todd D. Jick. They called them "The Ten Commandments" for executing change.

- Analyze the organization and its need for change.

- Create a shared vision and common direction.

- Separate from the past.

- Create a sense of urgency.

- Support a strong leader role.

- Line up political sponsorship.

- Craft an implementation plan.

- Develop enabling structures

- Communicate, involve people, and be honest.

- Reinforce and institutionalize change.

# CHAPTER 29

# MANAGEMENT LESSONS TO REMEMBER

## "Creative Destruction"

Corporate failures are part of the free enterprise system. The economist Joseph Schumpeter called capitalism "a process of creative destruction."

In the early part of the 20th century, hundreds of "mom and pop" auto companies existed. Today, only one healthy U.S. based company exists (Ford), with the two other firms attempting a comeback. Following are the largest U.S. corporate bankruptcies:

| Company | Assets (Bills.) |
|---|---|
| Lehman | $691 |
| Washington Mutual | 328 |
| WorldCom | 104 |

GM's June 1, 2009 bankruptcy filing with $91 billion in assets was the U.S.'s fourth biggest bankruptcy, and the largest industrial Chapter 11 filing ever. Chrysler's April 2009 files involved $39 billion in assets.

Economists cite many root causes why companies fail including misguided strategies (Mr. Nasser at Ford), poor management, outdated products, lack of financial resources, weak corporate governance, unions unwilling to recognize the new global competitive environment (autos, steel, rubber, airlines), and entry of new low-cost overseas competitors with no U.S. legacy cost. Board of Directors must often share the blame. In some cases, they are nominated by the CEO, and thus have an allegiance to him or her. Many are retired CEO's of large companies often past their prime. They enjoy the honor, financial rewards and comradery of being a Board member. No outside member should serve more than ten years on a company's Board to assure new blood. Excluding non-Ford family Board members and the CEO, only five of the Ford Board members in 2000 are still on the Ford Board of Directors presently (2010). [103]

Mr. Mulally has demonstrated that change management can succeed. However, the failure rate is very high, as discussed in the next section.

# Why Change Management Fails

Since filing for bankruptcy was not an option at Ford Motor Company, Mr. Mulally developed a detailed "One Ford" survival plan, although there are very few examples of major successful transformations in America. Two of the most prominent are Steve Jobs' rescue of Apple Inc. in the late 1990s and Lou Gerstner's revival of IBM.

What were the odds of success? In his thirty years of pioneering research concerning change management, Professor John Kotter has concluded "70% of all major change efforts in an organization fail." McKinsey & Company studies reached a similar conclusion that restructurings fail two thirds of the time. Further, in a May-June 2000 article in the Harvard Business Review entitled "Cracking the Code of Change" by Michael Beer and Nitin Nohria, they stated, "the brutal fact is that about 70% of all change initiatives fail." Lastly, a June 2010 article in the Harvard Business Review by Bain senior executives Marcia Blenko, Michael Mankins and Paul Rogers entitled "The Decision-Driven Organization" declared that a recent Bain & Company study "found that fewer than one-third produced any meaningful improvement in performance."

Professor Lawrence G. Hrebiniak of the Wharton School of the University of Pennsylvania postulated that change strategies fail because of:

- Lack of expertise in the execution of the new strategy.

- Executive inattention to the plan.

- Allowing the focus of the strategy to shift over time.

- Not communicating the plan to all the people.

- Individual resistance to change.

In a widely quoted articles on failed CEO's, Ram Charan and Geoffrey Colvin concluded in their June 21, 1999 Harvard Business Review dossier entitled "Why CEO's Fail" that "in the majority of cases-we estate 70%-the real problem...is bad execution." They also outlined five self-test signs for failures: How is your performance? Are you focused on the basics of execution? Is bad news coming regularly? Is your Board doing what it should? Is your team discontented?

Robert S. Kaplan and David P. Norton in their well-known 2001 book entitled "The Strategy-Focused Organization" concluded that there are several reasons for process failures including the following:

- Lack of senior management commitment.

- Too few individuals involved.

- Keeping the scorecard at the top.

- Too long of a development process.

The next section outlines the potential lessons that could be learned from the meltdown of the "Big Three."

## Management Lessons to Remember

The U.S. automotive industry, the most important component of the American manufacturing sector, almost self-destructed during the last years of the first decade of the 21$^{st}$ century. The blame game has started for this humiliating defeat of American icons. However, it centers primarily on the industry leaders who fell asleep at the wheel while they had reached the apogee.

- Believing that they will forever have the market to themselves. U.S. auto companies had almost 100% market control for almost seventy years, lasting into the 1960's. They believe that Shangri-la would last forever with insatiable auto demand, no outside competitors, and virtually no price competition. Further, the U.S. had the largest auto industry in the world, and the U.S. was the wealthiest nation on this planet. The country was virtually insurmountable from overseas. Lastly, U.S. companies had economies of scale nobody could match, and the entry barriers were very high. Thus, they ignored emerging competition. **The lesson learned: Shangri-la seldom lasts forever.**

- Living an insulated life in a provincial city and not paying attention to the outside world. They had no idea about Japan Inc.'s mindset; it was an enigma.

There was this "we were the victors" (the historic WASP attitude), and "Nobody Can Beat Us" (growing up in post World War II West Germany, we accepted this American attitude as completely normal). Had Detroit studied General MacArthur's account of the Japanese people (dedication to education, high work ethic, perseverance, Japan Inc. mentality, etc.) or hired an epigrapher, they might have paid more attention to the Japanese in the late 1960s. **The "no-brainer" lesson is: pay attention to emerging competition.**

- Ignore the causes of declining shares. If a company's market share keeps declining year after year, as it happened to the "Big Three," there must be a fundamental reason for this trend such as poor: quality, reliability, styling, competitive prices, etc. **The lesson is: stop coming up with excuses, stop ignoring the warning signals, and face reality. Reassess the entire business strategy (Mr. Mulally' approach).**

- Hiding behind protectionist barriers. During the 1980's, "voluntary" Japanese import restraints, capped imports at about two million units annually. U.S. auto companies achieved record earnings during the roughly ten-year period, but did little to develop highly competitive small cars. **Lesson learned: if an industry has enough clout in Washington to gain import protection, take the precious time to strengthen the product portfolio. Secondly, do not assume that protection will last forever.**

• Growing via acquisitions. A Towers Watson survey summarized in the December 20, 2010 edition of the Wall Street Journal stated: "Many North American and European companies expect to resort to mergers and acquisitions to drive growth." This was the historic mindset in the auto industry. They mostly ignored the core business, and expanded into noncore sectors. "The grass is greener" theory is as old as capitalism. This eventually weakened the foundation of the "Big Three" by spending billions on acquisitions. The modern era of "Big Three" noncore acquisitions probably started in 1961 when Ford Motor Company bought Philco Corporation, which was a well-known consumer electronics and defense related company (consumer portion sold in 1974; The Aerospace component incorporated into Ford Aerospace Corporation in 1976). As outlined in chapters 7 and 8, Ford, GM and Chrysler ignored their historic core belief and launched into a noncore acquisition binge` never before witnessed in the auto industry. Between 1961-2000, the "Big Three" concluded roughly 50 acquisitions. The exact amount of this unwise strategy will never be known because in many acquisitions the cost was not announced. However, a $40-$50 billion price tag is not inconceivable including billions in write-offs and operating losses ($50 billion is equivalent to at least 15-20 "all new" vehicle programs, or roughly 50 new assembly plants to fight the imports). Had the U.S. automobile companies instead focused on their fundamental enterprise, there would be no need to say today Sayonara, Auf Wiedersehen or Annyong-Hi Kashipshio (Korean) to their overseas competitors since they would not have gained a strong foothold in America. **Lesson learned: focus on your core business.**

- Milk the most profitable vehicles. However, cash cows don't last forever (SUV's and big trucks) because of economic meltdowns, rapidly increasing gasoline prices or imports entering into such high-margin sectors. The auto companies generated billions and billions in profits from the cash cows for several years during the 2000s. They ignored the passenger car business, especially the emerging small-car segment. **Lesson learned: have a balanced portfolio (Mr. Mulally's philosophy).**

- Planning for the future no matter how dark the horizon. Ford's aggressive product development actions during the economic meltdown saved Ford Motor Company from joining GM and Chrysler into Chapter 11. **Lesson learned: continue an aggressive product development program during recessions to be prepared with competitive products when the economic cycle turns positive (Ford Motor Company's "One Ford" strategy).**

- Waiting too long to replace a company's most important core products. The Model T, which was introduced in 1908, was dethroned in 1926 after GM introduced a more competitive car. Sales dropped significantly, but

Ford was unprepared to introduce the new Model "A" and had to close its plants for six months for retooling. The same happened to the Ford Taurus. The futuristic jellybean styling was an instant success, and Taurus competed effectively against the bland Toyota Camry and Honda Accord. For several years, it was the best selling car. In 1996, instead of evolutionary styling changes, Ford chose a revolutionary exterior which was unrecognizable from its original version. However, unlike the Japanese auto producers, who nurture their winners, Ford failed to keep the Taurus competitive. The focus in the early 2000s was on the cash cow SUV's and trucks. Eventually, the Taurus was sold only to rental fleets, which is the death-blow for any product. The Taurus name was eventually dropped when its replacement was introduced (upon arrival at Ford in 2006, one of Mr. Mulally's first actions was to insist that the Taurus name must not be discarded after hundreds of millions of dollars had been spent in creating Taurus' name recognition. The 2010 Ford Taurus is a worthy successor to the original Taurus) **Lesson learned: don't neglect your core products**.

• Aggressively initiating a fundamental reengineering when a company is faced with insurmountable problems. According to Michael Beer and Nitin Nohria of Harvard University, a company has essentially two change choices: under Theory "E," "shareholder value is the only legitimate measure of corporate success." With

Theory "O," the "soft" approach to change, "the goal is to develop a corporate culture and human capability through individual and organization learning." **Lesson learned: implement restructuring actions before it reaches the point of Ford's problems in 2006, or GM's and Chrysler's bankruptcy.**

• Creating chaos as a way of life. For example, Ford Motor Company had five Reinvention Plans–Ford 2000, 2002 Revitalization Plan, 2005 Restructuring Plan, 2006 Way Forward Plan, and "One Ford" Plan (GM had at least five). **Lesson learned: do the restructuring all at once, and do it correctly.**

• Being totally focused on world leadership at any cost. Toyota's "We Can and We Will" slogan (we <u>will</u> be number one) is the perfect example. This ambition led to the company's current problems. Toyota believed in the 1980s song "We are the World," and neglected product safety in their drive to dethrone GM from its perennial world's number one position in 2008, a position GM held for over 75 years. **Lesson learned: another "no-brainer," pay attention to your products; your customers don't care about your slogans. They want safe vehicles.**

• Entering into union agreements, which can't be sustained in the long-term. The "new boys on the block" do not have a unionized workforce and legacy costs. Unless a company is in Chapter 11, it is almost impossible to gain "give-backs" from powerful unions. Harley-Davidson's September 2010 labor strategy can't be utilize by most major industrial companies. They threatened the unionized-employees with plant relocation to the South if they don't approve a cost-cutting contract. **Lesson learned: the only solution is to work with the union leadership in tough times to gain some "give-backs" since it is impossible to totally discard an existing contract and "start from scratch" (unlike in China, rank and file members elect union leaders in the U.S.).**

- Fighting the continuing power grab in Washington. The bureaucrats have little affection or even interest in the survival of the auto industry. They love new job-killing regulations; it is a job protector for them. For the auto industry, it is dealing with a whole alphabet of agencies such as the EPA, NHTSA, etc. with never-ending costly rules. Being humbly deferential to these powerful auto "czars" will lead to defeat. **Lesson learned: involve all stakeholders, Congressional delegations, the unions, etc. to lobby aggressively for reasonable rules.**

- Allowing, "bean-counters" to gain a disproportionate power base, especially in a manufacturing industry. The finance people control all numbers, and generally focus first on cost, and secondly on product competitiveness. **Lesson learned: there must be a reasonable balance among all internal stakeholders.**

- Being unreachable when facing serious safety problems. Akio Toyoda, Toyota's CEO was called "no-show Akio." Similarly, CEO Tony Hayward's widely publicized yachting adventure during BP's Gulf oil spill crisis, and his "getting my life back" comments, and the difficulty in gaining access to him sealed his fate (he, unlike Mr. Toyoda, lost his job). (Ford had a full-court public strategy during the Ford Explorer Firestone tire problem, even closing assembly plants to divert tires to fearful customers.) **Lesson learned: as the CEO, face the music to regain public trust.**

- Entering into direct competition with your dealers. As part of "Ford 2000," Ford established the "Auto Collection" Plan, which put Ford in direct competition with its dealers. Even after terminating this unwise strategy, it took years for Ford to regain the trust of its dealers who invest millions of dollars into their franchise. **Lesson learned: stick to your business as the manufacturer, and treat the dealers as valuable partners.**

- Spending several billion dollars acquiring a manufacturing business without thorough due diligence. Ford was in a bidding war with GM for Jaguar and was not allowed to visit Jaguar facilities in the United Kingdom prior to closing the deal. Ford of Europe's top manufacturing executive, Bill Hayden, was "horrified" when he visited the Jaguar plants after the acquisition was consummated. **Lesson**

**learned: buying manufacturing facilities sight unseen may not "get one's money's worth."**

- Imitating a competitor's acquisition strategy does not necessarily assure success. The best examples are the forays during the late 1980s and the late 1990s by Ford and GM. Most of the roughly dozen Ford acquisitions, excluding The Associates and possibly Hertz, involving in excess of $20 billion were failures. In addition, Ford probably had to commit $10-$15 billion in incremental funding to sustain the often loss-operating luxury brands. In an undated 2000 article on Forbes.com, Jerry Flint stated that "Ford pumped $6 billion into Jaguar over the past decade," and an August 2006 article in Bloomberg Business Week stated that Ford's cost and investment in Jaguar alone was more than $10 billion. This excludes the additional huge losses after the articles appeared. **Lesson learned: losing billions of dollars of shareholder wealth could be risky to a CEO's future (ask Mr. Nasser, Juergen Schrempp of Daimler AG or the former Porsche CEO who tried to buy giant VW AG and who was ousted when VW turned the table and bought Porsche).**

- Use of quantitative slogans to rally the troops has pitfall. Several years ago, all GM executives wore buttons with the number "28" to convey that General Motors' objective was to achieve a 28% U.S. market share. This goal appeared unrealistic to auto analysts and the buttons eventually disappeared. (Today's GM share is under 20%). The "Ford 2000" slogan "to be the world's leading automotive company" was as unrealistic as GM's "28" buttons. Further, the 2006 Ford "Way Forward" slogan "change or die" was too emotional. **Lesson learned: slogans can rally the troops, but they must be realistic and long lasting.**

• The auto business is a very cyclical business closely tied to the U.S. economy. One blogger put it perfectly in describing the auto industry: "Time can be good or it can be cruel." During its over one hundred year existence, there have been around 9 growth spurts followed by 9 trough swings. According to GM's IPO video presentation, the initial sales peak was between 1913-1929 followed by deep sales decline between 1929-1932. Following are the Ford Motor Company's U.S. cyclical sales patterns during the last 85 years:

AVERAGE ANNUAL FORD U.S. SALES (millions)

| | |
|---|---|
| 1925/1926–1.4 ⟶ | 1927/1928–0.5 |
| 1949/1950–1.5 ⟶ | 1951/1952–1.2 |
| 1956/1957–2.0 ⟶ | 1958/1959–1.6 |
| 1978/1979–3.5 ⟶ | 1980/1981–2.2 |
| 1989/1990–3.3 ⟶ | 1991/1992–3.0 |
| 1999/2000–4.2 ⟶ | 2001/2002–3.8 |
| 2006/2007–2.7 ⟶ | 2008/2009–1.8 |

As Robert Lutz, former Chairman of GM North America stated in a January 2003 speech at the Automotive News Congress, "every Golden Age comes on the heels of trying times...the Age of Enlightenment followed the Dark Ages." Tom Peters summarized it as follows: "That Which

Goethe Up and Up and Up Doth Goethe More Up and More Up and More Up Forever and Ever and Ever."

It is a normal human tendency to be euphoric during boom times. However, it often leads to financial losses because of the high breakeven level which evolved during the boom times; it leaves companies unprepared when the trough cycle commences. **Lesson learned: be prepared for the down cycles, which happen like the annual hurricanes in Florida.**

# CHAPTER 30

✻ ✻ ✻

# WHY "ONE FORD" ACCOMPLISHED ITS GOALS

## Happy Days Are Here Again

Ford's comeback is in full strides; it didn't take millennia to climb up the ladder of success. Only Carlos Ghosn achieved similar results in such a short time when he rescued Nissan. Why has the "One Ford" corporate makeover succeeded when most change managements fail? Was it what Bank of America CEO Brian Monihan calls "day-to-day, hand-to-hand combat?" It appears that Mr. Mulally embraced all the elements Professor Kotter identified in his extensive change management research (kotterinternational.com), and in his well-known book entitled "A Sense of Urgency."

• **Acting with urgency**. With adrenaline flowing, and in less than two months after Mr. Mulally's arrival at Ford–working 24/7 and never off duty– he and his top associates completed the most comprehensive "change" plan strategy in Ford's almost 110-year history. The Ford team struck like a thunderbolt in nanoseconds by stepping up to the diamond for a game of survival. Mr. Mulally is the courier of "How to Succeed in Business With Really Trying" (it's a take-off of the wonderful 1967 movie celebrating "the great American corporate way"–How to Succeed in Business Without Really Trying.") Mr. Mulally's strategy encompassed every aspect of the problems Ford faced as outlined in chapter 14. Tom Peters, on his website, referenced Mickey Drexler of J. Crew's fame who wrote an article in the September 20, 2010 edition of the New Yorker which outlined his business philosophy including: bias for instant action, impatient but not brutal, relentless, vibrate with energy, offense and not defense, communication all the time, and willing to act (Mr. Mulally's strategy).

- **<u>Developing the guiding coalition</u>**. In preparing the "One Ford" vision, Mr. Mulally involved all affected internal and external stakeholders in face-to-face meetings. This included the UAW as well as Ford's bankers. Being a student of human behavior, it appears that Mr. Mulally has been able to set aside the historic internal turf wars because the "One Ford" team seems to be working effectively as a group. Mr. Mulally continuously stressed the urgency of the required painful actions. Importantly, it was critically important that all stakeholders understood the rationale for the survival plan. It was also desirable to appoint a reinvention "czar" to focus on restructuring of the company. This indicated that the company is totally committed to the rebuilding plan. In Ford's situation, Mr. Mulally became the de facto "czar" because of his outstanding leadership abilities.

- **Developing the change vision**. Although Mr. Mulally was a freshman in the highly complex automotive industry, he had done his homework before he developed his "One Ford" makeover vision by meeting with all stakeholders, as well as auto industry analysts. He had such self-confidence about the success of "One Ford" that when Ford employees asked him in 2006 whether Ford would remain in business, he reportedly told them "we have a plan, and the plan says we are going to make it."[104] (It reminds me of Christopher Cross' song "All Right, Think We're Going To Make It.") The objective was putting Ford in forward gear again like driving a car, and to achieve operational excellence, and to outperform expectations. However, to actually accomplish the arduous and 24/7 reinvention milestones is like memorizing LeTolstoy's 150 year old and 1,475 page classic "War and Peace."

- **Communicating the vision buy-in.** Cheerleading is a uniquely American institution. Almost weekly, via television or newsprint interviews, the charismatic Alan Mulally is promoting Ford. He is a very effective "One Ford" cheerleader. He also visits Ford facilities to rally the troops. His motto is communicate, communicate, communicate.

- **Empowering broad-based action.** The "One Ford" plan attacked all elements of Ford's business, as reviewed previously. It involved internal and external stakeholders– employees, unions, suppliers, dealers, bankers, Washington, etc. Further, by totally reorganizing Ford's operating structure, Mr. Mulally eliminated potential barriers, which could undermine "One Ford." Road blocks is not a word in Mr. Mulally's vocabulary. Moreover, he developed an entirely new product strategy approach to directly challenge Asian competitors. For example, Ford's industry leadership in consumer technology is a "Ford First." Instead of being a follower, Ford is now a product leader, which has resulted in two consecutive years of U.S. market share increases.

- **Generating short-term wins** (to "silence critics and disarm cynics"). Although auto analysts continued to claim as late as 2008 that Ford is the weakest of the "Big Three," and its survival was in doubt, Ford was generating short-term wins such as the $23.5 billion survival loan, and the introduction of several highly competitive vehicles which stabilized Ford's 15 year long decline in U.S. market share. More recently, Ford was the runner-up in the prestigious Wall Street Journal "Innovative Technologies Consumer Electronics" category behind a company which invented a flexible computer screen! [105]

- **Don't let up.** The "One Ford" plan is in its fifth year and Ford is working toward dominus or grande dame status.

Mr. Mulally and his team are not unfurling the famous Bush "Mission Accomplished" banner, and, hopefully, don't believe their own press notices. With their exemplary work ethic, they are continuing to aggressively raise the envelope to achieve even further dramatic improvements, even if it impacts on short-term financial results such as the termination of the Mercury brand in late 2010. Mr. Mulally is challenging himself and Ford to ever tougher "change agents," especially related to new financial and product initiatives. However, as David Ristau of the Oxen Group stated in an October 2010 article "they (Ford) will only succeed further if they can continue on that path (best products)." In my opinion, this must include wresting the growth crown from Toyota, VW AG and Hyundai. Automotive News Europe reported on November 19, 2010 that Volkswagen AG plans to spend $71 billion between 2011-2105 to help leapfrog Toyota, and plans to hire 50,000 employees by 2015. Based on my association in the automotive industry since1964, it is a sum unheard in the annals of the auto industry. (VW plans to operate 11 plants in China within four years.) The $71 billion excludes roughly $14 billion the VW joint ventures in China plan to invest during the same period.

- **<u>Make change stick</u>**. The "One Ford" action plan is a permanent institution at Ford Motor Company; the umbilical cord to the "old" Ford has been cut forever, and, hopefully, it is not a temporary fad. Moreover, since

2006, there has been a "consistency of purpose" because the four fundamental principles outlined in chapter 17 remain unchanged. Mr. Mulally stated in a May 25, 2009 interview with Alex Taylor III of Fortune magazine, that he "uses a disciplined business review process that continuously assesses the business environment, updates our strategy and plan accordingly, and relentlessly drives execution and performance individually and as a team." Mr. Mulally's thinking is consistent with McKinsey's excellent April 2009 "Change Management" article in its quarterly publication: "change-management thinking extols the virtues of creating a compelling change story, communicating it to employees, and following it up with ongoing communications and involvement."

Mr. Mulally is fully involved on a day-to-day basis in "One Ford." His Thursday's Business Plan Review meetings, as well as the hundreds of performance charts, (updated daily) constantly keep the top executives abreast of Ford's worldwide developments. Mr. Mulally had experience at Boeing in executing complex turnaround plans; therefore, reengineering a company was not a new experience for him. Further, Mr. Mulally's position at Ford Motor Company was assured when William Clay Ford, Jr. aggressively brought to an end a nascent palace revolt after Mr. Mulally's arrival in September 2006.

Successful corporate transformations share several fundamental attributes according to "Eploring HR Management," a leading corporate transformation consultant.

- Creation of a clear and compelling vision, with visionary leadership the essence of a successful corporate transformation, together with alignment of the organization to the vision.

- A total-systems approach involving all elements of the whole organization.

- Comprehensive implementation process architecture.

Again, these are the "One Ford" core values. McKinsey & Company's extensive worldwide research regarding corporate transformations was described in detail in their April 2009 quarterly edition. Following are the key successful transformational aspects.

- Establish clear and high aspirations and targets. McKinsey claims that 90% of the transformations fail because they lack a well defined stretch targets. Importantly, the goals should have a clear plan not just for the short-term, but also a plan for the longer-term transformation.

- Exercise strong leadership from the top.

- Develop a clear structure for the transformation.

- Ensure "frontline" ownership of the change.

- Maintain high energy levels throughout the restructuring.

The "One Ford" reinvention plan contains the factors outlined above. Mr. Mulally has "true grit" (bold, brave, daring, courage, etc.), and is very passionate about it.

Moreover, it appears that he has the vigor and stamina to deal with the stress and complexity of his 24/7 jobs. Not all CEO's of giant companies can make such a claim. The CEO stories on pages B 2-3 in the December 7, 2010 edition of the Wall Street Journal included: stressed out, burned out, pressure cooker, rocky tenure, resignation.

Larraine Segil, in his book "The Many Faces of Leadership," outlined the ten traits of a dynamic leader based on his research of more than 250 companies; Mr. Mulally possesses these traits:

• Fearlessness

• Completion

• Commitment

• Inspiration

• Assuredness

• Penetration

• Intelligence

• Energy

• Integrity

• Perception

Also worth mentioning are the habits Dr. Stephen Covey discussed in his 1989 book "The 7 Habits of Highly Effective People" which sold more than 15 million copies:

1. Be proactive

2. Begin with the end in mind

3. Put first things first

4. Think win-win

5. Seek first to understand, then to be understood

6. Synergize (positive teamwork)

7. Sharpen the saw

Lastly, following are some of the "takeaways" from the 500-page book entitled "Breaking the Code of Change" edited by Michael Beer and Nitin Nohria.

• Reengineering has to be led from the top down although there is concern that CEO's lack the knowledge and skills to manage the reengineering process.

• Change management is impossible without the support of "followers."

• The proposed restructuring must have a clear vision.

• Changing the formal organized structure is central to the overall change process.

- Without a crisis, there can be no organizational change.

- Any significant change requires a process.

- Change must be ongoing and continuous.

Again, the "One Ford" restructuring plan reflects all the successful characteristics outlined above. David Ristau of The Oxen Group published the following comments about Ford on October 20, 2010: "We've all heard the E! True Hollywood Story about the star that rose to glory, nearly lost it all, only to make it all back again. It's the all-American turnaround story. In the business world, though, many times companies do not get the chance after near failure to turn things around. One company, though, is making the most of their chance and is developing some of the nicest and most sought after cars on the road today. That company is Ford Motors Co."

Ford Motor Company has weathered the storm through hard work, and by eliminating old Ford habits. They also know that there is no rewind to the "Big Three" 1950s and 1960s "paradise;" in fact, competition will be even tougher when the Chinese auto companies come forth to our shores in less than ten years. However, there is definitely "light at the end of the tunnel," and a new day in America–playing second fiddle is not acceptable for America. None of the 50 largest U.S. corporations have gone through such a successful process unless saved by Chapter 11 or government bailouts (banks). Moreover,

Ford's reinvention is not a passing fad: this American "fairy tale" is real.

Yes, it is "springtime for Ford Motor Company." Mr. Mulally didn't climb out on a limb with opportunistic, unproven, mystifying or new manifesto slogans. I literally spent weeks examining his performance and trying to unravel mysteries and looking for unknown "golden nuggets" or rocket science ideas which the "old" Boeing restructuring artist used to achieve the "One Ford" miracles. I was looking for precious diamonds in the rough, which no turnaround specialist had used before. Did he play the often used tricks to hide financial loses or liabilities off the book? Was this window dressing such as postponing paying bills? Did he force dealers to accept more vehicles to puff-up financial results? Did he make reckless wagers other than the $23.5 billion loan package? None of it happened. The best explanation for Ford out-competing the opposition is Jim Cramer's CNBC's pre-Thanksgiving (November 24, 2010) testimonial when he said that Ford is the "greatest comeback story of a generation, a business that just few short years ago many people thought was a wreck on the highway in a multi-car pile-up of an industry thanks to superior manufacturing, superior brand, superior management, and a superior attitude and state of mind."

There is no monarchistic mystery about Mr. Mulally's attack plan; it was simply a well-executed recovery plan led by an Albert Einstein type business genius. In deciphering the felix, it includes another word: <u>resilience</u> because it was an old-fashioned "Rosie the Riveter" roll-up your sleeves approach. Rosie was a World War II feminist icon; the "We Can Do It" poster showed a woman with her sleeves rolled up, with fist-raised and right hand on biceps to encourage women to work in the defense industry to beat Germany. (Uh, that's my homeland. I was the recipient of the bombs from Ford's B-24 bombers as a seven and eight year old, which I can't erase from my mind, even after 65 years. What ironic twist in life. I ended up working for the company that produced the squadrons of bombers that flew unopposed in 1944 and 1945 during daylight to the nearby city of Frankfurt causing indescribable destruction and death. (The bombings in our small town were not extensive, but kept us in the air-raid shelter many, many days and nights.) Moreover, I spent a few years as Director of Ford Aerospace in Newport Beach, California which was involved in producing the highly successful Gulf War Sidewinder missiles, satellites and a lot of secret stuff.)

# CHAPTER 31

❁ ❁ ❁

## WALKING ON THIN ICE

### Expert Opinions

Every 50 years or so, a business leader, previously not a household name in America like Jack Welch, Lee Ia-coccca, or Donald Trump, steps out onto the limelight and literally accomplishes the "Impossible Dream." There is no living CEO who became an "All-Star" in the two most important U.S. manufacturing sectors in the first decade of the 21$^{st}$ century. In the business world, he would be the equivalent of 20$^{th}$ century leaders such as Franklin D. Roosevelt, Harry S. Truman, Ronald Reagan, Winston Churchill, Margaret Thatcher, Nelson Mandela, M. Gandhi, Martin Luther King, Jr., and Vince Lombardi.

The name of this remarkable person is **Alan Mulally** who is piloting the rocket ship "Ford" to new heights. He is, however, on earth as the "One Ford" guiding light—the keeper of the lighthouse. What makes him such a great business leader and what inspires him? First, he has the traditional American "can-do" determination and the will to win spirit. He also has the resiliency which was epitomized by General Washington's daring crossing of the Delaware on December 25, 1776, by the 1969 moon landing, and by two of the most remarkable events in U.S. sports history–the two "miracles on ice" victories during the 1960 and 1980 Olympics by underdog college hockey players against the mighty and highly favored Soviet professional hockey teams who had been World and Olympic champions many times over. Mr. Mulally's odds of success were not much better when he joined Ford Motor Company in September 2006 because Ford has been collapsing as early as 2002. In a November 18,2002 article by Betsy Morris in Fortune magazine, she stated that "Ford didn't just fall from grace last year – it fell off a cliff."

John Grisham is often described as America's favored spy thriller storyteller. However, Mr. Mulally's "One Ford" story is a real old-fashioned "Yanqui" business thriller. He is not a "muddle through" leader; he respects his Asian rivals, but he is not in the business of bowing to them.

George F. Franks III, in an article in "Ezine Articles," describes what he considers great leadership characteristics, which Mr. Mulally easily meets:

• Knowledge

• Vision (and make it reality)

• Focus

- Decision making

- Communication

- Lead the troops in front

- Negotiation skills

- Humility

- Selflessness

As Bill Saporito stated in an August 15, 2010 article in Time magazine "if enthusiasm is measured in automotive terms, Mulally is 16 cylinders of it, pedal to the metal." Rick Newman of U.S. News & World Report called Mr. Mulally " one of the most successful CEO's in corporate America" in a July 30, 2010 article. Further, Rod Lache of Deutsche Bank called "Mulally's plan for success at Ford: "keep it simple." Mr. Mulally also meets other attributes of leadership included in Tom Peters and Nancy Austin's book "A Passion for Excellence" with credit to Robert Townsend who listed over 50 characteristics in his book "Further Up the Organization."

- Simplifies

- Trusts people

- Has strong convictions

- Decisive

- Arrives early

- Straight forward

- Openness

- Consistent and credible to the troops

- Plain office

Jack Welch, in his book "Winning" described "lack of candor the biggest dirty little secret in business...it basically blocks smart ideas, fast action, and good people communicating all the stuff they've got. It is a killer." Again, one of Mr. Mulally's fundamental strengths is candor–for himself and his associates. Ford's General Counsel, David Leitch, in an article in the August 9, 2010 edition of Time magazine stated that "Alan (Mr. Mulally) always saying that you can't manage a secret." His philosophy is: "if you need help, everyone who can help is present" (at his Thursday Business Plan Review meetings). The acid test came early in his new job, according to a May 25, 2009 article by Alex Taylor III in Fortune magazine, when Mark Fields, head of the Americas admitted a problem with the soon to be released Ford Edge. Mr. Mulally stated, "the whole place was deadly silent. Then I clapped...I really appreciate that clear visibility."

In Tom Peters' 561-page groundbreaking 1987 book "Thriving On Chaos," the management guru talked about leadership. Instead of "being driven by corporate staffs, the leader (should be) a lover of change and preacher of vision and shared values." Mr. Peters also is an advocate of eliminating bureaucratic rules, humiliating conditions, create a sense of urgency, practice visible management (a Mulally specialty), empower associates, and celebrate success. It may sound like a broken record, but these principles are Mr. Mulally's basic ways of doing business. Mr. Mulally, however, would probably not concur in Mr. Peters' belief of setting "conservative goals" although Mr. Peters stated that this is "not a plea for timidity."

# The Man With the Golden Touch

In the previously quoted article by Ram Charan and Geoffrey Colvin entitled "Why CEO's Fail," they described eight superior CEO qualities:

• **Integrity, maturity, energy.** Mr. Mulally has over forty years of highly successful top level manufacturing experience in two high-tech companies. He has more energy than the energizer bunny.

• **Business acumen.** Although he was a freshman five years ago, he learned quickly because he had done his homework. Further, he came to Ford Motor Company from a similar environment at Boeing where he was a superb technocrat. Thus, he had a deep understanding of how to reengineer a giant company. Thomas Edison said: "the three great essentials to achieve anything worth while are, first, hard work; second, stick-to-itiveness; third, common sense." This describes Mr. Mulally.

• **People acumen.** Mr. Mulally is a true team player; he has totally changed the culture at Ford Motor Company. Moreover, he is doing an extraordinary job leading the "One Ford" team with 164,000 employees. In announcing the death of counsel and speechwriter Ted Sorensen on October 31, 2010, NBC News stated that the late John F. Kennedy considered him his single most indispensable person, in addition to his brother Robert. Mr. Mulally considers all of his 16 direct reports indispensable. Moreover, he truly has molded a team, which I never noticed during my thirty years with the company. Shipmates were not a term too often used at Ford at that time, but we had many destructive fiefdoms. Moreover, Mr. Mulally is the exact opposite of the description of August Busch III in a book by Julie MacIntosh entitled "Dethroning the King." Supposedly, "he had only two moods: pissed off and suspicious."

• **<u>Organizational acumen</u>**. Mr. Mulally is a master organizer and a bold decision maker. He should receive an honorary degree in organizational management from MIT. His 300 plus performance review charts and his weekly Business Review meetings with his top 16 direct reports are only a few examples. He also shares results with internal and external stakeholders. Moreover, he is always in the "eye of the storm." He doesn't sit on a throne shouting orders; he is in the middle of the actions. His "One Ford" team doesn't have to shout "Where Are You? (Genesis 3:9). He leads the troops in front. In a book, which dealt entirely with successful partnerships, Michael Eisner in the Epilogue of his book "Working Together," states, "I'm still very much a believer in the need for leadership by one person and ultimate accountability." That appears to be Mr. Mulally's philosophy (probably Truman's "the Buck stops here"). Mr. Eisner also used the unusual German word "Tischordnung" which loosely translates one leader at the top.

- **<u>Curiosity, intellectual capacity, and a global mindset</u>**.
Mr. Mulally is a globetrotter; his base of operations is
the world. He leads a strenuous global life–one day in
Asia and the next day in Europe because 55% of Ford's
business originates outside the United States. No words
need to be wasted about his hunger for knowledge and
intellectual capacity.

- **<u>Superior judgment.</u>** Mr. Mulally has demonstrated his
intellectual gift with his historic accomplishments at Ford
in less than five years. He is like 24-karat gold–the highest
standard in the U.S. auto industry. CNN Money's editor
at large Paul La Monica calls Ford Motor Company "The
Big One" in Detroit.

- **<u>An insatiable appetite for accomplishment and results</u>**.
Mr. Mulally has demonstrated a never-ending mindset
to continue moving Ford to the top-tier of the world
automotive powers. In a November 2, 2010 report by
CNN Money's Paul La Monica, he cited a study by Kirk
Ludtke of CRT Capital Group "we have come to realize
that the company (Ford) is much more than a cost-
cutting story." In the same CNN Money dispatch, Mr.
La Monica quotes analyst Steve Dyer of Craig-Hallum
Capital "Mulally has worked wonders at Ford." Actually,
I am convinced that Mr. Mulally can walk on water! Phil
LeBeau, the outstanding auto analyst at CNBC, in a
one-hour special on November 10,2010 entitled "Ford-

Rebuilding an American Icon," stated it nicely: Mr. Mulally is "steel-nerved."

Folks, competitors are beginning to feel the pain because Mr. Mulally is raising the bar. For a change, in Dearborn, Michigan "Happy Days Are Here Again" (F.D.R.'s 1932 campaign song). Even Houdini could not have magically created the following heading from the November 15, 2010 edition of the Wall Street Journal "Toyota, Honda Lose U.S. Edge." Moreover, the December 6, 2010 issue of Automotive News cited the following quote from Lincoln Merrihew, managing director of Compete Automotive, a market research firm: "Honda is not riding the wave...outdated inventory system, sliding reputation among younger shoppers, declining buyer consideration." The January 6, 2011 headline from "Investment U Research" stated, "Honda Not Firing On All Cylinders." In addition, who could have conceived one year ago the January 10, 2011 title of a Bloomberg report from the Detroit Auto Show: "Detroit in the Driver's Seat." Only four years ago, the obituary had already been written for Ford, as well as GM and Chrysler. This was the time when the Asian competitors were on an unstoppable freight train eating U.S. automaker's lunch. However, despite the eye-catching headlines, I would urge the "Big Three" not to raise the victory flag too early. I am totally convinced that when the dust settles, the Japanese competitors will fully recover, and

<u>will definitely give the U.S. companies a run for their money again.</u>

- **<u>Powerful motivation to grow and convert learning into practice.</u>** Mr. Mulally has put into practice the restructuring theories he had refined at Boeing. Now that the basic building blocks have a sound foundation, his "Job One" is to motivate the employees of Ford to adopt a growth mindset after years of retrenchments which resulted in worldwide headcount reduction from roughly 400,000 to about 200,000 employees. Now is the time to push the freight train straight toward the Asian competitors who tried to run Ford off the road with pleasure. They didn't send "get well" cards when Ford Motor Company went under the knife in the operating room.

Rich Kargaard, the publisher of Forbes, in an article in the February 28, 2011 edition outlined "ten tips" for "Great Restructuring" winners:

- Design

- Cost

- Speed

- Service

- Logistics

- Talent

- Internal Communications

- External Communications

- Brand

- Purpose (integrity)

Mr. Mulally and his "One Ford" team have encompassed the "ten tips" listed above in their successful restructuring efforts.

# Grand Cordon

The Harvard Business School project "The Great American Business Leaders of the Twentieth Century" includes the following Ford Motor Company CEO's:

• Henry Ford

• Henry Ford II

• Philip Caldwell

• Donald Petersen

• Alex Trotman

The GM list includes, among others, William Durant (1910), the legendary Alfred P. Sloan, Jr. and Charles Wilson. Chrysler had several CEO's on the list including the former Ford CEO and subsequent Chrysler savior Lee Iacocca.

Without hesitation, a new name must be added to Harvard Business School "The Automotive Hall of Fame" when the list is updated. The name of the new candidate is **ALAN MULALLY.** He has brought a beacon of hope to American manufacturing and easily belongs in the super class of Steve Jobs, Jeff Bezos, J. Paul Austin (Coca-Cola), John Bogle (Vanguard), Mary Kay Ash, William Allen (Boeing), Arthur Andersen, Walter Annenberg, and Opra Winfrey. Moreover, if Ralph Edward's 1950s television shows "This Is Your Life" is ever relaunched, the first person to be invited should be Mr. Mulally. He is the "All-American" business leader young people can learn a lot from. Mr. Mulally's godsend performance at Ford Motor Company has clearly put him in the telescope of America's business leaders. My own Ford "Hall of Fame," reflecting over 47 years of intense focus on the worldwide automobile industry, includes the following post World War II Ford executives and alumni:

• Henry Ford

• Henry Ford II

• Ernest Breech

• Lee Iacocca

• Philip Caldwell

• Don Petersen

• "Red" Poling

• Ed Lundy

• Allan Gilmour

• Alan Mulally

• Robert Lutz

• Hal Sperlich

A rookie to watch as a future "Hall of Famer" is the relatively new Hyundai U.S.A. CEO John Krafcik, a Ford alumnus. Prior to his CEO position, he was vice president of

Product Development and is leading his company's phenomenal rise in America.

Today's miracle story is being written in Dearborn, Michigan, U.S.A; there appears to be no end of the tsunami of good news, and the "Stars Are Aligned" for Ford Motor Company. Ford's mantra under Alan Mulally is working to perfection. He is leading a paradigm shift in the U.S. auto industry. The title of Sam Cooke's popular 1960s song summarizes it nicely: "Ain't That Good News" because Ford is as original as the unique sounds of American Jazz, Bluegrass, Gospel, Country and Rock & Roll music. The "One Ford" change management approach will become the authoritative case study for future generations of business leaders because <u>CHANGE</u> is a permanent institution in the American free enterprise system.

Since I consider Alan Mulally the new Lord of the U.S. automotive industry, following is a summary of Lord Nelson's business philosophy, which he utilized when he achieved the famous victory at the Battle of Trafalgar in 1805 over Napoleon's navy (it is verbatim from Tom Peters' new book "The Little BIG Things." Mr. Peters stated that it is a summation of Andrew Lambert's book: "Nelson: Britannia's God of War").

1. Simple scheme

2. Soaring/bold/noble purpose

3. Engage others

4. Find great talent, at any age, let it soar!

5. Lead by love!

6. Seize the moment!

7. Vigor

8. Master your craft

9. Work harder-harder than the next person

10. Show the way, walk the talk, exude confidence! Start a passion epidemic!

11. Change the rules: Create your own game!

12. Luck

13. Be determined to come out on top, come hell or/and high water!

Speaking of the U.K., Mr. Mulally would have been honored with a title by the Queen for his achievements. (The late former Ford CEO Alex Trotman, a British subject, was knighted a Lord by the Queen a few years after his retirement. He presided during Ford's 1993-1998 "money no object" era, and didn't have to steer the company through a life and death struggle.) However, I am strongly opposed to this monarchy stuff. In America, where anybody can rise above his parents' class, if he or she has brains, is a hard worker, and has a little luck. (One of the reasons I left Germany was the country's historic class structure. I was born on the wrong side of the "railroad tracks" since my father was only a skilled tool and die maker.)

Lastly, since Mr. Mulally is an American business giant, the conclusion of this chapter lists seven American entrepreneurs, which Richard S. Tedlow considers "Giants of Enterprise" in his excellent 2001 book. Mr. Tedlow portrays these American masters as: empire builders, risk takers, innovators, experimentalists, visionaries–"all more hungry for success than they were afraid of failure...all men of extraordinary self confidence...genuine American genius."

In addition to, of course, Henry Ford, Mr. Tedlow included the following exceptional men on his crème de la crème:

- Andrew Carnegie (rags to riches)
- George Eastman (creation of mass marketing)
- Robert Noyce (toward a new business world)
- Charles Revson (consumer packaging goods)
- Sam Walton (All-American)
- Thomas Watson, Sr. (American salesmanship)

Considering that Mr. Mulally and his "One Ford" team turned around one of the biggest and most troubled giants in the world in less than five years, he would easily qualify for the 21$^{st}$ century "Giants of Enterprise List." While Mr. Mulally didn't create companies from dust as the men described above, he literally brought an American icon back from the deathbed, which is equally difficult.

# CHAPTER 32

❁ ❁ ❁

## NEWS FLASH

### Alan Mulally's Indy 500 Race

In 2011, the Indianapolis Motor Speedway celebrated its centennial. However, on a crisp day roughly five years ago in the Heartland of America, the "Indianapolis 500" announcer shouted: Gentlemen (and ladies, of course), start your engine:

• In the first row was "Team Japan" with three highly successful drivers. They won most recent races including a world number one position by the Toyota driver. The Japanese claimed that their cars never break down, and that they would whip the golden companies from the West who had their time in the sun, but lost their ways. However, as numerous recalls in 2010 and 2011 have shown, Toyota's cars didn't walk on water. In late December 2010 Toyota agreed to pay two more fines amounting to record $32.4 million for safety notification delays (maximum allowed by law). This is in addition to a mid-2010 $16.4 million fine. The latest fine involved periods (2004–2005 and 2007) when Toyota created Armageddon and demolished U.S. auto companies (the previous largest fine was a $1 million GM fine according to Automotive News). J.D. Powers & Associates in a late December 2010 survey of 25,000 new car buyers revealed a startling change in the perception of Toyota–19% of new vehicle shoppers avoided Toyota because of "bad reputation of manufacturer," and 15% cited "bad experience with the manufacturer." They will be schlepping this image with them for a while since, as U.S. auto companies learned, quality perception only changes slowly. Moreover, Toyota's workhorse, the world's top selling Corolla, is being left in the dust by new compact segment competitors such as the 2012 Ford Focus. Lastly, the ultimate insult was S&P's March 4, 2011 downgrade of Toyota's bonds while Ford's credit ratings are frequently being upgraded.

Despite all its problems, Toyota remains the world's largest automobile company with 8.42 million units in 2010, up 8% compared with 2009, followed by GM with 8.39 million units, an increase of 12%. In addition, Toyota has almost unlimited financial and technical resources. Furthermore, while Toyota lost almost two percentage points of market share in 2010 in the critical U.S. market, the company remains number one in the U.S. in terms of retail sales. Moreover, Toyota Corporation has the largest and most profitable dealer body in America.

Lastly, mid February 2011, NASA and NHTSA concluded that electronics were not part of Toyota's sudden acceleration problems, which the company celebrated in full page ads. The celebration didn't last long because one week later (February 24, 2011), Toyota recalled another 2.2 million vehicles. This brings the worldwide recall to 19.2 million units.

• The second row at the Indianapolis Speedway consisted of three luxury cars from Germany with fancy names like Mercedes, BMW and Audi. They were yodeling Achtung, Achtung, Achtung; we are the proud champions of Germany. They also told everybody that they had a head start because on the Autobahn (build by an evil mastermind in the 1930s) there are no speed limits (actually, only about 50% of the Autobahn is speed limit free).

• The third row included two upstarts from Korea who ranked last in all quality surveys until ten years ago. However, they have gotten their act together, and are now considered the hottest team in the auto industry.

• Way down in the last row was "Team America"–a failing business in the 2000's during record auto industry sales. It was very embarrassing for the U.S. entries to start in such a place, but they had become marginalized in their own market with declining market shares, poor quality, uncompetitive labor costs, and the most un-American blunder–they needed government money to build their race cars!

The Ford team barely qualified because experts claimed they were in the worst shape of the three U.S. racers. Furthermore, they had other problems; the young owner of the team, by the name of Bill Ford, had to replace himself as Crew Chief because he lost a lot of races lately. He admitted that he needed new blood, and made the startling decision to hire a Boeing pilot who knew nothing about building or driving racecars. Understandably, the crewmembers complained to Mr. Ford about the "new kid on the block," but the team owner told them that he would stick with the new man by the name of Alan Mulally "come hell or high water" (he might have remembered Rod Stewart's song "I'll Stand By You, in the Darkest Hour"). Since the owner had no money, he had to borrow $23.5 billion to pay for a new racecar, and a new strategy.

# Celebrations in Dearborn, Michigan

After roughly 375 of the 500-mile race, which seemed like a five-year adventure, the Ford team was still in last place and the pit crew became exasperated. Everybody had given up on them, even auto experts. However, they didn't know of the tenacity of the new racecar driver because most people never heard of him before. The competitors apparently didn't know that he was a "go-to" player which is defined as a competitor relied upon to make important plays, especially in clutch situations. They also didn't know that he promised himself before the race to follow the plaque in the New York Yankees' Clubhouse to "Play Like a Champion Today." In addition, he was already becoming a "CEO Rock Star" (December 2010 Automobile magazine), and that his team was "really on a roll" (AP auto writer Sharon Silke Carty in November 3, 2010 issue of Sarasota Herald Tribune) or that "he's been spectacular, and I don't think that's overstating it" (Steven Dyer of Craig-Hallum Capital). Moreover, in mid-December 2010, Mr. Mulally was named "MarketWatch 2010 CEO of the Year" "easily beating Steve Jobs, Vikram Pandit, Jeff Bezos and Reed Hastings." In addition, on January 6, 2011 Morningstar named Mr. Mulally "CEO of the Year". Also, CNBC's Maria Bartiromo on January 7, 2011 called Mr. Mulally "The Superstar of the Auto Business," and CNBC's "Mad Money" host Jim Cramer called him "the modern day Henry Ford" (January 12, 2011). Lastly, in Motor Trend's February 2011 edition, Mr. Mulally was ranked number one on the magazine's "2011 (world) Power list "being described as "the leader every automaker wants-and needs." Yes folks, a "New Star is Born."

Therefore, it was not surprising that slowly, but surely, he "kicked-up the game," and the spectators started trusting the new man. They witnessed one of the most remarkable and heart-stopping races they ever witnessed. The Ford team moved up and up with lightning speed, and crossed the finish line first after a grueling event. Yes, a fait accompli for an American icon with grand heritage; it was also a "New Morning in America," and a signature achievement. The Heartland spectators wouldn't stop screaming: USA, USA, USA! <u>The takeaway: don't underestimate America!</u> (Germany did it twice in the 20th century and my family paid the price with three killed in the war for such arrogance). Thus, through "blood, sweat, and tears" and no government handouts– the real American way–Ford has closed the circle from near bankruptcy to an honored place in America.

In a tribute to the many frontline soldiers, a plaque was placed in front of Ford's World Headquarters to remind future Ford leaders to learn from the past, and not to get cocky again and start the whole cycle of destruction with preposterous acquisitions.

The Ford community then proceeded to Ford's large auditorium to listen to a few speeches by Bill Ford, Alan Mulally and others. The highlight of the afternoon was a speech by Uncle Sam from Washington, D.C., U.S.A. According to Automotive News, Uncle Sam did "a little trash talking" when he celebrated GM's IPO at the NYSE. Sam arrived in Michigan by car after a grueling twelve-hour trip. Unfortunately, the proposed new 62 mpg EPA fuel economy regulations forced Uncle Sam to be driven to the Heartland of America in a modified golf cart. (Uncle Sam visited the UAW "Solidarity House" after the ceremonies for a glass of real champagne to celebrate the big winner of the bankruptcy fiasco–the UAW! Compared to the other stakeholders, who got shafted, the UAW has become the effective owner of GM and Chrysler via the VEBA Trust.)

Another highlight of the much - anticipated event was a speech about "Ford and the American Way of Life" (Attachment I). It included the evolution of the American character and a synopsis of the U.S. free enterprise system using "One Ford" as a case study. In the Heartland of America, these are important subjects, which the folks in Washington often consider old-fashioned talk. However, with the map of the U.S. now heavily red colored except for some Portuguese, Irish, Greek, and Spanish-like "progressive" states on the East coast (high-tax burden New York), and on the West coast (high-tax and bankrupt California), this looking down on "old fuddy-duddy" people with beliefs which made America great, must be accepted at their own peril!!

# CHAPTER 33

✖ ✖ ✖

## ALAN MULALLY'S SCORECARD

The following examples illustrate the sea change during the last five years under Mr. Mulally's leadership.

| Item | Ford's Situation In Mid-2006 | Ford's Status Today |
|---|---|---|
| Business Plan | Inconsistent | Consistent |
| Restructuring | Commenced | Completed |
| Automotive Profits | Heavy Losses | Solidly Profitable |
| Financial Services | Deteriorating | Strong |
| Balance Sheet | Deteriorating | Improving |
| Net Automotive Cash | Declining | Increasing |
| Operating Cash Flow | Declining | Improving |
| Capital Spending | Very High | Lower; Better Results |
| Breakeven Point | High | Competitive |
| Long-Term Debt | Increasing | Decreasing |
| Shareholder Return | Uncompetitive | Outstanding |
| Credit Status | Downgraded | Upgraded |
| Dividends | Eliminated In Late 2006 | None |
| Cost Structure | Uncompetitive | Improving |
| Health-Care Costs | Out of Control | Decreasing |
| Leveraging Global Assets | Poor | Outstanding |

| Item | Ford's Situation In Mid-2006 | Ford's Status Today |
|---|---|---|
| U.S. Market Share | Declining | Gaining Share |
| Product Planning Process | Uncompetitive | Leading Edge |
| Balanced Product Line-Up | SUV Focused | Broad Based |
| European Luxury Brands | Heavy Losses | Sold |
| Lincoln | Uncompetitive | Uncompetitive |
| Parts Commonality | Low | High |
| Heavy Emphasis on Incentives | Yes; Costly | Much Lower |
| Reliance on Fleet Sales | High | Decreasing |
| Residual Values | Low | High |
| New Products | Uncompetitive | Full Pipeline |
| Product Styling | Unappealing | Attractive |
| Product Technology | None | Leader |
| Product Quality | Deteriorating | Excellent |
| Product Reliability | Poor | Excellent |
| Warranty Costs | $3.5 billion | $2.2 billion |
| Product Recalls | Very High | Low |
| Mfg. Plant Flexibility | Low | Highly Flexible |
| Capacity Utilization | Declining | Very High |
| Productivity | Uncompetitive | Competitive |
| CEO Leadership | Improving | Outstanding |
| CEO Turnover | Revolving Door | None |
| CEO Succession Candidates | None | Several |
| Mgt. Bench Strength | Weak | Strong |
| Ford Culture | Destructive | Radically Improved |
| One Team Philosophy | Almost None | Strong Emphasis |
| Employee Morale | Lost Faith | Sky High |
| Labor Costs | Very High | More Competitive |
| Wall Street Reputation | Lost Respect | Highly Positive |
| Public | Indifferent | Highly |

| Item | Ford's Situation In Mid-2006 | Ford's Status Today |
|------|------------------------------|---------------------|
| Ford Dealers | Totally Unhappy | Respected Feeling Better |
| Ford Dealer Count | Very High | Decreasing |
| Ford Suppliers | Ranked Ford Low | Preferred Client |
| Emerging Markets | Missed Boat | Gaining Strength |
| Competitive Advantages | None | Making Progress |
| Competitive Threat | Very High | High |

# CHAPTER 34

✖ ✖ ✖

## EPILOGUE

Until approximately 1965, the U.S. manufacturing sector, including the automotive industry, was the pride of Americana especially in the "Rust Belt." (Coming off the boat from Germany penniless in 1957, I will never forget the sight of the American "Strassenkreuzer" exemplified by the 1959 Cadillac with its huge fins.) Today, only 19 enterprises on Fortune's top 50 list are manufacturing companies. [106]

Books such as "The Reckoning" and "The End of Detroit" predicted the "Untergang" (collapse) of the "Big Three" and the obituaries had been prepared. It almost became a reality, and an entire era in America would have come to an end. Ford, GM, and Chrysler sank to the bottom of Lake Michigan because of a lack of focus on the core business, unwise and costly acquisitions, uncompetitive labor costs (UAW kowtowing), products consumer did not want anymore, together with perceived poor product quality, uncompetitive fuel economy, and generally unattractively styled vehicles. In addition, the "Big Three" ignored emerging competitors, especially from Asia.

Ford Motor Company has gone through tumultuous ups and downs in its almost 110 year history. Yet, the company remains one of the top twenty global enterprises. [107] Ford contributes importantly to the U.S. manufacturing sector because of its large steel, aluminum, copper, glass, rubber, zinc, plastic, electronics, and fabric purchases from U.S. sources. In addition, Ford is one of the biggest U.S. exporters, a large generator of patents, one of the largest employers of well-paying jobs, is in the forefront of technological advances with an annual research and development budget of $5 billion, has $28 billion in Automotive liquidity, has over 200,000 stockholders, is honored for its total commitment for diversity and charitable contributions, and Ford is also the largest taxpayer in many communities.

Mr. Mulally joined Ford in September 2006 when the company had reached a state it had not experienced since the late1920s and 1945. At its lowest point in 2006, Ford's market value had declined to less than $5 billion (on December 31, 2010 it was $58 billion). A shake-up was urgently required; it was not an assignment for the faint of heart. It appears Mr. Mulally's philosophy was no pain, no gain. Otherwise, Ford would have followed GM and Chrysler into Chapter 11.

**The most exciting headline from Dearborn, Michigan, U.S.A:** America is witnessing one of the most remarkable corporate survival stories in U.S. history under the leadership of Alan Mulally and his united "One Ford" team. Even Mr. Mulally called the rebirth of Ford "the most fantastic turnaround in human history" (Daren Fonda's November 3, 2010 article in SmartMoney). The pendulum can't swing back to the first 25 years of the 20th century when Ford was the master of the auto world under the legendary Henry Ford! However, the genesis is in the right direction and the famous Ford logo with its iconic products is reverting to its glory days.

Mr. Mulally is the modern-day incarnation of Alfred P. Sloan who led GM to its historic zenith, and who ended Ford's dominance of the U.S. auto industry in the late 1920s. The battle-hardened Mr. Mulally created a new vision for the company; he is a class apart. Mr. Mulally has orchestrated a lightening fast recovery of a newly proud American institution, and never deviated from his original 2006 strategy. He is a man with a Midas touch, and he is responsible for one of the few "feel good" U.S. business stories in recent years. As Daren Fonda stated in an November 3, 2010 article in SmartMoney," Mr. Mulally has been "turning a firm potentially destined to the junkyard into a profitable company with a rising market share and some hot-selling products."

Clearly, Mr. Mulally is the new American business icon–the "merchant of good news." He is doing all the right things right. He has vision, Fuehrung (leadership) and knows how to "turn the trick" into reality. Furthermore, he is fastidious, enthusiastic, and his management style inspires his associates to achieve the impossible; that's the sign of a great leader. He is as smooth as the maestro directing a large symphony orchestra at the renowned Metropolitan Opera. He is also urbane, decisive and analytical. Lastly, he is omnipresent with a game plan Vince Lombardi would have been proud of. However, he does not exhibit the notoriety and brashness of Lee Iacocca, Renault-Nissan CEO Carlos Ghosn, Sir Richard Branson or Donald Trump.

Mr. Mulally appears to be an embodiment of the Amerikaner I encountered as a boy after U.S. forces occupied my hometown of Bad Nauheim, Germany on March 29, 1945. The officers and soldiers were professional, confident, exuberant, optimistic, and fearless. They exhibited a "take-charge" attitude, and had a purpose and direction to defend Europe during the Cold War. [a] The U.S. soldiers were also defending "the American Way of Life" which is exactly what Mr. Mulally said in his August 15, 2010 Time magazine interview–"we are fighting for the soul of American manufacturing." As Automobile magazine stated in naming Mr. Mulally "2010 Man of the Year," "Mulally is living proof that a single, extraordinary leader with vision and determination really can make all the difference in an organization." [108] In my opinion, he is an equal to Steve Jobs of Apple Inc., who returned in 1997, and is generally considered the genius behind the biggest turnaround in U.S. corporate history. In its December 6, 2010 edition, Fortune magazine named Mr. Mulally its "Business Person of the Year – Reader's Choice." He beat 32 other contenders including Warren Buffett, Michael Duke (Wal-Mart CEO), Ellen Kullman (CEO of DuPont), Steve Jobs, and many others. Akio Toyoda (CEO of Toyota), eat your heart out, and don't under-estimate my beloved America. Mr. Mulally was also runner-up as Fortune's 2010 "Business Person of the Year" behind Netflix's revolutionary techno-guru CEO Reed Hastings (600 employees). Mr. Mulally created a tour de force.

Mr. Mulally and his management team have saved an iconic international business giant, and an important piece of Americana. In a January 12, 2011 one-hour special from Ford's F-150 plant in Dearborn, Michigan, CNBC's Jim Cramer called Ford the "miracle of Detroit." Moreover, unlike GM and Chrysler shareholders, who lost their money in the bankruptcy process, the Ford common stock and bondholders retained the hope of a return of shareholder wealth, which is already taking place. CNBC's Jim Cramer included Ford in his September 20, 2010 report among his top eleven American manufacturing companies (Ford was the only auto company on the list).

Mr. Mulally appears to exhibit many of Mr. Churchill's leadership traits such as: vision, decisiveness, take-action, energy, creativity, courage, self-belief, integrity, collaboration, charisma, and communication (www.winston-churchill-leadership.com). Similarly, he also seems to possess some of Mr. Truman's characteristics--disciplined, realistic, systematic, precise and decisive. This, of course, sounds like apotheosis, or as Shakespeare once defined it: "the observed of all observers."

Ford has advanced from Second Division to the Champion League by achieving solid profits during depression-level auto industry sales. However, another two to three years will be required to assure that "One Ford" is a permanent institution and has legs because, in my opinion, the only truly competitive advantage the company has is Mr. Mulally and his "One Ford" executive team! (In our capitalist system, they can easily walk out of Ford's World Headquarters for other jobs, especially since they have proven their metal.) Hopefully, this great team will not be carried away by "irrational exuberance." Most importantly, Ford should not start "bulking up" on growth through acquisitions. The company should adopt a "Constitutional Amendment" and unwavering commitment to forbid "wheeling and dealing and strategic transformational M&A deals," ala the late 1980s under Don Petersen or during the late 1990s under Jacques Nasser. Ford Motor Company must avoid flashbacks to this period.

The race for survival must continue in this world of constant "car wars" and the company must stay at the battle station with powerful ammunition; shining stars don't last forever. Fortunately, Ford Motor Company has a deep executive bench. The company's playbook must now switch from a survival to a profitable growth offensive to assure that its best days are still ahead (the international hit says it all: "I Love You, You're Perfect, Now Change"). This is the tenet of Toyota, VW and Hyundai who have an expansionary mindset. Further, keep your eyes on your key cross-town rival. GM's fourth new CEO in two years, Dan Akerson, announced on September 17, 2010, that he is trying to instill "an attacker's culture." [109] Perhaps the most sincere compliment for "One Ford" has come from GM, which is becoming a Ford "wannabe." "New General Motors CEO Dan Akerson outlined his own plans in a press conference on Thursday, and they're (unsurprisingly) Ford-like: to implement a clear, unified global strategy that allows GM to contain costs, be nimble, and to go on the offensive against competitors. Sound familiar?" [110] Wow, what a reversal of roles from my time in the auto industry!! Everybody is trying to catch Ford's magic elixir!

Professor John Kotter, in his book "A Sense of Urgency" framed it well: "an organization that can sustain a high sense of urgency over time has the potential to become a high-performance machine, where results go from good to great and beyond. Mr. Mulally has repaired Ford Motor Company and built a top-quality management team, which inspires confidence. However, in my crystal ball of the 2015 auto industry Zukunft, everybody will again be chasing Toyota, which will be running on all cylinders. The line of fire will also be directed at Hyundai, which will be the unstoppable shark. In addition, GM will be a formidable competitor once more, and VW AG claims that it will be the new auto industry shining star by 2018 (third place in 2010 with sales of 7.1 million units). Within five years, new kids on the block will be Chinese auto companies that will flood the world with low-cost and attractive cars.

Ford has slipped to number five position worldwide from its historical number two ranking, and only is number three in U.S. retail sales, and barely ahead of fourth-place Honda. The future will be a tougher battle than in 2010. Therefore, what is Ford's long-haul competitive edge and tour de force? To move up to the rank of top tier companies, what will be Ford's encore, especially with setting apart new segment products? Secondly, what is the company's formula by 2015 to differentiate itself from the top world auto companies?

Nothing is endless except our ever-growing fiscal debt. As Wall Street Journal's Dan Neil stated in a major article in the January 15-16, 2011 edition, "no company, no one, stays on top forever." Rick Newman of U.S. News & World Report advised Ford in an October 2010 article," this is not the time to turn on the cruise control." The no-brainer Holy Grail is for the "red, white and blue" to run the engine at 150 mph, and to move to a hyper offensive profitable growth posture considering that the World Bank is projecting a worldwide middle class of one billion by 2030 compared with 400 million in 2005 (January 2011 National Geographic).

(a) A one hour documentary entitled "Turning American: A German Immigrant's Story" was shown on all four Michigan PBS stations several years ago. It included my recollections living during and after World War II in Germany and life in America. The day the Americans occupied our town about 20 miles north of Frankfurt on March 29, 1945 is still so vivid in my mind as if it happened yesterday. The remembrance haunts me to this day as well as my lifetime shame for the crimes committed by Nazi Germany although I was only eight years old. When American soldiers literally attacked my 90-pound mother as she tried to give some water to the captured German soldiers lined up in front of Hotel Geyer, it opened my eyes that we were not free anymore (readers will rightfully question who is really free in a dictatorship, especially under Nazism).

White bed sheets were displayed from many homes and hotels as a sign of surrender along the Hermann Goering Strasse (main road to Frankfurt). The people in my hometown accepted the Einmarsch (entry) of the Americans calmly and without despair. There was no crying; residents stood in line in the afternoon at city hall to quietly collect their monthly food ration stamps as if nothing had happened! However there was jubilation from the hundreds of forced laborers, primarily from France, who were free again. The soldiers threw candy bars from the tanks; the old people told us not to touch it because it was poisoned! We picked it up anyway.

Contrary to the Soviet Union's occupation of East Germany, there were no large-scale rapes of women and no brutality in the U.S. zone. However, our Army Stadtkommandant was a self-important dictator. He seized hotels and villas on 24-hour notice and commandeered all local sports facilities (soccer, golf, tennis, etc.). He also imposed a curfew. In addition, small groups of people couldn't assemble anymore. Nobody was allowed to leave the city, and everybody was considered a Nazi (the majority of Germans including the educated elite supported Hitler and millions voted for him). There were frequent humiliating Razzias (sweeps) of homes and apartments searching for guns. When Germans complained of living in an occupied land, Germany's greatest post World War II Chancellor Konrad Adenauer told them "who do you think won the war?" according to 2002 Time's 75th anniversary edition of "Person of the Year."

Life in Germany between 1945–1947 was very difficult although bombs were no longer raining down on us. The infrastructure was destroyed. Trains stopped running and power stations lacked coal. Many people froze to death, especially during the severe winter of 1946-1947. Furthermore, there was large-scale starvation. Average daily rations in 1945 and 1946 totaled roughly 1,000 calories per day, which is equivalent to a few slices of bread, two small potatoes and some soup (we used to rummage through the garbage cans of hotels occupied by Americans looking for lard). There was no hope for a new future, and many people believed their life was no life anymore.

The streets of most cities were cleared of the rubble from the destroyed buildings by the end of 1945. Women did most of the work because the men were either killed in the war or POW's. Once Germans were allowed to travel again, they went to farmers in surrounding villages to trade in their previous belongings for a sack of potatoes. Moreover, there was an active black market, especially for cigarettes and nylons. Against strong objections from older people, who considered it humiliating, we used to pick-up American cigarette buds from the streets and traded them for candy at the POW hospitals, which held 5,000 German injured soldiers.

Most major German cities were demolished by the day and night bombings, which resulted in a severe housing shortage. This was compounded by the influx of over 10 million Vertriebene (expellees) from historic German territories confiscated by Poland and Czechoslovakia after World War II.

However, within one year, and contrary to Iraq, local elections were held in West Germany. Moreover, the elected officials were not puppets of the U.S. occupation administration. Again, unlike in Iraq, Germans worked day and night to rebuild the country in the three Western sectors. This led to West Germany's Wirtschaftswunder of the 1950s

through 1970s. The 1948 Waehrungsreform (currency re-
form), with U.S. encouragement, created the catalyst for
West Germany's economic rebirth. Importantly, and suddenly, the stores had merchandise again because now
we had real money, which the storeowners had faith in.
Every person received 40 DM ($10) to start life again.

Slowly, life returned to a more civilized state, and we regained more personal freedom within three years after
World War II. Unlike the 18 million people in the Soviet zone
of occupation, the roughly 55 million Germans in the three
Western sectors (U.S., British, and French) could look to the
future again with hope. Fraternization was allowed again
and thousands of GI's married German Fraeuleins. What
mesmerized us were American movies (German movies
were not allowed because all World War II period films had
a war or patriotic theme). We couldn't believe our eyes–
big cars, big houses, skyscrapers, beautiful, well dressed,
well fed, and happy people. Wow, all the ladies looked
like Cleopatra. The music was also out of this world, especially Harry James, Benny Goodman, the Dorsey Brothers and Glen Miller. We often listened to the Frankfurt AFN
(American Forces Network), which played upbeat sounds.

America was an unreal world to our eyes, especially after
American soldiers showed their German girlfriends Sears
Roebuck's 300 plus page color catalog. It left an indel-
ible impression on me as a preteen, and largely led to my
decision ten years later to immigrate to this dream place

called America. As the lyrics of Elvis Presley's famous song stated, "Follow That Dream Wherever It May Lead" (it led to the "Promised Land.") (I came off the boat in February 1957 without an education or solid English language skills, no job, no money nor relatives or friends in America. I pledged to myself never to return to Germany as a loser, which everybody had predicted. It was an all or nothing gamble. However, I had a burning desire to succeed in my new life, no matter the hardships during the first year, and without asking for government handouts. Eating cheap rice puffs 24/7, sleeping on a chair for lack of furniture and with the sound of rats outside the door of an inexpensive apartment, with no heat nor shower, "Sometimes I Felt Like a Motherless Child a Long Way From Home"–American spiritual.)

Although long forgotten in today's Germany, the United States of America acted with great compassion considering Nazi Germany's crimes committed during World War II.

- Treated German POW's fairly and released most of them in1946. The Russians worked and starved millions of German POW's to death.

- Sending over 1.7 million CARE packages to West Germany between 1946-1949 (the parents of my dear friend in Frankenmuth, Michigan, Donald Weber, were one of the donors). This was all part of the American "do-good" spirit.

- Providing millions of German children in the American zone of occupation with warm meals, such as oatmeal for two years in view of the starvation in post-World War II Germany (it was my only warm meal of the day).

- Launching the 1948 airlift to sustain 2.1 million Berliners after Stalin blockaded West Berlin, which potentially saved Western Europe from Russian domination.

- Granting approximately $150 billion in foreign economic aid to Western Europe according to John Steele Gordon's perceptive book, "An Empire of Wealth, The Epic History of the American Economic Power."

- Arranging, in conjunction with the United Kingdom and France, for German experts in the three western zones to prepare a federal constitution, which went into effect in September 1949. It sowed the seeds of democracy in West Germany, and is the anchor today of a powerful, peaceful and western-oriented Germany.

- Advocating West Germany's full independence in 1955 and NATO membership during the same year. There was great concern in Europe of a rearmed West Germany only 10 years after World War II. I can categorically state that militarism is truly dead in Germany today; it is not ingrained in German society anymore. (In my six years in the U.S. National Guard, I failed my rifle tests.) It is my opinion, the German Soldaten are not carrying their weight in defending the West against terrorism, especially considering the country's economic and political power, as well as the size of the population (80 million), the largest in Western Europe. Wehrpflicht or conscription is only six months in Germany, and soldiers can't be forced to serve in battlegrounds against their will! Twice as many draft-age conscripts fulfill their military obligations by serving in "alternative" services such as hospitals. Germans used to call Americans Kaugummi soldiers (chewing gum or soft) for supposedly being mellow compared with World War II German frontline Soldaten. Today, it is reversed; U.S. soldiers do all the tough fighting.

Primarily as a result of the U.S. philosophy toward its former enemy, West Germany was able to embrace the four essential freedoms President Franklin D. Roosevelt talked about in his 1941 State of the Union address:

• Freedom of Want

• Freedom of Fear

• Freedom of Speech

• Freedom of Worship

Today, Germans take these four freedoms for granted and they can sing Louis Armstrong's immortal song: "What a Wonderful World." I will remember forever who was instrumental for this precious gift—the people of the United States of America.

# ATTACHMENTS

## Attachment I

• Ford and the American Way of Life

☐ The Decline of America?
☐ The Positive Aspects of America
☐ Hip, Hip, Hooray for America

## Attachment II

• The Rulers of this Century

☐ Overview
☐ Economic Powerhouse
☐ Chinese Automobile Industry
☐ Not Everything Is Coming Up Roses

# ATTACHMENT I

✼ ✼ ✼

## FORD AND THE AMERICAN
## WAY OF LIFE

### The Decline of America?

Ford Motor Company, with is dangerous headwinds in mid-2006, and subsequent survival also symbolizes the story of America. Both are intrinsically linked. Having worked on four continents during my business career, two names always became closely associated with the United States of America–Ford and Coca Cola (today, names like McDonald, Apple and Microsoft are also on the list).

Throughout its illustrious history, the U.S. was "Numero Uno," and a unique institution unmatched in the world. Ford Motor Company was in a similar position. Unfortunately, both lost their footings. It appears that America is currently following the steps that led to the collapse of the British Empire after World War II–out of control spending, an enormous welfare state, and huge borrowings from overseas. The historic Yankee optimism seems to be fading, and replaced by clouds of discouragement.

The famous American writer Henry David Thoreau once stated, "nothing is so much to be feared as fear." John Steinbeck in his book "America and Americans" stated, "now we face the danger in which the past has been most destructive to the human: success–plenty, comfort, and ever-increasing leisure. No dynamic people have ever survived these dangers" (written 45 years ago!).

Books now appear such as "The End of the American Century" by Stephen Schlossstein, or Dr. Jerome R. Corsi's, "The Late Great USA," which was on the New York Times Bestseller List (one chapter is entitled, "The U.S. in Twilight"). Cullen Murphy, in his book, "Are We Rome?" stated that America might follow Rome's demise because of our "corruption and arrogance." The former Comptroller General of the United States, David M. Walker, in a powerful speech on August 7, 2007 in Chicago, drew a parallel between the fall of the Roman Republic and the present situation in America. Mr. Walker claims that the collapse of ancient Rome was due to: "Declining moral values and political civility at home, an over confident and overextended military in foreign lands, and fiscal irresponsibility by the central government. Sound familiar?" Professor Garrett G. Fagan of Pennsylvania State University, in a brilliant 48 part video lecture series entitled "The History of Ancient Rome" stated that there are no universal answers why the Roman Empire in the West collapsed in 476 AD while the Eastern Roman Kingdom survived as the Byzantine Empire until 1453. Professor Fagan outlined some of the potential reasons for the demise of the Roman Empire including moral decadence, public corruption, a divided country and a wide gap between the rich and poor. Other experts included a lack of will and a rapidly growing bureaucracy as Roman problems. These issues are similar to the problems we are facing including our ever-increasing deficit, which continues our downward spiral of self-destruction. We literally live on Chinese money, and may eventually become their slaves. Is this the way to chase the American dream? House Majority leader John Boehner stated a day after the January 25, 2011 State of the Union speech by President Obama "the fact is, we are broke."

What is America all about? Morris Berman, in his book "The Twilight of American Culture," summarized the root of the problems relating to the decline of American civilization: "social inequality, increasing entitlements, decreasing intellectual ability (crumbling school systems), violent crimes and spiritual death, but we do not know until after the fact." Other headlines in recent years included "Danger Time America," "Empire's Collapse," "Is America Over a Barrel," and "The End of Exceptionalism." Sadly, a November 12, 2010 lead article in the Wall Street Journal summarized our present state of world status: "U.S. Wields Less Clout at Summit" (Group of 20 meetings in Seoul in November 2010). The "Situation Room with Wolf Blitzer" on November 12, 2010 reported, "there is a tendency to be more dismissive of the U.S." On the same day, Wall Street Journal's influential editorial page writer Stephen Moore stated on CNBC's "Kudlow Report" that "we (the U.S.) have lost our way." Furthermore, Bret Stephens of the Wall Street Journal stated it painfully on November 16, 2010: "we are now at risk of entering a period-perhaps a decade, perhaps a half-century—of global disorder, brought about by a combination of weaker U.S. might and even weaker U.S. will." Lastly, as early as 1987, according to Tom Peters' book "Thriving On Chaos," the U.K. Financial Times stated: "Can America Make It? A huge trade imbalance, a sliding currency, falling real wages and a dismal productivity record." The latest humiliation arrived in February 2011 when the Deutsche Boerse announced plans to acquire the NYSE.

In a two hour special entitled "Prophets of Doom" (History Channel, January 5, 2011), the panelists concluded that America would decline and meet its end. They cited as contributing factors: financial insolvency, living beyond our means, societal disintegration, infrastructure disrepair, collapsing home values, terrorism, etc. They were also concerned about overpopulation, depletion of natural resources, water shortages and a projected forthcoming energy crunch in America. I don't subscribe to this "End of Plenty" theory although the projected 8 billion world population by 2025 will require the expansion of cropland, continued increase in yields, and, hopefully the end of such silly EPA mandates to use ethanol in cars.

In a series of lectures in 1787 entitled "Decline and Fall of the Athenian Republic," Sir Alexander Tytler, Professor of History at the University of Edinburgh in Scotland, stated that great civilization progress through the following cycles:

- "From bondage to spiritual faith;

- From spiritual faith to great courage;

- From courage to liberty;

- From liberty to abundance;

- From abundance to complacency;

- From complacency to apathy;

- From apathy to dependence;

- From dependence back into bondage"

It appears that the U.S. is in the early stages of the abundance/complacency/apathy phases. Moreover, a large percentage of the U.S. population is in the dependency phase. We face a plethora of monumental challenges, and we don't have many friends. They have long forgotten America's billions in economic assistance after World War II, when the United States was the Bellsheep. In addition, Elvis Presley's famous gospel song means nothing to them: "When the Storms of Life Are Raging, Stand By Me."

Although America's achievements during the last 125 years have been astounding, anti "red, white and blue" sentiment is at an all-time high. As early as the 1890s, books appeared in Europe, such as the "American Invaders" and the "Americanization of the World" according to John Steele Gordon's compelling book "An Empire of Wealth: The Epic History of American Economic Power." People outside America often resent our dominance and claim that "Uncle Sam" uses his hegemonic strength recklessly and abuses its military power by intervening overseas needlessly. They also consider us too:

• Imperial ("Yankee" imperialism)

• Arrogant ("Bring it on" military philosophy)

• Powerful (too many footprints every place)

• Bullying

• Hyper-energetic

• Confrontational

• Disdainful of international organizations

• Braggadocios with no humility (Tocqueville also stated it)

• Faultless

• Shrill rhetoric during international crises

• Focused on get-rich quick versus the European get-rich step by step philosophy

• Uncaring about the environment

• Imposing our dominant culture on the rest of the world

• Overbearing in selling our style of democracy (some call it naiveté)

We also have racial problems, have inequality of wealth, are obsessed with moneymaking, have no self-restraint, are vastly overweight, and exhibit a certain degree of superficiality. Some also claim that we:

• Have bad manners

• Our moral values are deteriorating ("morally deficient")

• Are a litigious society

• Have exaggerated national pride

• Are addicted to shopping and don't know the word frugality

• Are too deep into debt ($14 trillion vs. $291 million in 1960)

• Have a gambling epidemic

• Are a gun toting society

• Are overmedicated

Following is my perception of the evolution of the characteristics of American society:

| CHARACTERS | 1840s | 1900 | 1945 | TODAY |
|---|---|---|---|---|
| -Poor Race Relations | Yes | Yes | Yes | ½ Yes |
| -Violet Society | ½ Yes | No | No | Yes |
| -Materialistic/Greedy | Yes | Yes | Yes | Yes |
| -Chauvinistic | No | No | Yes | Yes |
| -Decline in Moral Values | No | No | No | Yes |
| -Lack of Safety Net | Yes | Yes | ½ Yes | ½ Yes |
| -Health Care Crisis | Yes? | Yes? | No | ½ Yes |
| -Significant Wealth Gap | No | Yes | No | Yes |
| -Mediocre Public Schools | Yes | Yes | Yes | Yes |
| -Litigious Society | No | No | No | Yes |
| -Shopping Addiction | No | No | No | Yes |
| -Lack of Interest in Democratic Process | No | ½ Yes | ½ Yes | Yes |
| -External Threats | No | No | ½ Yes | Yes |
| -International Unilaterism | Yes | Yes | No? | Yes |
| -Interventionist Militarism | No | ½ Yes | Yes | Yes |
| -Government Fiscal Irresponsibility | No | No | No | Yes |
| -Powerful Unions | No | No | Yes | Yes |
| -Deindustrialization | No | No | No | Yes |
| -Large-Scale Outsourcing | No | No | No | Yes |
| -Lobbying Influence | No | No | No | Yes |

Comparing the traits of a primarily rural 1840s American society (only 15% urban) with only 23 million inhabitants to today's America of 310 million people, and a hard charging, high-tech industrial society with its ever-increasing job insecurity, moral decay (highest teen pregnancy among key Western countries) and serious external threats, is not an "apple to apple" comparison. Nevertheless, many of the positive American ethoses of the 1840s still resonate across Americana. However, the1840s society did not exhibit some of today's negative traits, which is not unusual because values evolve in a fluid democratic society.

Comparing the 1945 society with today's America, it appears that over 65 years ago there were fewer negative traits. (People also had a "sense of purpose.") Maybe that is why we said in postwar Germany, that America was Shangri-la and the streets were paved in gold (that's what lured me to America in 1957 at the age of 20). (We can't be transported to another time and maybe I am nostalgic, but I believe that the fabulous1950s and 1960s were a more idyllic time than today's hectic lifestyle despite the Soviet Union's menacing nuclear threat during the Cold War. Today, however, we are confronted by China, which is a powerful economic and military adversary.)

Another serious problem is the public school system in America, which ranks consistently low in international math and science scores. Powerful and unresponsive teacher unions, the general lack of parent engagement in the education of their children, and widespread public indifference are the possible causes.

Wealth disparity is another problem. The December 1, 2010 edition of the Wall Street Journal, using data from economist Edward Wolf of New York University, stated, that "the top 20% of Americans now own more than 85%

of the wealth in the U.S." As early as 1770, the top 20% of the population owned about two-thirds of the wealth in America, according to John Steele Gordon's excellent book, "An Empire of Wealth, the Epic History of American Economic Power." During Alexis De Tocqueville's visit in 1831 to the U.S., which led to one of the most important books ever written about America, "Democracy In America," he observed "I know of no other country where the love of money occupies as great a place in the hearts of men or where people are more deeply contemptuous of the theory of permanent equality of wealth." When asked in 1900 what the greatest menace of the new century is, President Schurman of Cornell University stated: "the exaltation, worship, and pursuit of money as the foremost good like," according to Mark Sullivan's provocative book, "Our Times." For example, "in 1890 the richest 1% of families controlled about one-half of the country's wealth and the richest 12 percent had 86%," according to Noel Jacob Kent's informative book, "America in 1900."

In its July 21, 2007 edition, the Financial Times stated that the United States is "growing richer and less equal." Further, "income inequality in the U.S. is at its highest since that most doom-laden of years: 1929" (April 8, 2008 Financial Times). Moreover, Paul Starr, in his book "Freedom Power," claims that the economic elite increasingly dominates U.S. politics; they seem to have the grasp of an octopus. It seems that Wall Street owns Washington whether under Republican or Democrat power.

Brink Lindsey, of the Cato Institute, in his remarkable book, "The Age of Abundance," claims that the rise in inequality can be attributed to "demographic and cultural changes." He included fewer married couple households, high divorce rates, increasing rates of out-of-wedlock births, and movement of women into the workforce as well as a more ethnically diverse society (Hispanics) with lower levels of socioeconomic achievement thus they are more economically unequal. The IMF stated that technology worsens inequality by increasing wages of highly trained people relative to the compensation of unskilled workers. President Bush, in an October 11, 2007 interview with the Wall Street Journal, stated "our society has had income inequality for a long time. Skills gaps yield income gaps." However, as William Gross of PIMCO stated in his February 2011 "Investment Outlook" letter, "how can bond traders make ten, one hundred, one thousand times more money than an engineer or social worker, given their dismal historical performance?" We need to build stuff in America instead of shuffling paper.

It appears that the super rich in America live in Shangri-la and buy such things as a $104 million sculpture and $107 billion Picasso painting (January 7, 2011 Wall Street Journal), a $52,500 Louis Vuitton handbag (September 8-9, 2007 Wall Street Journal), $8,000 bottles of wine and $100,000 custom-made beds (CNBC Television "Business News," August 26, 2007), $11.5 million bird book (December 8, 2010 Wall Street Journal), a $23 million small marble statue (December 8, 2010 CNN), $110 million painting (January 17, 2011 issue of Forbes), $700,000 power boats (September 14, 2007 CNBC "On the Money"), and $5 million-$10 million diamonds (December 9, 2007 CNBC "High Net Worth"). The lifestyle of some billionaires, America's new aristocracy, sounds like the life of the Roman nobility in the A.D. 100s or of the wealthy noblemen during the Feudal Age. However, as Professor Claude S. Fischer stated in his new book "Made in America," expanding wealth is a central force in American history."

Why are the stars aligned for the super wealthy? Knight Kiplinger outlined in "World Boom Ahead" the root causes for the increasing income inequality:

- It is linked to education; the pay premium for people with higher education is increasing at a rapid rate

- The continuing entrepreneurial boom is a major contributor to the widening gap

- Strong executive pay

- The number of affluent, highly educated dual earning couples is increasing

The present state of our affairs, however, faces severe headwinds. We are approaching transcendental challenges—a watershed period and "perfect storm," including potentially a new epoch of world power reorientation.

- The world is not our complete fiefdom anymore; the financial and political nucleus is shifting, and our influence in major crises is diminishing. The sphere of emerging autocracies, flush with money, such as China and Russia, is increasing and are potential Achilles heels for America. These are nations, which infringe on democracy and are striving for global emporium, and are aggressively challenging America's agenda.

- Ever increasing dependence on unreliable foreign oil. (Except for Mexico, Iraq and Norway, the other top producers are essentially autocratic regimes.) The present situation in America is even worse than during the 1973 oil crisis. For example, former friends such as Iran and Venezuela are now our foes. The headline in the January 24, 2011 edition of the Wall Street Journal summarized the situation: "Power in Energy Sector Shifts From the West." Moreover, OPEC revenues increased ten fold from the $80 billion ten years ago. As Donald Trump stated on a January 12, 2011 Fox News program with Neil Cavuto, "OPEC is draining the blood out of our country...they have unbelievable lobbyists (in the U.S.)." Moreover, contrary to the 1970s when Western Oil companies controlled oil reserves, today state-owned entities control the vast majority of oil reserves.

- A nonchalant and "who gives a hoot" frightening degree of complacency exists in America about our cloudy outlook. Sadly, many people seem to believe in the famous 1940s song "Manana" (Tomorrow) is soon enough for me." In addition, the "I want it all," lack of sacrifice, "something for nothing" and "live in the moment" mentality is becoming prevalent. Further, not many people seem to be anguished that we are bankrupting future generations that is due to the parallel fiscal and trade deficits, which are partially financed by unreliable overseas foes, such as China. The profligate spending will be exacerbated by the added financial burden when many of the 78 million baby boomers start retiring soon.

• Many Americans seem to be drifting with no clear vision and road maps for tomorrow except to enjoy life to the fullest today which bodes ill for our future.

• Continued gains by Radical Islam to destroy the Western world.

• Lackluster leadership in Washington. Can we ever find another transformative figure like George Washington who exemplified the principles of sacrifice, character and leadership? Moreover, today's motto in Washington seems to be the more laws they can pass the more power they have.

• A rapidly growing underclass, primarily consisting of tens of millions of unskilled and semi-skilled workers who are unemployable because of bleak job prospects. These workers often do not have the training, aspirational Kultur, or the desire to move upward into "new economy" jobs.

- Our personal freedom is under attack because of the ever-expanding government intrusion into our lives and into business affairs. It appears that there are not many government restraints left, and some authors already call the U.S. a "nanny state."

During the first sixty years of the 20th century, the U.S. had a carte blanche and was omnipotent and everybody was wooing the United States. America was the master of the universe and Yankeeism was widely admired and we had virtually no economic challengers. It appears that the U.S. was the world's best friend although heavily influenced by our generous economic aid. Today, America no longer has that total pre-eminence in the world. Our foes cheer the end of American triumphalism, and the power shift away from the United States to our archrivals. It is "sexy" to "talk down" America in Europe and the Middle East. There is great joy in many places that we are facing an epochal struggle, and our power is receding relative to the expanding strength of other nations, such as China, Russia and OPEC. The U.S. sphere of influence including moral leadership is declining in Latin America (rising socialism in many countries), Asia (because of China's influence), Africa (replaced by China) and the Middle East (Iraq War and growth of Radical Islam).

## The Positive Aspects of America

Yes, most of us don't live in Shangri-la or Camelot, and we can't follow the old American instrumental "Wrap Your Troubles in Dreams." Our paramount standing is slowly being overtaken by China. Nevertheless, I believe in this country, and as Lee Greenwood's great lyrics clearly state "I Am Proud to be an American."

Roger Pilon of the Cato Institute summarized America's beginning: "In 1776, America's Founders gathered in Philadelphia to draft the Declaration of Independence, which dissolved the political ties that had bound the American people to Great Britain. A new nation was thus born, free and independent, the United States of America. Eleven years later, in 1787, after American patriots had won our independence on the battlefield, many of the men who had met earlier in Philadelphia, plus others, met there again to draft a plan for governing the new nation, the constitution of the United States. In 1789, after the plan had been ratified, the new government was established."

White Anglo Saxon Protestant (WASP) Yankees formed America. These settlers are mainly responsible for the success the U.S. has achieved during the first 200 years since the founding of the first permanent English settlement in Jamestown, Virginia in 1606. Today, the WASP credo remains the key element of the identity of Americans and still infuses our culture. Subsequently, Catholics, Quakers and Jews followed, as well as others, such as Huguenots who were fleeing religious persecution in Europe.

The westward movement affected the American character ("go West young man, go West"). The template for subsequent generations of Americans is rooted in the frontier spirit, which inspired the "American Way of Life." The American fur traders also helped open the West although their mindset was on hunting beaver, buffalo, sea otters, etc. and buying pellets from the Indians. According to Eric Jay Dolin's 2010 book entitled "Fur Fortune, and Empire," the Hudson Bay Company (1670), and Jakob Astor's American Fur Company (1808) were leading corporations in the fur business.

The impetus of the manifest westward movement was the desire for greater opportunities and a yearning for material possessions as well to have more "elbowroom." The settlers believed in themselves—they were courageous, hard working, left the safety of civilization and risked everything they had. This exemplifies what is today called "rugged individualism." The pioneers were mostly self-educated and unskilled. They were often confronted with unique problems not encountered in the civilized world. To survive and to prosper, they had to have an adaptive and inquisitive mind—"Yankee tinkering"—still a common character in America today.

The rapid westward expansion between 1820 and 1850 led to transformational events. It soared to new heights in 1846 when "the nation was obsessed with territorial expansion, despite the external conflicts it could cause," according to Margaret C. S. Christman's interesting book, 1846: Portrait of the Nation." The U.S. achieved victory in the Mexican War with the Treaty of Guadalupe Hidalgo in 1848; the U.S. received more than 500,000 square miles of territory according to Kenneth C. Davis' 2010 book entitled "A Nation Rising." The Treaty led to Mexico ceding Arizona, California and New Mexico as well as the annexing of Texas. The British ceded Oregon during this period. (Today, the former territories of California and New Mexico constitute Arizona, Utah, Nevada, New Mexico, California and parts of Wyoming. In 1867, the U.S. acquired Alaska from Russia for two cents per acre.) When General Scott rode into Mexico City in 1847, it was the first time the U.S. flag had flown in the capital of a defeated foe. New York Morning News editor John L. O'Sullivan declared in 1845 that it was America's "Manifest Destiny" to control all of North America because of our "political and economic superiority." The westward expansion was completed in 1959 when Hawaii became the 50th State.

Professor Frederick J. Turner of the University of Wisconsin presented a paper on July 12, 1893 at Chicago's World Fair, entitled "Significance of the Frontier in American History." Professor Turner stated that what is defined as the "American Character" was profoundly influence by the movement into the frontier. He claimed that it created the great American spirit of confidence, independence, individual liberty, restless and nervous energy as well as the searching for new opportunities. Importantly, Professor Turner also theorized that the westward movement allowed Americans to create their own character and thus moving away from the influence of Europe, which had been the dominant power during the previous two hundred plus years. Professor Turner synthesized that wilderness life is the genesis of the American character:

• The availability of free land made Americans optimistic.

• The hardship of the frontier made them self-reliant and individualistic. Professor Landes, in his important book, "The Wealth and Poverty of Nation," similarly stated that frontier life became a "seedbed of democracy and enterprise. Equality bred self esteem, ambition, a readiness to enter and compete in the marketplace, a spirit of individualism and contentiousness; it also created technical self-sufficiency."

• As the frontier settlement advanced, it carried with it individualism, democracy and nationalism.

• Frontier life led to the desire to get by with a minimum of government.

The philosophy of enterprise dates back to Jamestown in 1606 when the first for profit company was established; this was the beginning of America's commercial heritage.

The philosophy is also consistent with President Abraham Lincoln's remarks on March 2, 1864 to the New York Workingmen's Democratic Republican Association. According to James Cornelious of the Abraham Lincoln Presidential Library he stated: "property is the fruit of labor–property is desirable, is a positive good in the world; that some should be rich, shows that others may become rich, and hence is just encouragement to industry and enterprise. Let not him who is houseless pull down the house of another; but let him labor diligently and build one for himself."

The United States consists of a mosaic of people. One hundred percent are immigrants or their descendants (almost 34 million immigrants arrived between 1820-1972, according to World Book Encyclopedia). Most of them left because Europe had a stratified society. As memorialized in the folk song, they were all "Bound for the Promised Land," including myself. (My American wife keeps telling me that I only listen to the "music of the past" including the beloved African-American spirituals.) Not until roughly thirty years ago, did highly educated people, especially scientists, researchers and entrepreneurs, started to immigrate in large numbers to America. They come to the United States because of the immense leading-edge technological opportunities and venture capital available in the United States of America.

America should be respected for its open-door policy, its religious freedom, its unmatched generosity, its institutions and traditions, its dynamic nature, and as Ralph Waldo Emerson wrote in an essay about "American Civilization" in the April, 1862 edition of the Atlantic, and reprinted in "The American Idea, The Best of the Atlantic Monthly," "America is another word for opportunity." People still queue up to come to America by the countless millions—the Promised Land. This includes twelve to twenty four million illegal immigrants who have entered the U.S. during the last twenty-five years for a better life. Thousands continue to cross into the U.S. illegally each day. Over 40 million first generation immigrants live in the U.S. today or seven million more than in 2000. More than one million people become naturalized citizens each year compared with 100,000's in 1960s. According to "Diversity News," over 15 million people applied for the U.S. government's green-card lottery (5.5 million in 2005). One hundred thousand immigrants become U.S. citizens each year on July 4.

Americans can keep their heads high because the United States of America:

- It is not an empire builder, and never established permanent colonies.

- Rescued Europe from fascism over 60 years ago.

- Saved Greece and Turkey from communist subversion.

- Single-handedly financed Western Europe's recovery after World War II through the Marshall Plan, and didn't remain as a military conqueror, unlike Rome.

- Was in the frontline guiding West Germany and Japan to democracy after WW II.

- Saved South Korea from a communist takeover.

- Through the "Reagan (an American original) Doctrine" in the 1980s, the Soviet Union collapsed which liberated the Soviet Union satellites. (It was like the famous Southern gospel song "When the Saints Go Marching In.")

- Displayed a high degree of selflessness by providing hundreds of billions of dollars in foreign—unmatched in history.

- Pioneered the digital revolution 30 years ago, and started the biotech revolution at the same time.

I am an eternal student of America who has lived in all four corners of this great country. Moreover, I have studied the country from an outside and inside perspective. I readily admit that the "American Empire" is presently facing countless challenges and that the outlook is cloudy. I believe, however, in America's resilience. This makes the story of Ford Motor Company's remarkable recovery from turmoil in 2006 to the top of the class and respectability an American story. It is also the story of the United States of America.

America's staying power has been tested many times during violent winds, starting with the War of Independence, and more recently during the 20th century.

- World War I

- 1929 Stock market Crash

- The Great Depression

- World War II

- Korean War

- 1961 Cuban Missile Crisis (John F. Kennedy's finest hour)

- Vietnam War (the enemy, however, claimed victory)

- 1973 Oil crisis (OPEC brought home the bacon)

- 1990 Gulf War (the senior Bush dropped the ball)

- 9/11 World Trade Center Disaster (my comments can't be printed)

- Iraq War (foolish or necessary?)

- Afghanistan War (foolish or necessary?)

America's traditional character of courage and determination was severely tested during the early years of World War II when the United States was confronted with mammoth historic national and international challenges. The war economy created an expanding middle class and 17 million jobs and over 60% of women were working. According to a rebroadcast of an actual news report from November 17, 1945, "the average income of workers virtually doubled between 1941 and 1945 to $2,390 (DirectTV,

November 17, 2007, XM channel 801, 40s"). (In attempting to understand the American psyche during World War II, I have listened frequently to this channel because it re-broadcasts the news of the day in the 1940s. The news also contained a "War Report." In addition to mentioning Allied victories, the news also mentioned German and Japanese battle victories on that day using such words as "the Japanese continued their conquering ways" or the "German air force made a surprise attack." It leaves me speechless that there was this freedom of speech in America. In Germany, the state-owned Deutschland Sender controlled all the one-sided news. If somebody wanted to hear a balanced picture, he had to listen to the British BBC, which was illegal.)

# Hip, Hip, Hooray for America

The United States has many other positive traits, as summarized below:

- Despite strident anti-Americanism around the world, America remains a magnet to the world and still welcomes "your tired and poor."

- We live in an open society. Also, the U.S. is still a young country, yet it has the longest continuing democracy in the world without imperial rule. Moreover, compared with the rapidly aging populations in Europe and Japan, the U.S. has a young population.

- The American people:

  ☐ Live in "the land of the free and the home of the brave."

  ☐ Are proud to live in the United States (80% believe that the U.S. is the greatest country in the world; they don't go on overseas "apology tours" and are not ashamed of their country).

  ☐ Are individualistic. We have 310 million different opinions, which is why some political scientists claim that the U.S. doesn't have an agenda.

  ☐ Never imposed their will on anybody.

  ☐ Have unbelievable vitality.

  ☐ Enjoy freedom of worship (religious minorities are not subject to persecution and are able to practice their religion).

☐      Have a pervasive sense of responsibility. The U.S. has never wavered from this commitment. (America lost 406,000 soldiers in World War II, with another 600,000 wounded in fighting fascism. America lost 37,000 soldiers during the Korean conflict and 38,000 in Vietnam.)

☐      There is no such thing as the divine right of birth. "Perseverance, energy and talent are the key to success in America" (guide for newly arrived German immigrants in 1840 based in Steven Ozment's book "Mighty Fortress"). Further, as the Declaration of Independence stated: "We hold these Truths to be self-evident, that all Men are created equal, that they are endowed by their Creator with certain unalienable rights, that among these are Life, Liberty and Pursuit of Happiness."

☐      Volunteer on a massive scale for good causes, and are compassionate.

☐      Have demonstrated empathy for underdogs.

☐      Are extremely generous (a lifetime cause celebre). The United States of America provides over $40 billion in financial aid annually to poor countries. (The OPEC countries, with $900 billion in yearly oil revenues have a despicable charity record.) Moreover, according to Giving USA, philanthropic giving in the U.S. totals roughly $310 billion annually. Further, according Charities And Foundation, American charitable giving totals over 1.5% of GDP (in Germany it is equal to approximately 0.2% of GDP and less than 0.2% in France).

☐      Live in a multicultural society.

☐      Are resilient and have great survival skills.

☐      Are innovative and risk-takers and entrepreneurial, which is an inspiration to young people around the world to copy the model. However, our system of capitalism is not perfect and often focuses on near-term results. The latest example is Pfizer's decision to cut its R&D budget by discharging over 5,000 employees and initiating a major share buy-back program to lift its stock price, which analysts strongly supported (February 2, 2011 Wall Street Journal).

☐      Reward those who have the talent, energy and perseverance. One of my favorite songs of the 1950s by Les Paul and Mary Ford says it clearly: "How High the Moon" is the horizon for go-getters.

☐      Have no rigid class system and provide upward mobility opportunities regardless of race, religion or national origin.

Stephen Schlossstein in his book "The End of the American Century," mentioned other key elements of the American character: "An uncompromising ideological commitment to representative government and individual freedom and liberty.

☐ An incredible diverse and resilient society capable of unmatched entrepreneurial energy, vitality and skill.

☐ A market second to none in responsiveness, flexibility and unparalleled inventiveness.

☐ A vibrant multi racial society and ability, because of these, to attract the very best people regardless of nationality, irrespective of class and religion and race from all over the world."

- A fundamentally positive characteristic is the parity of women in the United States. America has always been in the vanguard and a trailblazer of this movement. This is especially important considering the anti-modern culture and lack of freedom and basic rights of women in extreme Muslim countries. World War II brought millions of women into the workforce. However, even by 1970 they represented only 8% of medical degrees and 5% of law degrees. Since then, a paradigm shift has taken place, and women have effectively broken the "glass ceiling." Today, women are close to parity in degrees conferred in the important fields of medicine (46%) and law (49%). Women have also achieved significant advancements in the business world, with Ford Motor Company a prime example of the new powerful role of female business executives.

- The U.S. has the top universities in the world, which helped the U.S. capture more Nobel laureates than any other country since World War II. According to a major study by Shanghai Jiao Tong University, the United States of America has 17 of the top 20 universities in the world.

- America has the world's top medical centers, although we constantly hear about the "breakdown" of the U.S. health-care system.

- The U.S. has a mega of cultural institutions—over 5,000 well-stocked libraries plus the leading museums in the world.

- In commerce, U.S. unstructured laissez-faire capitalism, entrepreneurialism and business model has resulted in:

    ☐        The triumph of capitalism, and free-market principles, with the newest members being China, Russia and India although they practice their own form of capitalism.

    ☐        World leadership in leading-edge enterprises, technological sophistication and a future-oriented focus.

    ☐        Constant search for new ideas as exemplified by the U.S. led digital and biotech revolution during the last thirty years.

    ☐        Ability to attract the brightest talent from around the world, especially to Silicon Valley.

- The U.S. has a growing population (400 billion by 2050), and an abundance of natural resources. It is also one of the major food baskets of the world exporting roughly $120 billion annually.

In commerce, nothing exemplifies the American character of "tinkering geniuses" more than the venturing and nurturing of embryonic enterprises. No country in the world has the venture capital system, which exists in the United States. Microsoft, Apple, Google, eBay, Yahoo, Dell Amazon, YouTube, MySpace, Facebook, PayPal, etc., etc. are the most recent venture capital success stories (CNBC reported on September 9, 2007 that "400,000 people make their living on eBay").

Technical innovations and creative entrepreneurship is the lifeblood of the United States, which constantly creates new economic opportunities. U.S. Research & Development expeditures total 2.6% of GDP compared with 1.4% in China and 2.5% in Germany. America is the global technology pacesetter, which is part of the American character and dates back to the 19th century, including the following firsts:

• Telegraph (1844)

• Telephone (1876)

• Phonograph (1877)

• Electricity (1879)

• Skyscrapers (1884)

- Airplanes (1903)

- Mass-production of cars (1908)

- Transistors (1947)

- Moon landing (1969)

In recent years, America's competitive society has created leading-edge technology enterprises, which have produced a potpourri of innovative and useful products. This continues to demonstrate America's penchant for innovation with large contributions from immigrants (especially from Asia) and even college dropouts, such as Steve Jobs, Bill Gates or Mark Zuckerberg of Facebook. On June 18, 2007, the most venerable daily U.S. business journal–the Wall Street Journal summarized recent developments: "thirty years ago, the U.S. led digital revolution commenced with the introduction of the personal computer, the Apple II. In its wake came the MacIntosh, Windows and America On Line; Play Stations and Xboxes; Palm Pilots and digital cameras; Ipods and Smart Phones and Internet; and now Iphones." This ability is a fundamental U.S. asset.

We can't relive the booming 1950s and 1960s. Yes, the United States faces challenging headwinds. However, America is not passé; we can soar again, and have a "Rendezvous with Destiny," a term used by Franklin D. Roosevelt in 1936 and by the late President Reagan. I believe in America, and totally agree with Chuck Berry's 1960s song: "I am happy living in the U.S.A." Even after being here for over 55 years, I am still intoxicated about the United States of America. (During my many years stationed overseas on business, it felt wonderful coming back home to America. As the words in A. Dvorak's symphony states "Goin'Home, Goin'Home To Stay.") It may sound corny, but I love this country and to paraphase Stevie Wonders' greatest hit "You'r (America) the Sunshine of My Life." GOD BLESS AMERICA.

# ATTACHMENT II

✠ ✠ ✠

## THE RULERS OF THIS CENTURY

### Overview

China's 1.3 billion people represent about 19% of the world's 7 billion inhabitants (3 billion in 1960), and roughly 7% of the earth's land area. (10% of the planet's arable land according to the January 2011 issue of National Geographic.) One thousand years ago, the Song Dynasty was the most advanced nation in the world. As late as 1820, China had the biggest economy in the world, according to a 1995 study by Angus Maddison entitled, "Monitoring the World Economy 1820-1992." [111] The great American orator and reformer, Wendell Phillips, stated around 1870 that the Chinese are: "a race as bold, as indomitable, as indestructible as the Yankees." Professor Niall Ferguson of Harvard University claimed in an extensive article in the November 20-21, 2010 edition of the Wall Street Journal entitled "In China's Orbit" stated "by 1820 U.S. per capita GDP was trice that of China; by 1870 it was nearly five times greater."

The new 21st century de facto superpower clearly will be China. Two separate headlines in the January 12, 2011 edition of the Wall Street Journal tell the story: "China Shows Its Growing Might." Equally menacing, "New Move to Make Yuan a Global Currency." China even tested a new stealth fighter (reportedly developed with secret U.S. technology) during Robert Gates' January 2011 China visit, which the U.S. had previously predicted wouldn't be on the scene until 2020! To me, this was a frightening display of "assertive Chinese nationalism," especially by its military leadership. Moreover, four headlines in the January 18 & 19, 2011 edition of the Wall Street Journal also tell the new Chinese story: "The New Era of U.S.-China Rivalry," "Dealing With an Assertive China," "Beijing's Influence Grows;" and "China Flexes Its Clout." This police state doesn't even make an attempt to keep the genie in the bottle, which demonstrates how self-assured they are! In my opinion, Communist China wants nothing less than to celebrate "We Are the World." The latest Chinese squeeze play against the West is export restrictions of the all-important rare-earth metals.

A subheading in Professor Ferguson's essay cited above summarized the outlook crisply:" After 500 years of Western predominance...the world is tilting back to the East." In its November 2010 issue, Forbes named Chinese President Hu Jintao the most powerful person in the world, ahead of President Barack Obama! The November 22, 2010 edition of the Wall Street Journal stated that China's standard of living has "grown at a rate where they double every decade...a rate of growth...that is unprecedented." Fred Smith Chairman and CEO of FedEx, stated in the December 20, 2010 CNBC Squawk Box program that China is "assertive and aggressive." As Hitler did, China limits personal and religious liberty, which the Communist regime perceives as a threat to its dictatorial power (remember the tanks at Tiananmen Square in 1989). Despite President Hu Jintao's lip service at the joint United States-China January 19, 2011 presidential press conference stating "work still needs to be done in China in terms of human rights," China is actually retrenching regarding human rights. They are not concerned about the political heat from the West for their human rights record. As Secretary of State Hillary Rodham Clinton stated in an important speech on January 14, 2011, China censors bloggers, harasses or imprisons political activists, denies freedom of worship and sends legal advocates to prison for representing clients who challenge the government's positions. In my opinion, China seems to becoming more belligerent as its economic and military power reaches new heights!! We have to watch our back because China holds all the leverage, and now has the upper hand against the West.

It appears that China has no inhibitions dealing with unsavory and pariah regimes and trading with tyrants and murderous regimes such as Iran, North Korea, Burma,

Zimbabwe, Angola and Sudan where Arab Islamist militias commit large-scale and unspeakable genocidal campaigns against black Christians. China reportedly has invested an estimated $6 billion in Sudan's oil infrastructure. Supposedly, there are several hundred thousand Chinese in Africa working on Chinese projects. The Chinese appear to be the new colonists in Africa. Promoting human rights and democracy in these countries is of no concern to them. On the day of Chinese President Hu Jintao's official U.S. state visit (January 19, 2011), the Wall Street Journal revealed that a Chinese company signed a $2 billion deal in North Korea, one of the "Axis of Evil's" members. It demonstrated China's "in your face" diplomacy. I have no doubt that China is watching with satisfaction as the United States is bankrupting itself with wars in Iraq and Afghanistan while China is buying-up critical commodities and natural resource companies around the world including in our own backyard (Canada). (Boone Pickens stated on the February 28, 2011 Bloomberg "Surveillance Midday" program that China is tying-up $200 billion in oil around the world.) As Gideon Rachman, Chief Foreign Affairs commentator of the prestigious Financial Times stated in the January/February 2011 edition of Foreign Policy magazine," America's appeal also might be diminished if the country (U.S.) is no longer so closely associated with opportunism, prosperity, and success."

The power is clearly shifting to China, and they could eventually control our destiny and dictate terms to America. They have hundreds of billions in U.S. dollar assets, and U.S. Treasury bills. Chinese institutions threatened to use what they call the "nuclear option" to commence a massive sell-off of their vast U.S. dollar and government bond holdings if the U.S. imposes trader barriers on Chinese goods. On November 7, 2007 China threatened to "dump" its U.S. dollar holdings after Congress announced plans for tough safety regulations. They consider their U.S. holdings as a "bargaining chip." If they implement the strategy, this would seriously disrupt our financial markets. It is unlikely that China would throw us under the bus and doubtful they would use the "nuclear option" because China's job creation and rapidly rising wealth is heavily derived from the export sector. Nevertheless, China seems to have no inhibitions to demonstrate its new global power. China is not impressed by our continuing gesture of friendship and efforts to achieve détente. The U.S. acts like "babes in toyland" vis-à-vis China. The Zeit fuer Zaertlichkeit (time for being nice) is gone.

Communist China is becoming assertive militarily and is expanding at an alarming rate (a CNN "Lou Dobbs Tonight" panel on September 9, 2007, concluded that China is using the funds it is generating from U.S. trade to build-up its "blue water" fleet). Reportedly, China is conducting extensive military and industrial espionage in America.

The United States-China Economic and Security Review Commission concluded in 2007 "Chinese espionage now comprises the single greatest threat to U.S. technology."

There are 2.3 million people in China's military compared with approximately 1.6 million in the U.S., according to an MSNBC report (January 20, 2011 Dylan Ratigan Show). There is a frightening and growing military threat from China directed at the United States. Their objective is to weaken and undermine America, and to infiltrate our Allies (a Major General of Taiwan was recently arrested for spying for China).

Another emerging threat to the "American Way of Life" is the growing alliance between Russia and the People's Republic of China–a marriage of convenience between two rising giants who are aggressively buffeting us. Both countries are actively pursuing a shift in the world order away from America. Their value systems are contrary to our democratic ideals and they would have no inhibitions to bring us to our knees. Russia is like the Phoenix rising again from the ashes and is re-emerging after the humiliating defeat of the Soviet Union during the Cold War, followed by the chaos of the 1990s including Russia's financial collapse in the late 1990s. Today, Russia is again a resurgent political, economic and belligerent military power and is slowly returning to Stalin's "Polizeistaaat" (dictatorship). It still has the historic dream of dominating Europe; the time under a new modern-day Czar called Putin. They consider the West, especially America, as their natural enemy. Former President Gorbachev recently called Russia an "imitation" democracy.

Russia has started to re-assert its military power and the saber rattling of the defeated Soviet Union has returned. Since Putin took over in 2000, Russian military expenditures have quadrupled, according to an October 14, 2007 report on ABC Television's "World News Sunday." Russia has put its long-range bombers back on regular patrol for the first time since the breakup of the Soviet Union. Russia has developed a new class of nuclear submarines and a new generation of nuclear missiles. MacLean, the respected Canadian newsweekly, asked in its September 3, 2007 issue, if Putin is creating a "neo-fascist, ultra-nationalist monster that may soon lurch out of control?" Moreover, the publication is asking, "can anyone control the forces the Russian president has unleashed?"

## Economic Powerhouse

China is the envy of the West, and is steaming ahead with a burning desire to succeed. In my opinion, their global intention is to replace the U.S. as the number one world military, political and economic power. The engine, which drives the train, is the economy. China's economy is firing on all cylinders. U.S. and Europe seem to be out of steam. China is hungry and dynamic and its economic model is working well. China has the dynamism America had a century ago!

China's economy has been growing at an average annual rate of approximately 10% during the last 30 years and the sky is the limit with this unfettered growth (10.3% in 2010). Lee Kuan Yew, the Minister Mentor of Singapore stated in the December 20, 2010 issue of Forbes that China can maintain its 10% annual growth rate for at least another decade. One number tells the whole story in a nutshell: "Six of the world's 10 largest ports are now in China, up from two in 1999" (Fortune, November 15, 2010). The chairman of the Board of Governors of the Federal Reserve System, Ben Bernanke, stated in a December 15, 2006 speech in Beijing "the emergence of China as a global economic power is one of the most important developments of recent decades." This encapsulates China today, which surpassed Japan as the world's second largest economy in 2010, and now is the world's largest exporter ahead of German (in 2000, China ranked sixth in

GDP). Clearly, the epicenter is shifting to China, and they have achieved "The Impossible Dream." For example, in 1975 China's GDP was $161 million compared with a U.S. GDP of $1.6 trillion. By 2010, China's GDP had increased to $5.9 trillion (Japan $5.5 trillion and $14.7 trillion for the U.S.). Goldman Sachs forecasts that China will overtake the U.S. in terms of GDP in 2027. However, China's 2010 GDP per capita at $7,400 ranks only number 128 in the world ($47,000 U.S. per capita in the U.S.).

The world is racing to this mega country and is welcomed by a business-friendly government although 71% of U.S. companies in China cite regulations as the top hurdle doing business there (CNBC, January 19, 2011). Moreover, "U.S. firms decry China's Heavy Hand" (January 19, 2011 Wall Street Journal). Nevertheless, almost 22,000 "foreign funded" enterprises were established during a 12 months period in China, according to a Chinese language newscast on CNBCW Television's "Managing China," on August 22, 2007. Moreover, total foreign direct investment in China in 2009 totaled about $90 billion, and is projected at $100 billion in 2010. U.S. investment in China ($50 billion) represents only approximately 5% of China's total foreign investment. The Secretary General of the WTO stated on a January 27, 2011 program on CNBC from Davos "China is the assembler of the world."

The Chinese economic miracle exceeds the vitality of the "Wirtschaftswunder" Germany and Japan experienced, starting in the early1950s. The nexus of the Chinese growth is the sweeping market-oriented reforms the late Chairman Deng Xiaoping introduced about thirty years ago. In the process, China has created a middle class of over 300 million. China has a working-age population of over 820 million; the unemployment rate is only about 4%. China achieved its economic rebirth in a single generation. Plutus, the Greek God of wealth, would have been proud of China.

China seems to practice 18th and 19th century mercantilism (a nation's wealth increases by exporting goods). China had a trade surplus of about $275 billion in 2010, compared with $10 billion in 1990 and $84 billion in 2000. This is resulting in a serious anti-Chinese campaign in the United States. About 19% of U.S. imports are from China; U.S. exports to China constitute only 7% of American exports. Astoundingly, China's worldwide exports increased from $195 billion in 2000 to $1.5 trillion in 2010 (CIA World Factbook).

China's foreign currency reserves total a world record of over $2.9 trillion compared with $125 billion about 25 years ago. China holds $1.2 trillion of U.S. Treasuries ($400 billion five years ago). China holds all the trump cards. The emerging power of China and other major emerging countries can also be illustrated by Michael Milken's comments, Chairman of the Milken Institute, on December 14, 2010 CNBC's Closing Bell that the stock market value of the U.S., Europe and Japan has decreased from 94% to 63% now, and eventually to 40%.

In an outstanding report from Beijing on November 16, 2010 in the Wall Street Journal by Jason Dean, Andrew Browne and Shai Oster entitled "China's State Capitalism Sparks a Global Backlash," they stated that "central to China's approach are policies that champion state-owned firms and other so called national champions, seek aggressively to obtain advanced technology, and manage its exchange rate to benefit exporters." In Secretary Clinton's January 14, 2011 speech in Washington, she stated China must "end unfair discrimination against U.S. and other foreign companies or against their innovative technologies; to remove preferences for domestic firms."

The quality of life is extremely poor in China, but it is instrumental in providing China with significant competitive advantages:

- A dedicated and hard-working labor force similar to the first class worker bees in Japan and South Korea. In addition, China has extremely low manufacturing labor costs of about $400 per month.[112] This is the linchpin of China's export success, and the foundation of its competitive edge.

- Highly educated employees. China consistently ranks in the top of worldwide high-school science and math tests scores (Finland, Singapore and South Korea usually in the top five; the U.S. is around number 20).

- Virtually no fringe benefits such as health-care and pensions, which add an additional 34% to U.S. manufacturing sector labor costs. According to Ben Bernanke's December 15, 2006 speech in Beijing, "only about 14 percent of the population in China is covered by health insurance, and pension plans apply to only about 16 percent of the economically active population." [113] (This is contrary to Bismarck who established the first modern welfare state in the 1870s, which many other countries subsequently followed.)

- No labor unions comparable to the West. However, employment laws enacted in late 2007 provide Chinese "unions" with a slightly enhanced role. Moreover, in 2010, for the first time, workers in auto parts plants and electronic factories have openly challenged the central government's authority and conducted strikes without the government-controlled labor union's approval.

- Anecdotal evidence appears to indicate that Chinese companies can quickly ramp up production.

- Currency manipulation; the yuan is tightly "managed" and kept artificially low which gives Chinese exporters a price advantage on world markets. According to a November 8, 2010 article in Barron's by Leslie P. Norton, the Chinese yuan is overvalued "by as much as 40%." President Obama stated during the January 19, 2011 joint press conference with President Hu Jintao "trade must be conducted on a level playing field."

- Lax safety and environmental standards reminiscent of similar conditions during the 19th century in the West. China appears to have little interest in climate change because this modus operandi gives China a distinct competitive advantage. The January 15, 2008 edition of the Wall Street Journal stated, "in China, workers making goods for American consumers have long borne the brunt of a global manufacturing system that puts cost cutting ahead of safety." The November 20, 2007 PBS "News Hour with Jim Lehrer" included an extensive interview with Loretta Tofani of the Salt Lake Tribune who had written a series of articles about "American Imports, Chinese Death." She described the unbelievable safety and environmental conditions and environmental mayhem in Chinese factories. During his state visit to China in late November 2007, President Nicholas Sarkozy of France called for "more balanced trade and environmentally sustainable development" (November 25, 2007 CNN Television). According to an August 9, 2007 report on CNN, "pollution kills 400,000 people annually in China." A World Bank report claims that 750,000 people die yearly in China from pollution. A 1998 World Health Organization report stated that China has seven of the worlds ten most polluted cities. (China recently introduced new product safety and anti-pollution regulations.)

- Artificially cheap capital according to the European Union. Also, an extensive array of illegal export subsidies. A major study presented in 2008 at the prestigious U.K. Royal Economics Society by Nottingham University concluded that China provided its companies with $310 billion in "production subsidies" between 1995-2005. Further, according to the January 12, 2011 edition of the Wall Street Journal, the Chairman of the Export- Import Bank stated that the Chinese "are not playing by the rules." In his 1776 book "Wealth of Nations," Adam Smith warned against government subsidies.

- An ocean of credit lines by Chinese state-owned banks to China's IBM-size telecommunications-equipment manufacturers not available to European competitors (EU Commission January 2011 findings).

- Inadequate intellectual property protection; this leads to large-scale piracy in China. President Obama used the word "theft" in describing the problem during his press conference on January 19, 2011 with President Hu Jintao. The February 9, 2011 edition of The Street.com claims that the U.S. is getting tough on China industrial spying. It's a pipe dream—we filed a mere dozen or so trade secret or industrial espionage cases during the last ten years. The AP reported on February 10, 2011 that China's Internet hackers stole sensitive Western oil company information and that Internet crime is "pervasive." Supposedly, the hackers are linked to China's military. (According to Gavin Weightman's 2007 book "The Industrial Revolutionaries," there were foreign spies in 18th century Britain "to unearth the secrets of Britain's industrial success.")

- Asia is also flooding the U.S. and Europe with counterfeit products; 81% come from China. The associated loss of American jobs is estimated at 750,000 according to the U.S. Chamber of Commerce on CNN "Lou Dobbs Tonight" (August 22, 2007). Reportedly, Chinese counterfeiters cause $20 billion in lost annual profits in the U.S. and $135 billion in lost sales (January 20, 2011 Fox News "Happening Now"). Further, the October 8, 2007 edition of Automotive News stated that the Chinese government "gives lip service to intellectual property rights." The February 2, 2011 headline really tells the Chinese economic warfare against the West: "U.S. Firms, China Are Locked In Major War Over Technology" (effectively stealing the inventions of other nations).

Over 100 years ago, America was on top of the world–the power to be feared. However, even at that time, Samuel Gompers, the first President of the American Federation of Labor, when asked what is "the greatest menace of the new Century?" he stated that he "was concerned about oriental competition against American labor," according to Mark Sullivan's landmark book, "Our Time" published in 1926. Unfortunately, it has become reality today because our power is receding. China's leaders clearly understand that industrialism equals wealth equals military power equals influence equals world domination and equals destruction of political enemies.

The template of the Chinese economic strategy is the "playbook" Japan utilized successfully starting approximately 50 years ago. China is even copying the renowned Japanese Ministry of International Trade and Industry (MITI). It was MITI, which established strategic industrial priorities in cooperation with the nation's key industrial enterprises (automobiles, machine tools, semiconductors, etc.). Chinese government officials direct the country's economic development through five-year plans, but reportedly, there is slow movement away from central planning.

(Japan's economy recorded average annual GDP increases of roughly 8% in the 1950s to the mid 1980s. Futurists predicted continued rapid economic growth for the 125 million Japanese people. However, the bubble burst in 1989 and the economic engine has sputtered along at only 2.0% average annual rate between 1988-1997 and at roughly the same rate since then. The Japanese industrial strategy included virtually free capital, low wages in the early years, and manipulation of the yen although there is very little interference today. The economy was booming with full employment. Japan utilized non-tariff barriers to protect the domestic industry, and focused totally on an export-oriented strategy including export subsidies. There was also a lack of pollution controls, which I experienced myself on trips to Japan. The highly successful Japanese strategy resulted in severe economic frictions between the U.S. and Japan, similar to what is happening today between the U.S. and China. Today, the Japanese are strongly attacking Korea for its currency intervention. The headline in the October 16, 2010 edition of the New York Times portrays Japan's new face: "Japan goes from Dynamic to Disheartened." Further, according to the December 15, 2010 edition of the Wall Street Journal, China surpassed Japan in R&D spending in 2010. Surprisingly, Germany is showing signs of solid recovery with unemployment at the lowest level since 1992.)

In September 2010, China's State Council announced the seven strategic sectors the country will focus on during the 2011-2015 Five Year Plan. Reportedly, by 2020 it is China's aim to be the world's technology leader. Clearly, the following are the industries of the future.

• Alternative-fuel cars

• Alternative energy

• Biotechnology

• Information Technology

• High-end manufacturing

• Advanced materials

• Environmental protection

China is becoming the global manufacturing center, and is encouraging its companies to expand abroad, which is already a major thrust. According to the September 27, 2010 edition of Fortune magazine, China already has three of the top ten global corporations compared with two each for the U.S. and Japan. Further, according to the May 10, 2010 issue of Forbes, China is the home of two of the top six global companies in terms of profits and market value! Moreover, in 2010, "Chinese companies completed 3,235 acquisitions valued at $190 billion... more than other nation except the U.S." (January 3, 2011, Wall Street Journal, page R1). Similar to the classic 1966 "Cold War" comedy "The Russians Are Coming, The Russians Are Coming," the next battle cry in the world will be a real story: "<u>The Chinese are Coming, the Chinese are Coming</u>." Volvo was the first major Chinese overseas automotive acquisition. This was followed by the mid-2010 purchase of GM's giant Saginaw Steering Gear unit with 8,300 employees and 1,000 patents by China's Pacific Century Motors. The Wall Street Journal rightfully described it as "A Landmark Deal for this Era" in its November 9, 2010 edition. Concurrently, according to the New York Times (January 19, 2011), China provides "state subsidies to favored domestic companies" and the Chinese "so-called indigenous laws (are) meant to favor homegrown businesses."

As Japan did about 40 years ago, the next step is for China to climb the technology ladder. Airbus is already building a factory in China, and Cessna announced that it is building a new plane in China because of significantly lower costs than in the U.S. The Wall Street Journal reported on November 16, 2010 that China "unveiled a mockup of a large passenger jet to compete with Boeing and Airbus." It appears that the Chinese are not afraid to enter into industries with historically high entry barriers. Therefore, within less than ten years, China will move from textiles and toys (as Japan did), and export sophisticated, high-quality, technological advanced products and automobiles. China has the human resources to continue its economic growth. China graduates about 500,000 engineers annually, while the U.S. graduates roughly 78,000 (128,000 Chinese presently study in the U.S.). According to Fareed Zakari's excellent article in the October 18, 2010 issue of Time magazine, the number of students enrolled at Chinese universities increased from one million in 1997 to 5.5 million in 2007.

## The Chinese Automotive Industry

The world was astounded in 2009 when Chinese automotive sales exceeded U.S. levels for the first time in history. China sold almost 14 million vehicles compared with U.S. sales of about 10 million units (the lowest level since 1967). It was a seismic event! In 2010, Chinese auto sales totaled 18.1 million; they are projected at 19 million in 2011. As late as 1980, Chinese vehicle output totaled only 200,000 units, increasing to 500,000 units by 1990. By 2002, sales increased to 3.3 million, and reaching 4.6 million in 2003. By 2007, sales advanced to 9.2 millions.

The Chinese automotive industry consists of about 80 manufacturers. [114] The November 1, 2010 article in Fortune magazine entitled "China Charges into Electric Cars cited a Booz & Company report which claims that China has about 120 auto companies. The chairman of Ford's partner in China, Changan Automobile Company, stated that about 160 makers produce cars in China according to a dispatch from China by the Wall Street Journal (October 25, 2010). This compares to 12 in the United States. Domestic auto companies' control roughly 30% of the market; with BYD the largest locally owned company. However, as shown below, foreign companies play the leading role through their joint ventures with domestic auto companies. [115]

| Company[a] | 2009 Market Share |
|---|---|
| VW/FAW [b] | 13.0% |
| GM/SAIC | 9.0 |
| Toyota/FAW Group | 7.5 |
| Hyundai/Beijing Automotive | 7.0 |
| Honda/Guang Zhou | 6.5 |
| Nissan/Dongfeng | 6.0 |
| BYD (independent) | 5.0 |
| Cherry (independent) | 5.0 |
| Kai | 3.2 |
| Suzuki/Changan | 2.8 |
| FAW | 2.6 |
| Geely (independent) | 2.6 |
| Ford/Changan | 2.6 |

[a] Only lists key Chinese partners
[b] Also has major venture with Shanghai Automotive Industry Corporation

The Chinese auto market increased by over 20% annually between 2005 and 2009. What is a sustainable level? Straight-lining extrapolations would generate sales of 59 million units by 2017, which is unrealistic. J.D. Powers & Associates and Goldman Sachs project average annual growth rates of 7% to 8% during the next decade, which translates into 29 million by 2020. J.D. Powers & Associates estimate China auto sales of 19.2 million by 2017. [116] According to a November 16, 2010 Reuters dispatch, Bain & Co. projects growth of 13-15% per year over the medium term. Daimler AG chairman Dieter Zetsche stated on October 23, 2010 that "China sales might reach 20 million to 30 million vehicles by 2020" according to an October 25, 2010 article in the Wall Street Journal. GM, in its IPO road show video, projected significant gains in China's vehicle sales as the country's GDP per capita continues to increase. GM cited the sales growth in Japan (1957-1967), Korea (1984–1999) and Taiwan as examples for their predictions. An executive of Beijing Automotive Industry Holding Company projected 40 million sales by 2020 (January 13, 2011 Automotive News website).

According to the CIA website, China's GDP per capita is roughly $7,400 compared with $47,000 in the United States; thus, there is significant room to grow for China, as well as in India ($2,800 GDP per capita). The November 24, 2010 edition of Automotive News Europe stated that Borgwarner CEO Timothy Manganello predicts China auto capacity at 30 million by 2020, with some forecaster projecting 40 million! McKinsey & Company estimated the China's car market could grow tenfold between 2005 and 2030. At 2005 sales of 5.8 million, this would result in sales of 58 million units by 2030. [117] To test the McKinsey predictions, the following table details U.S. vehicle registrations and licensed driver trends since 1960. [118]

| Year | Population (Millions) | Licensed Drivers (Millions) | Vehicles Registered (Millions) |
|------|------------|-----------|-----------|
| 1960 | 180 | 87 | 74 |
| 1970 | 204 | 108 | 108 |
| 1980 | 227 | 145 | 156 |
| 1990 | 248 | 167 | 189 |
| 2000 | 281 | 191 | 218 |
| 2010(e) | 308 | 220 | 250 |

China's middle class is growing rapidly. However, the estimates for the number of middle class families in China vary by hundreds of millions. The highest estimate is 817 million, which was projected by the Asian Development Bank. [119] "Shanghalist" estimates the middle class at 700 million by 2020. [120] An article in "ArticlesBase.com" estimated China's middle class at 400 million in less than 20 years. [121] McKinsey forecasts a Chinese middle class by the early 2020's of 520 million compared with 290 million in 2011. [122] McKinsey & Company predicts "nearly 70 percent of Chinese people will live in and around cities by 2015, up from 43% in 2006." [123]

China's household wealth is increasing at lightning speed. An October 2010 Credit Suisse Report projected China's household wealth to double to $35 trillion by 2015. Presently, China is only behind the U.S. and Japan.

At a middle class of 450 million by 2030, and a vehicle to population ratio of 0.8 cars per inhabitant (U.S. ratio in 2010), the Chinese auto market could generate 36 million units by 2030. At a more realistic 0.40 ratio (U.S. ratio in 1960) because China is still a developing country, annual sales could total 18 million, which appears too low. Carl Hahn, the former VW CEO, who had the vision in the late 1970's to lead VW into China, predicted at a Seoul Forum in 2010 "China will rank first among all nations for the rest of this century, until India overtakes it." [124] (India's population is projected at 1.6 billion people by 2050 compared with 1.2 billion today.)

However, even achieving "only" 25 million vehicles sales annually should be judged in the context of the following:

- China's continuing need for a highway infrastructure. According to the "Business Wire" website, China had 22,000 miles of highway in 2008, and a projected 31,000 miles by 2010. The long-term forecast is 53,000 miles. Fareed Zakari's Time article cited previously stated that China's physical infrastructure has been "built with a speed and on a scale never before seen in human history." (President Dwight D. Eisenhower launched the "Federal Interstate Highway System" in 1956. It is the world's largest highway with 47,000 miles.)

- The hundreds of billions of dollars required building the necessary roads.

- The billions of additional foreign reserves required importing crude oil (China imports about 60% of its oil requirements).

- Serious traffic congestions in major cities. Beijing is already restricting the number of car license plates it issues annually.

- China toppled Japan in 2010 to become the world's number two economy. Secondly, China dethroned Germany to become the world's leading exporter in 2009. However, China remains a relatively poor country; it ranks 128 in terms of GDP per capita according to the CIA website. Moreover, according to ABC World News report with Diane Sawyer on November 15, 2010, "China still has 700 million people living in poverty earning less than $2 per day."

Historian Victor D. Hanson stated in a September 2010 column at his website: ... "they (the Chinese) must deal with a new era of coming suburban blues, worker discontent, unions, environmental discretion and regulation, an aging and shrinking population and greater personal appetites, social protest, and nonconformity-in the manner that industrializing Western nations did as well in the early twentieth century." [125]

Rapidly rising minimum-wage levels might eventually reduce China's competitive labor cost advantage. Nevertheless, 1992 Nobel Economics Laureate Gary S. Becker stated in the September 29, 2010 edition of the Wall Street Journal, "China's prospects for continued growth ... are strong." [126]

Lastly, in the euphoria of celebrating yearly sales records, and the associated significant capacity expansion-taking place (projected at 40 million by Bain & Co.), industry forecasters often visualize a boom going on for eternity. While the present record auto sales in China are not unreasonable, bubbles do happen from time to time:

• The tulip bust of 1637.

• The 1999 book by James Glassman and Kevin Hassett during the dot-com period predicting a DOW of 36,000 (the record reached 14,165 on October 9, 2007).

- The collapse of the overheated U.S. housing market in 2008.

- The meltdown of U.S. auto sales. Between 2000-2007, U.S. vehicle sales averaged 17.2 million, which auto experts believed was the new plateau. Since then, sales averaged 11.6 million units.

The modus operandi of China's next phase of its automotive policy could include:

- Significantly strengthening domestic auto companies, and increasing their share of the Chinese market from 30% to over 60%.

- The Chinese government will create global giants through forced consolidation because China has to many small auto companies.

- China will force foreign companies to share their technology with their domestic partners. It is happening already. For example, according to a front-page article in the November 18, 2010 edition of the Wall Street Journal, the Chinese railroad equipment companies are utilizing the Japanese and German high-speed train design technology acquired through their joint ventures with them and competing against their partners in China and around the world. The Chinese simply call it "re-innovating" foreign technology. The Chinese are also geniuses at reverse engineering. Concurrently, China is pushing to be the EV (electric vehicle) leader. According to the December 6, 2010 issue of Automotive News, the Chinese government is pledging $15 billion over the next ten years to develop EV's.

• Continue to encourage strong domestic auto companies to acquire international auto firms.  The poster boy is Volvo.

• Launch aggressive plans within less than ten years to flood the world with cars (it is a no-brainer forecast because that's exactly what Germany, Japan and South Korea did once they established a domestic base). The December 15, 2010 Automotive News website stated that "China's SAIC raised $1.5 billion to help fund (its) own brand."

The Chinese State Council has already targeted the auto industry as a strategic industry. Therefore, within 15 years, the Western countries' battle cry will change from "are we successful against Japan," to "are we prevailing against China?"

In a September 27, 2010 editorial, Keith Crain, Editor-in-Chief of Automotive News stated "it's feasible that some-where down the line, the Chinese might feel empowered to nationalize the industry, leaving all Western companies out in the cold." [127]

## Not Everything Is Coming Up Roses

China's economic success during the last 30 years has been unprecedented in history. However, it is in sharp contrast to its political system under the Communist Party. Has the relative prosperity, which improved the lives of hundreds of millions of Chinese, weakened their resolve for the next phase–personal freedom? Is the Chinese march to economic dominance irreversible? Are there barriers to China's continued economic explosion? In addition to possible disastrous natural calamities, potential impediments, which could slow the Chinese economic train, might include:

- An inflexible "Five-Year Plan" mentality among the highly centralized and authoritarian Chinese bureaucracy (fast-paced globalization is radically changing world trading patterns). To date, however, China's officials have shown bureaucratic agility in responding to changing world economic conditions.

- U.S. and European Union (E.U.) imposition of extensive trade barriers to counter Chinese exports. To date, the Chinese yawn when they hear U.S. warnings about market access and the yuan manipulation.

- The continued deep recession in the U.S., which is China's biggest single export market. The Chinese Commerce Ministry already warned that China would be "devastated" by such a development.

- Can China continue its breakneck economic expansion indefinitely by copying Western products? China does not seem to have too many homegrown, cutting-edge, world-class products of its own, but has made major strides recently. In the meantime, China will save billions of dollars in R. &D. costs.

- Potential collapse of the highly speculative Chinese stock market (reportedly, over 100,000 new accounts are being opened daily). The Chinese fervor is reminiscent of the time 15 years ago when the once invincible and overoptimistic Japanese bubble burst–the economy, urban real estate and the stock market (the Nikkei index declined from over 40,000 to 10,000). Other contributing factors to the Japanese decline could have been the frequent changes of the prime ministership, political corruption and high levels of business failures.

- Significant economic growth often leads to expectations of personal freedom. How long can the Communist government contain this potential powder keg?

- Karl Marx predicted 160 years ago that industrialization would result in rivalries between social classes. It would eventually lead to Communism–a classless society and the "dictatorship of the proletariat." However, the society in Communist China is not classless. Therefore, will China's love affair with capitalism eventually lead to social unrest among 700 million Chinese who live outside urban areas and who earn $400 annually (ABC "World News" December 9, 2007)? They are not fully participating in the present economic boom.

- Persistent large-scale embezzlement and corruption by government officials.

- Continued unresponsiveness to human rights, including press freedom, and Internet censorship. Similar to Nazi Germany during the 1936 Berlin Olympics, China put on its best face during the highly successful 2008 Olympics, but as in Germany, repression and harassment commenced after the games.

- Growing economic hardship as a result of rampant inflation, which is reaching high levels. (One of the reasons for the 1989 Tiananmen Square uprising was a protest over rising inflation which had caught the rulers' off-guard.)

- Potential turmoil among the 20 million Chinese Muslims, similar to the Muslim unrest in Southern Thailand, the Southern Philippines and Chechnya.

- Possible energy and water shortages (especially in the arid North), and breakdown of the electric power grid as a result of the rapidly growing economy. (China recently announced a $12 billion irrigation project according to the January 31, 2011 edition of the Wall Street Journal.)

• Military confrontation with the U.S. over Taiwan. Against what country is the frightening military build-up aimed at? I believe the target is the United States.

• Turmoil within the Communist leadership, but on a much greater scale than witnessed during the infighting among the political elite at the time of the Tiananmen Square uprisings (the hardliners won).

No single event would cause an economic catastrophe, but a convergence of external, social and economic factors could lead to turbulence. However, unlike in Western democracies, China's ruling Communist Party could employ ruthless tactics to minimize problems, as evidenced by their Tiananmen Square response.

# BIBLIOGRAPHY

(1)   Neil, Dan. "A Stab at a European Sport Sedan-From Ford." The Wall Street Journal, February 5-6, 2011, p. D10.

(2)   Palmer, Jay. "Ford, A U.S. Auto Maker Hitting on All Cylinders." The Wall Street Journal, WSJ.com, August 8, 2010.

(3)   Fonda, Daren. "CEO Interview: Ford's Alan Mulally, "SmartMoney Magazine, November 3, 2010 (posted on website November 13. 2010).

(4)   Saporito, Bill. "How to Make Cars and Make Money Too." Time Magazine, August 9, 2010, p. 36.

(5)   MSNBC November 23, 2010 Special "Ford: Rebuilding an American Icon."

(6)   Forbes, Steve. Forbes Magazine. Quote from August 2010 Ford Motor Company "@Ford" Publication, p. 24.

(7)   Cramer, Jim. CNBC Mad Money, Quoted in August 2010 Ford Motor Company "@Ford" Magazine, p. 24.

(8)   Quote from Rebecca Lindland, IHS Automotive, in August 2010 Edition of Ford Motor Company "@Ford Magazine, p. 24.

(9)   Bernasek, Anna. "Who the Admired Admire." Quote from Howard Schultz of Starbucks About Alan Mulally Fortune, March 22, 2010, p. 126.

(10) Ingrassia, Paul. "Ford's Renaissance Man." Wall Street Journal, February 27-28, 2010, p. A13.

(11) Ibid., p. A13.

(12) Taylor, Alex III. "Ford's Comeback Kid." Fortune, May 25, 2009, p. 45-51.

(13) Brown, Peter. "Mulally's Magic Works; GM, Chrysler Are Looking Up." Automotive News, April 27, 2010.

(14) Iacocca, Lee with Whitney, Catherine. "Where Have All the Leaders Gone?" Scribner, a Division of Simon and Schuster, Inc. (2007), p. 184.

(15) Johnson, Mark W., Clayton M. Christensen and Henning Kagelmann. "Reinventing Your Business Model." Harvard Business Review, December 2008.

(16) Lacey, Robert. "Ford, The Men and Machine." Little, Brown and Company (1986), p. 571.

(17) Olson, Mathew S., Derek Bever and Seth Versey. "When Growth Stalls." Harvard Business Review, March 2008, p. 59.

(18) Brinkley, Duglas. "Wheels for the World." Viking, Published by the Penguin Group (2003), p. 162.

(19) Vlasic, Bill. "Detroit Goes From Gloom to Economic Bright Spot." New York Times (NYTimes.com), August 13, 2010.

(20) _____. "Fortune Global 500." Fortune, July 26, 2010, p. F-1.

(21) _____. "Largest Corporations in the U.S." Fortune, May 3, 2010, p. F-1.

(22) _____. "Factors Underlining the Decline in Manufacturing Employment Since 2000." Congressional Budget Office, December 23, 2008, p. 1.

(23) Ward, William A. "Manufacturing Productivity and the Shifting U.S., China and Global Job Scenes." 1990-2005, Clemson University, Center for International Trade, August 4, 2005, p. 1.

(24) _____. "U.S. Manufacturing Sector." American Manufacturing Trade Action Coalition," 2010, p. 1.

(25) Ibid., p. 4.

(26) _____. "1994 Facts and Figures." Automobile Manufacturers Association, Detroit, Michigan (1994), pp. 8, 20, 49, 51.

(27) _____. "A Look Back at GM, Chrysler and the American Auto Industry." Executive Office Of The President, April 21, 2010, p. 4.

(28) Menk, Deb and Kim Hill. "Auto Industry Contributes Significantly to U.S. Economy, Employment." Center for Automotive Research, Ann Arbor, Michigan, April 22, 2010, p. 1.

(29) Vlasic, Bill. "Detroit Goes From Gloom to Economic Bright Spot." The New York Times, August 13, 2010, p. 3 (website).

(30) _____. "A look Back at Chrysler and the American Auto Industry." Executive Office of the President, April 21, 2010, p. 1.

(31) Menk, Deb and Hill Kim. "Auto Industry Contributes Significantly to U.S. Economy, Employment." Center for Automotive Research, Ann Arbor, Michigan, April 22, 2010, p. 1.

(32) _____. "U.S. Automotive Industry Employment Trends." U.S. Department of Commerce, March 30, 2005, p. 3.

(33) _____. "Endangered Species: Factory Jobs." Center for Automotive Research, Ann Arbor, Michigan, November 26, 2007, p. 34 (reported in Automotive News).

(34) Webb, Alysha. "Beating the China Price." Automotive News, September 24, 2007, p. 48.

(35) Meredity, Robyn. "The Elephant and the Dragon, the Rise of India and China and What It Means For All Of Us." W.W. Norton & Company (2007), pp. 79, 84.

(36) Tayor, Alex III. "Sixty to Zero." Yale University Press (2010), p. 241.

(37) Brinkley, Douglas. "Wheels for the World." Viking, Published by the Penguin Press (2003), pp. 661-662.

(38) Liker, J. "The Toyota Way: 14 Management Principles from the World's Greatest Manufacturer." (2004), Wikipedia, Toyota Motor Corporation.

(39) Prestowitz, Clyde V. Jr. "Trading Places, How We Allowed Japan to Take the Lead." Basic Books, Inc. (1988), p. 252.

(40) Taylor, Alex III. "How Toyota Lost Its Way Conquering the Auto Market." Fortune, June 26, 2010, p. 108.

(41) Christensen, Clayton. "The Innovator's Dilemma." Harper Business Essentials, an Imprint of Harper Collins Publishing (1997), p. 186.

(42) Ingrassia, Paul. "Crash Course, the American Automobile Industry's Road from Glory to Disaster." Random House (2010), p. 115.

(43) Treece, James. "Ford Rebounds to Riches." Automotive News 2003 Commemorative Edition, Ford 100, June 16, 2003, p. 256.

(44) _____. "Customed Focused Strategy." 1999 Ford Motor Company Annual Report, p. 8.

(45) Taylor, Alex III. "Sixty to Zero." Yale University Press (2010), p. 161.

(46) Brinkley, David. "Wheels for the World." Viking, Published by Penguin Group (2003), p. 749.

(47) ICMR Center for Management Research. "Ford CEO Mulally Battles Red Tape." May 9, 2007 (www.newsmax. com). David Killey. "The New Heat on Ford." June 4, 2007 (www.businessweek.com).

(48) Brown, Peter. "2003 Commemorative Edition, Ford 100." Automotive News, July16, 2003, p. 3.

(49) Ingrassia, Paul. "Ford's Renaissance Man." Wall Street Journal, February 27-28, 2010, p. A13.

(50) Saporito, Bill. "Can Alan Mulally Keep Ford in the Fast Lane?" Time Magazine, August 15, 2010, p. 84 (www.Time. com/Detroit).

(51) Cash, Nancy. "The Ford Century." Ford Motor Company, 100 Years, Tehabi Books (2002), p. 17.

(52) Taylor, Alex III. "Sixty to Zero." Yale University Press (2010), pp. 185-186.

(53) Taylor, Alex III. "Chrysler's Speed Merchant." Fortune, September 6, 2010, p. 78.

(54) Porter, Michael E. and Nitin Nohria. "What Is Leadership?" Handbook of Leadership Theory and Practice, Harvard Business School Publishing Corporation (2010), pp. 436, 454, 461.

(55) Taylor, Alex III. "Ford's Comeback Kid." Fortune, May 25, 2009, pp. 44-51.

(56) Christensen, Clayton. "The Innovator's Dilemma," Harper Business Essentials, A Harper Business Book (2003), p. xiii.

(57) Murray, Alan. "The Wall Street Guide to Management." Harper Business (2010); Quote is from Mr. Murray's August 21, 2010 article in The Wall Street Journal entitled "The End of Management."

(58) MacDuffie, John Paul, and Fujimoto, Takahiro. "Why Dinosaurs Will Keep Ruling the Auto Industry." Harvard Business Review, June 2010, p. 25.

(59) Johnson, Richard. "Japanese Save Billions by Attacking the Basics." Automotive News, December 5, 1994.

(60) Johnson, Mark W., Clayton M. Christensen and Henning Kagermann. "Reinventing Your Business Model." Harvard Business Review, December 2008, p. 53.

(61) LaReau, Jamie. "2010 Automotive News All-Stars." July 12, 2010, p. 12.

(62) Saporito, Bill. "How To Make Cars And Make Money." Time Magazine, August 9, 2010, p. 36.

(63) Solheim, Mark. "Detroit Motors Back." Kiplinger's Personal Finance, January 2008, p. 95.

(64) Maglano, George. "2007 Global Automotive Conference." Tokyo, Global Insight, May 23, 2007.

(65) LaReau, Jamie. "The New Ford Has Learned to Think Small." Automotive News, August 9, 2010, p. 18.

(66) Groysberg, Boris, Andrew N. McLean and Nitin Nohria. "Are Leaders Portable?" Harvard Business Review, May 2006, p. 98.

(67) Saporito, Bill. "Can Alan Mulally Keep Ford in the Fast Lane?" Time Magazine, August 15, 2010, p. 2.

(68) Porter, Michael E. and Nitin Nohria. "What Is Leadership?" Handbook of Leadership Theory and Practice," Harvard Business School Publishing Corporation (2010), pp. 436, 454, 461.

(69) Lorsch, Jay. "A Contingency Theory of Leadership." Handbook of Leadership Theory and Practice, Harvard Business School Publishing Corporation (2010), pp. 415, 418, 439.

(70) Brinkley, Douglas. "Wheels for the World." Viking, Published by Penguin Group (2003), p. 495.

(71) _____. "2010 All Stars." Automotive News, July 12, 2010, pp. 11-13.

(72) Taylor, Alex III. "Ford's Comeback Kid." Fortune, May 25, 2009, p. 50.

(73) _____. "2009 All Stars." Automotive News, July 6, 2009, pp. 1, 24-28.

(74) Crain, Keith. "100 Leading Women in the North American Auto Industry." Automotive News, September 13, 2010, p. 4W.

(75) Harris, Donna. "GM's IPO Filing Calls Ally Partnership a Risk." Automotive News, August 23, 2010, p. 26 (Lexis Nexis News).

(76) Meners, Jens. "Chinese Takeout." Car & Driver, October 2010, Volume 56, No. 4, pp. 31-32.

(77) Muller, Joann. "Can China Save GM." Forbes, May 10, 2010, p. 74.

(78) Langlois, Shawn. "Ford Ramps Up Business Plans for India." Market Watch, August 26, 2010.

(79) Choudhury, Santanu, and Anirban Chowdhury. "Ford Plans 8 New Models to Drive Sales in Growing Indian Market." Wall Street Journal, August 27, 2010, p. B3.

(80) LaReau, Jamie. "Booming Brazil Benefits Ford." Automotive News, August 23, 2010. (www.autonews.com).

(81) _____. "UAW Head Says Auto Workers Should Share in Industry Upside." www.autonews.com, August 30, 2010.

(82) Naughton, Keith. Ford Said to Reverse Plans to Make SUV in Kentucky for Export." Bloomberg, September 9, 2010, p. 2.

(83) _____. "2009 Market Data Book." Automotive News, May 25, 2009, p. 3.

(84) _____. "GM Accelerates Its Reinvention As a Leaner, More Viable Company." GM News, April 27, 2009, p. 1.

(85) Ibid., p. 2.

(86) ACEA. "Total Europe New Passenger Car Registrations by Manufacturer." January 15, 2010, p. 3.

(87) Crain, Keith. "GM Is Starting to Sound Like Peyton Place." Automotive News, September 13, 2010, p. 12.

(88) Gardner, Greg. "Ford Sales Will Top GM by 2010, Economist Says." Detroit Free Press, September 30, 2009, (ggardner@freepress.com).

(89) _____. "Ford Projected to Gain U.S. Share, Overtake GM." Automotive News (Reuters), July 16, 2009 (www.autonews.com).

(90) Muller, Joann. "Can China Save GM?" Forbes, May 10, 2010, p. 74.

(91) Child, Charles. "A Skewed Look Fordward." Automotive News, January 3, 2000, p. 20 FS.

(92) "Ford and Changan May Expand." Zachs Equity Research, September 7, 2010, p. 1.

(93) Bary, Andrew. "GM Is Back." Barron, March 1, 2010, p. 20.

(94) Woodall, Bernie. "Ford's Fleming Says He Is Happy With Mazda's Tie-Up." Reuters, September 9, 2010.

(95) Wernie, Bradford. "Chrysler's Sales Rise In a Down Market." Automotive News, September 6, 2010, p. 23.

(96) Ingrassia, Paul and Joseph B. White. "The Fall and Rise of the American Automobile Industry." Simon & Schuster (1994), pp. 67-68.

(97) Kino, Ron. "Mature Audiences." Motor Trend.com, October 2010, p. 110.

(98) Zetsche, Dieter. "Chairman's Letter." 2009 Daimler AG Annual Report, p. 1.

(99) _____. "2009 Volkswagen Annual Report." P. 14.

(100) Toyota, Honda, Nissan Websites.

(101) Taylor, Alex III. "Ford's Comeback Kid." Fortune, May 25, 2009, p. 50.

(102) Fitzpatrick, Dan. "BOFA Chief Shares His Vision Finally." Wall Street Journal, September 14, 2010, p. C1.

(103) 2000 Ford Motor Company Annual Report. pp. 30-31; 2009 Ford Motor Company Annual Report, p. 5.

(104) Taylor, Alex III. "Ford's Comeback Kid." Fortune, May 25, 2009, p. 51.

(105) Totty, Michael. "The Winners, Category by Category." The Wall Street Journal, September 27, 2010, p. R2.

(106) _____. "The Largest U.S. Corporations." Fortune, May 3, 2010, pp. F 1-2.

(107) _____. "World Leading Companies, Top 50 in Sales." Forbes, May 10, 2010, p. 104.

(108) DeMatio, Joe. "2010 Man of the Year, Alan Mulally, CEO of Ford Motor Company." Automobile Magazine, November 2009.

(109) Mayne, Eric. "Akerson Keen to Instill 'Attacker's Culture' at GM." Wardauto.com, September 17, 2010, p. 1.

(110) Rosevear, John. "Ford's Turnaround Continues to Impress." Motley Fool Stock Advisor, September 18, 2010, p. 4.

(111) Maddison, Angus. "Monitoring the World Economy, 1820-1992." OCED, Paris, France (1995), pp. 21, 30, 39.

(112) Barta, Patrick, and Alex Frangos. "Southeast Asia Linking Up to Compete With China." Wall Street Journal, August 23, 2010, p. A2.

(113) Bernanke, Ben. "The Chinese Economy: Progress and Challenges." Chinese Academy of Social Sciences, Beijing, China, December 15, 2006, p. 1.

(114) Peaple, Andrew. "China Takes Wheel From Auto Sector." Wall Street Journal, September 17, 2010, p. C10.

(115) Hunkar, David. "Top Auto Companies In China, India." Seeking Alpha, May 2, 2010, p.2. Data is credited to J.D. Powers & Associates.

(116) Denning, Liam. "Car Makers Face Twists In China's Open Road." Wall Street Journal, September 10, 2010, p. C12.

(117) _____. "Automobile Industry In China." Wikipedia, p. 1.

(118) U.S. Department of Commerce.

(119) _____. "Report Claims China's Middle Class Numbers 800 Million." Virtual Review, August 30, 2010, p. 1.

(120) _____. "China's Middle Class Will Reach 700 Million by 2020." Virtual Review, August 30, 2010, p. 2.

(121) _____. "Reaching China's Middle Class." August 20, 2009, ArticlesBase.com, p. 1.

(122) _____. "Middle Class Is Burgeoning." China Daily, September 17, 2010, p. 1.

(123) O'Brien, Elizabeth. "A Chinese Spending Spree." SmartMoney, October 2010, p. 20.

(124) _____. "Visionary Who Saw A Sleeping Giant Sees a Century of Chinese Auto Domination." Automotive News, July 12, 2010, p. 26.

(125) Hanson, Victor Davis. "Notable & Quotable." Wall Street Journal, September 21, 2010, p. A 21. (Quote from September 18, 2010 website of Pajamasmedia.com).

(126) Becker, Gary S. "China's Next Leap Forward." Wall Street Journal, September 29, 2010, p. A21.

(127) Crain, Keith. "Lots of Risks and Rewards In China." Automotive News, September 27, 2010, p. 12.